Fodor's 92 Hong Kong

Fodor's Travel Publications, Inc.
New York and London

Fodor's Hong Kong

Editor: Carolyn Price
Contributors: Shann Davies, Linda K. Schmidt
Art Director: Fabrizio La Rocca
Map Editor: Marcy Pritchard
Cartographer: David Lindroth
Illustrator: Karl Tanner
Cover Photograph: James Griffiths/Magnum

Design: Vignelli Associates

Special Sales

Contents

Maps

Foreword

While every care has been taken to ensure the accuracy of the information in this guide, the passage of time will always bring change, and consequently, the publisher cannot accept responsibility for errors that may occur.

All prices and opening times quoted here are based on information available to us at press time. Hours and admission fees may change, however, and the prudent traveler will avoid inconvenience by calling ahead.

Fodor's wants to hear about your travel experiences, both pleasant and unpleasant. When a hotel or restaurant fails to live up to its billing, let us know and we will investigate the complaint and revise our entries where the facts warrant it.

Send your letters to the editors of Fodor's Travel Publications, 201 E. 50th Street, New York, NY 10022.

Highlights'92 and Fodor's Choice

Highlights '92

Hong Kong's tourist industry is very much back on track, with almost six million visitors in 1990, more than 10 percent over the previous year, and, despite the decrease during the Gulf War, every expectation of a further increase in 1992.

The competition to accommodate visitors to Hong Kong also continues to grow. In 1991 almost 3,000 new rooms were opened in a wide variety of hotels. These included the luxury town house of the **Ritz-Carlton,** the super-elegant **Island Shangri-La,** the vast new-town **Kowloon Panda,** and an array of three-star properties located in areas a little off the main tourist track, such as Yaumati in Kowloon and North Point on Hong Kong Island.

The hotel boom continues into 1992, along with many extensive new mall complexes that contain an assortment of shops, restaurants, and entertainment facilities, which are proving as popular with visitors as local residents.

Ocean Park is a popular lure for both audiences and regularly introduces new attractions. In 1991 it was a **Shark Tunnel,** where visitors walk through the shark tank, which proved a great success, and now the park is building a 70-meter **Sky Tower** for some spectacular views from the ascending observation cabin.

Both the **Hong Kong Park** and **Science Museum,** which opened in 1991, offer some world-class exhibits of flora, fauna, and man-made marvels. In addition, visits are now possible to the **Mai Po marshes** bird sanctuary.

Macau is even busier adding facilities and attractions. Construction proceeds for its **international airport,** scheduled for completition in 1993, and the hotel supply is growing. The **Emperor New World** opened in late 1991, leading the way for a clutch of new properties. These include a **Holiday Inn** and the **Westin resort** on Coloane Island, where Macau's first **golf course** is expected to be completed in mid-1992.

The resort and two other hotels will have their own casinos, and the **Jockey Club** has adopted year-round racing. It is also building a wharf for ferries direct from Hong Kong to the track.

Meanwhile, in Macau's festivals grow in stature and diversity. Fans of pyrotechnics flock to the **international fireworks festival** each year, and the **Music Festival** now includes such venues as a Colonial courtyard, a Baroque church, and the 19th century country villa in Lou Lim Ieoc gardens. As for performers, Teresa Berganza and Ileana Cotrubas appeared in 1990, while Jean Pierre Rampal opened the 1991 festival.

Fodor's Choice

No two people will agree on what makes a perfect vacation, but it can be fun and helpful to know what others think. We hope you'll have a chance to experience some of Fodor's Choices yourself while visting Hong Kong and Macau. For detailed information on individual entries, see the relevant sections of this guidebook.

Special Moments

Hong Kong The view of Hong Kong and Kowloon when coming in by plane

The dazzling view of Hong Kong from the Peak

The harbor, night or day, for the soul of Hong Kong

The passing scene from the top deck of an island tram

Sung Dynasty Village, for a glimpse of ancient China

The colorful tableaux of legends and mythology at the Aw Boon Haw (Tiger Balm) Gardens

Macau Protestant Cemetery near Camões Museum

Taste Treats

Hong Kong The pizza at Il Mercato at Stanley Market

Dim sum lunch—anywhere

The taste of Peking duck skin and the smell of beggar's chicken

A marketstall Chinese breakfast of *congee* (rice porridge) at Kowloon Park Road/Haiphong Road, Kowloon

A Chinese dinner at a garish floating restaurant at Aberdeen Harbour

Buffet dinner at Furama Hotel's revolving rooftop restaurant

Afternoon tea in the grand lobby of the Peninsula Hotel

A drink in the Regent Hotel's lobby bar, with panoramic views of the harbor.

Macau African chicken at Henri's

The cottage loaf of bread served before meals at Flamingo, at the Taipa Resort

Museums

Hong Kong The Railway Museum at Tai Po

The Aw Boon Haw Villa jade collection

The photography collection at the Hong Kong Museum of History

Space-age shows at the Space Museum

Macau   The Maritime Museum, one of Asia's finest

Excursions

Hong Kong   The view of the coastline from the Ocean Park cable car

Crossing the harbor on the Star Ferry—second class, at water level

A tram ride all the way from Kennedy Town to North Point

A bus ride around the island to Repulse Bay or Stanley

Macau   Driving a mini-Moke

The double-decker bus ride over the bridge to Taipa Island

A pedicab ride for leisurely sightseeing

Special Events

Hong Kong   Candlelight parades in honor of the mid-Autumn moon and at the Dragon Boat Festival in June

Bun Festival (May) on Cheung Chau

Horseracing at Happy Valley track

Macau   World-class excitement at the Grand Prix

The Good Friday Passion Parade, the first weekend of Lent

Temples and Shrines

Hong Kong   The Temple of 10,000 Buddhas, Shatin, with its gilded, mummified Holy Man

Po Lin Buddhist Monastery, on Lantau Island

Wong Tai Sin Temple for fortunetelling, racing tips, and cures

Macau   A-Ma Temple, dedicated to the goddess of the sea

Dining

Hong Kong   Chesa (*Very Expensive*)

Gaddi's (*Very Expensive*)

Au Trou Normand (*Expensive*)

Lai Ching Heen (*Expensive*)

Jumbo (*Moderate*)

Peking Garden (*Moderate)*

Rangoon (*Inexpensive*)

Macau   A Lorcha (*Inexpensive*)

Lodging

Hong Kong   Mandarin Oriental (*Very Expensive*)

The Peninsula (*Very Expensive*)

Regent (*Very Expensive*)

Omni The Hong Kong (*Expensive*)

Kowloon (*Moderate*)

Ramada Inn, Kowloon and Hong Kong (*Moderate*)

Harbour View International House (*Inexpensive)*

Macau   Hyatt Regency and Taipa Island Resort *(Expensive)*

Pousada de Sao Tiago *(Expensive)*

Nightlife

Hong Kong   Bar City in New World Centre, Kowloon

Macau   Crazy Paris Show at Lisboa Hotel

Street Markets

Hong Kong   Jade Market, Kansu Street, Kowloon—the world's only jade market

Night Market at Temple Street, off Jordan Road, Kowloon

Bird Market on Hong Lok Street, near Mongkok MTR station

"Poor Man's Nightclub" at the Macau Ferry Terminal, Central, 8 PM to midnight

Luen Wo Market, near Fanling in New Territories

Parks and Countryside Walks

Hong Kong   Tai Lam Country Park, open country just minutes from Kowloon

Dragon's Back in Shek O Country Park

Lantau Island, Shek Pik to Tai O

Victoria Park, Causeway Bay, to watch early morning practitioners of t'ai chi ch'uan (shadow boxing)

Macau   Camões Gardens

For Free

Hong Kong A ride up the "glass bubble" elevator at Hopewell Centre to see the city lights at night

Any Chinese temple

Street markets and back lanes

The Hong Kong Zoological and Botanical Gardens

For Children

Hong Kong Ocean Park, a huge marine park with dolphin shows and cable car rides

Peak Tram, for the thrill of the steep ascent

Space Museum, to feel what it is like to take a ride through space

Lai Chi Kok Amusement Park, for games, sideshows, and rides

Aw Boon Haw (Tiger Balm) Gardens

Sung Dynasty Village, to see the lion dance and fortunetellers

Shopping for a new Walkman cassette player and blue jeans

Macau The games room at the Lisboa Hotel

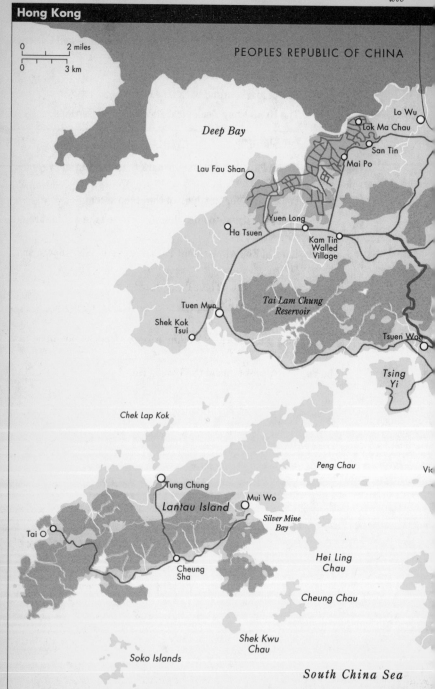

Hong Kong

0   2 miles

0   3 km

PEOPLES REPUBLIC OF CHINA

Deep Bay

Lo Wu

Lok Ma Chau

San Tin

Mai Po

Lau Fau Shan

Yuen Long

Ha Tsuen

Kam Tin
Walled
Village

*Tai Lam Chung
Reservoir*

Tuen Mun

Shek Kok
Tsui

Tsuen Wan

*Tsing
Yi*

Chek Lap Kok

Peng Chau

Vic

Tung Chung

Mui Wo

Lantau Island

*Silver Mine
Bay*

Tai O

*Hei Ling
Chau*

Cheung
Sha

Cheung Chau

*Shek Kwu
Chau*

Soko Islands

South China Sea

N

Crooked Island

Sheung Shui

Fanling

Wu Kau Tang

Plover Cove Reservoir

Grass Island

Taipo

Kam Shan

Tolo Channel

Pan Chung

Tolo Harbour

NEW TERRITORIES

Chek Keng

Shatin

Sai Kung

High Island

Ho Chung

Kau Sai Chau

Sung Dynasty Village

Port Shelter

Lai Chi Kok Amusement Park

Basalt Island

KOWLOON

Kowloon Bay

Yau Tong

Junk Bay

Tai Wan Tau

Victoria

Victoria Harbour

Tei Tong Tsui

HONG KONG

Tung Lung Chau

Stanley

Lamma Island

Stanley Peninsula

Po Toi Islands

World Time Zones

+12 +13 -9 -10 -11 -10 +11 +12

-4 -3 25

MONDAY
SUNDAY

International Date Line

-7 -5 -4

-6 -5

-5 -4 -3

-3

Numbers below vertical bands relate each zone to Greenwich Mean Time (0 hrs.).
Local times frequently differ from these general indications,
as indicated by light-face numbers on map.

+11 +12 - -11 -10 -9 -8 -7 -6 -5 -4 -3 -2

Algiers, **29**	Berlin, **34**	Delhi, **48**	Istanbul, **40**
Anchorage, **3**	Bogotá, **19**	Denver, **8**	Jerusalem, **42**
Athens, **41**	Budapest, **37**	Djakarta, **53**	Johannesburg, **44**
Auckland, **1**	Buenos Aires, **24**	Dublin, **26**	Lima, **20**
Baghdad, **46**	Caracas, **22**	Edmonton, **7**	Lisbon, **28**
Bangkok, **50**	Chicago, **9**	Hong Kong, **56**	London (Greenwich), **27**
Beijing, **54**	Copenhagen, **33**	Honolulu, **2**	Los Angeles, **6**
	Dallas, **10**		Madrid, **38**
			Manila, **57**

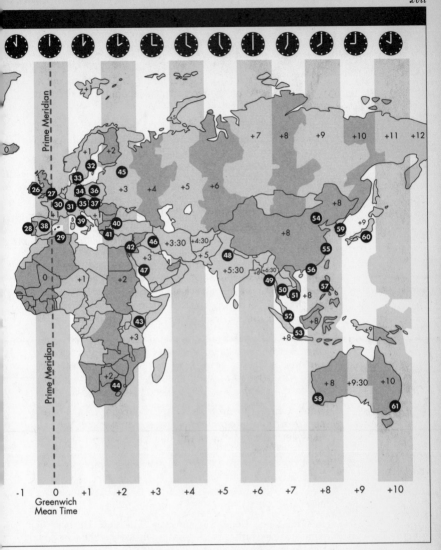

Mecca, **47**
Mexico City, **12**
Miami, **18**
Montreal, **15**
Moscow, **45**
Nairobi, **43**
New Orleans, **11**
New York City, **16**

Ottawa, **14**
Paris, **30**
Perth, **58**
Reykjavík, **25**
Rio de Janeiro, **23**
Rome, **39**
Saigon, **51**

San Francisco, **5**
Santiago, **21**
Seoul, **59**
Shanghai, **55**
Singapore, **52**
Stockholm, **32**
Sydney, **61**
Tokyo, **60**

Toronto, **13**
Vancouver, **4**
Vienna, **35**
Warsaw, **36**
Washington, DC, **17**
Yangon, **49**
Zürich, **31**

Introduction

When you fly to Hong Kong, try to get a window seat on the aircraft; the landing will take your breath away.

As the prelanding announcement is being made, you will probably still be out over the gray South China Sea. As you get closer to the coast of China, you will spot a few small, rocky islands, tiny fishing boats, and sailboats in the channels leading into Hong Kong Harbour—the most spectacular harbor you will ever see.

The final approach into Hong Kong's Kai Tak Airport is sudden and rather startling. If you come in over the sea, you follow the channel between Hong Kong Island and the mainland, on wings that seem close enough to touch the boats or the windows of the skyscrapers rising above the hills. If you fly in over Kowloon, the plane will seem dangerously close to the scrub-covered hills, and you will see children playing in schoolgrounds, and perhaps even read the advertisements on the sides of buses.

Close up, the streets are a jumble of brightly colored signs, most written in Chinese characters, and always crowded. Like ant hills that have been stirred up, the streets are filled with streams of people relentlessly going about their business—the restless, urgent need to make money.

Hong Kong is the ultimate capitalistic society, almost desperate in its urge to produce, earn, sell, and spend. You will find yourself caught up in this momentum, and wondering whether at heart the place is Western or Oriental. At first sight the character of the city will seem entirely Western, but this is only the veneer. Underneath the surface you will soon discover that Hong Kong is essentially Chinese, in heart and spirit.

In Cantonese, Hong Kong means "Fragrant Harbor," a name inspired either by the incense factories that once dotted Hong Kong Island or by the profusion of scented pink *bauhinias*, the national flower.

Hong Kong is both a British Crown Colony—one of the few left—and a "dependent territory" of Great Britain. Since New Territories, a major section of the colony, is leased from China, Hong Kong is also part of China.

Hong Kong is located on the southeast coast of China, at the mouth of the Pearl River, on the same latitude as Hawaii and Cuba. By air, it's 2¾ hours from Beijing, 17 from New York, 12¼ from San Francisco, and 13 from London.

It consists of three main parts: Hong Kong Island, roughly 32 square miles; Kowloon, 3.5 square miles; and New Territories, about 365 square miles.

The name Hong Kong refers to the overall colony as well as to its main island, Hong Kong Island, which is across the harbor from Kowloon. The island's principal business district is officially named Victoria, but everyone calls it Central. Also on the island are the districts of Wanchai, Causeway Bay, Repulse Bay, Stanley, and Aberdeen.

Kowloon includes Tsimshatsui, Tsimshatsui East, Hung Hom, Mongkok/Yaumatei, and the area north to Boundary Street. New Territories begins at Boundary Street and extends north to the border of China, encompassing the container port, the airport, most of the major factories, and the outlying islands.

Hong Kong is 98% Chinese. Other nationalities include British, American, Indian, and Japanese. Although the official languages are English and Cantonese, many other languages and dialects are spoken here, including Mandarin, Hakka (the language of a group of early settlers from China), Tanka (the language of the original boat people who came here some 5,000 years ago), Shanghainese, and Chinglish (a mixture of Cantonese and English). Some 30,000 Filipinos live and work in Hong Kong, so you're also likely to hear Philippine languages, especially near the Star Ferry and Statue Square park.

Buddhism, Taoism, ancestor worship, Christianity, and animism are the major religions, and you'll see signs of them everywhere. Pragmatism and money-making are such a part of the way of life here that you can almost call them religions, too. The distinctions are often blurred because Chinese people tend to be eclectic in their beliefs. It is not uncommon for the same Hong Kong citizen to put out food and incense for his departed ancestors at Spring Festival time, invite a Taoist priest to his home to exorcise unhappy ghosts, pray in a Buddhist temple for fertility, and take Communion in a Christian church.

Hong Kong is a delightful place to visit. It has the best shopping in the world, if you work at it; great Chinese food; mountains, beaches, harbors, and parks; and exotic festivals. You can experience firsthand an economic feat of superhuman proportions: some 5.7 million people living and working on 400 square miles of land with few natural resources other than a deep harbor on the Chinese coast. You can also experience history in the making, as the British prepare to hand over Hong Kong to the People's Republic of China when the New Territories lease expires in 1997. Feelings about this changeover are mixed, and most people are more than a little apprehensive, especially in the wake of 1989's brutal suppression of the democracy movement in China.

Hong Kong is not entirely dependent on Britain, which pays only 25% of the colony's defense budget. The Hong Kong government picks up the rest of the tab. Britain, however, still makes most of the important decisions for Hong Kong, which is Britain's largest Asian market—a captive market for such British-made products as buses and railway cars. Hong Kong also trades with China, the United States, and Japan.

Part of Hong Kong's phenomenal success stems from its ties to the British government, which has given it political stability and a strong judicial system. These attributes have attracted local and foreign capital. The decision to make Hong Kong a duty-free port and a trading center was British. The territory has also benefited from Chinese entrepreneurial skills, hardworking Chinese refugee labor, and, of course, the harbor.

Hong Kong is also economically and politically dependent on China for markets, resources, and cooperation. China is Hong Kong's fourth largest trading partner, providing most of the food—including 1.8 million squealing pigs a year. About half of the water consumed in Hong Kong comes from China, which also provides the colony with relatively inexpensive pots, pans, blankets, sweaters, textiles, and beds.

I n past years, Hong Kong has also been aptly described as "a pimple on China's behind" and "a gem in China's navel." Both descriptions fit—almost. The Communist Chinese have been very embarrassed by Hong Kong's blatant capitalism. But China has been earning an estimated 40% of its foreign exchange in Hong Kong, about U.S.$6 billion to U.S.$8 billion a year. Many Hong Kong businesspeople have also invested in China and, more particularly, in China's new Special Economic Zones. The largest, Shenzhen, is on Hong Kong's northern border. Financially, Hong Kong is worth more to China than it is to Britain.

Hong Kong is shamelessly capitalistic. But though it is the world's foremost example of a laissez-faire economy, it has many socialistic policies. Although Hong Kong has no minimum wage laws and no unemployment insurance, it has compulsory workmen's compensation laws, minimum working-age regulations, and nine years of compulsory education. About 2.5 million people—almost 50% of the population—live in government-subsidized housing. Government hospitals provide near-free medical care—an ambulance ride, X-rays, 14 stitches, an overnight hospital stay—and medicines cost less than U.S.$10.

Hong Kong is far from the classic image of a "colony" or a sweatshop based on cheap labor. It has an infant mortality rate lower than that of either Britain or the United States, more secondary students per capita than Britain, and one of the highest protein-consumption rates in the world. It also has hardly any unemployment.

Hong Kong has not just survived, it has thrived. It has the world's fourth largest financial center, third largest diamond and gold trading center, and the largest market for 24K gold jewelry. It is the busiest container port, and the world's largest manufacturer of toys, textiles, clothing, watches, clocks, and radios.

Major North American, European, and Japanese computer companies compete for customers here, sometimes at prices less than at home because of lower mark-ups, no sales taxes, and no duties. Computers not only keep track of customers and orders in Hong Kong, but they are also used to cut cloth into dresses in the most cost-efficient manner, to design machines, and to do other complicated tasks.

Hong Kong has hundreds of banks providing capital or facilitating financial transactions. Many publishing houses are in Hong Kong because world copyright and trademark registry are protected under British law, while costs are low. In addition, the government avoids interfering with editorial content (aside from pornographic and libelous material).

Some companies have departed, however, because of the incredibly high rents of the late 1970s and early 1980s— among the highest in the world for commercial and postwar residential property. Relatively new, modest (by American standards), three-bedroom apartments can cost as much as HK$25,000 a month, or more than U.S.$3,000.

Real estate is not only a principal money-maker for many Hong Kong citizens, it is the largest single source of revenue for the government. Ever since British Hong Kong began, the government has controlled practically all the land. People can buy buildings only on long-term leased land.

Hong Kong makes no pretense about being a democracy. It isn't. But it is more sensitive to its citizens than most "democratic" countries in Asia. Only illegal immigrants and criminals need fear the police.

Hong Kong's top political leader is the governor, who represents the British sovereign. In the absence of a "Colonial Office," the British foreign secretary is answerable to Britain's Parliament. Next in line to the governor are the chief secretary, financial secretary, and attorney general. The highest-ranking body is the 17-member Executive Council, which combines the functions of a cabinet and top advisory board. The Legislative Council enacts legislation, allocates funds, debates policy, and questions the administration. Since September 1985, as part of the plan to prepare the territory for self-rule under China in 1997, the Legislative Council has included 24 indirectly elected members.

The first semblance of popular government came with elections held in 1952 for seats on the Urban Council, which takes care of beaches, playgrounds, cultural centers, and garbage collection. In 1982, elections were held for the 18 newly created District Boards. After the District Boards were filled, the partially elected Regional Council, the rural version of the Urban Council, was created.

Citizen participation also takes the form of lively letters to the editors of newspapers and participation in open-line radio talk shows. Questions are usually answered by the government official concerned. District Offices have regular "Meet the Public" programs for citizens to make criticisms and offer suggestions directly to District Board members. Some 320 citizen advisory boards and councils give advice. Demonstrations and petitions to the governor also take place freely. Political stability, however, is a critical factor because it affects the entire economy.

Initially, Hong Kong's earliest visitors were believed to be boat people of Malaysian-Oceanic origin who came here about 5,000 years ago. They left geometric-style graffiti, which is still visible on rocks in Big Wave Bay (on Hong Kong Island) and Po Toi Island. The earliest structure found so far is the 2,000-year-old Han Dynasty tomb at Lei Cheng Uk. More than 600 years later, the Tang Dynasty left lime kilns full of seashells—an archaeological mystery because there are no clues indicating how or why the lime was used.

There are also records from the 13th century, when Sung Dynasty loyalists fled China with their child-emperor to escape the invading Mongols. The last of the Sung Dynasty emperors, a 10-year-old boy, is said to have spent a night in the late 1270s near what is now the airport. One of his men is credited with naming Kowloon, which means "nine dragons" (he counted eight mountains that resembled dragons, and added one for the emperor, who was also considered a dragon). The boy was the only Chinese emperor believed to have set foot in what is now Hong Kong. However, many of his courtiers settled here. Today, anyone visiting Po Lin Monastery, high in the mountains of Lantau Island, will pass Shek Pik reservoir, where innumerable Sung Dynasty coins were found during the reservoir's excavation. You can also get a feel for life during the period by visiting Sung Dynasty Village, a reproduction of a Sung village, in an amusement park in Laichikok near Kowloon. The village is small, but it demonstrates the highly developed Sung civilization with spirit and charm and is well worth a visit.

Western traders first appeared in the Hong Kong area in 1513. The first were Portuguese, soon followed by the Spanish, Dutch, English, and French. All were bent either on making fortunes trading porcelain, tea, and silk, or saving souls for their respective religions. Until 1757, the Chinese restricted all foreigners to neighboring Macau, the Portuguese territory 40 miles (64 km) across the Pearl River estuary. After 1757, traders—but not their families—were allowed to live just outside Canton for about eight months each year. (Canton, now known as Guangzhou, is only 20 minutes from Hong Kong by plane, or three hours by train or hovercraft.)

Trading in Canton was frustrating for the foreigners. It took at least 20 days for messages to be relayed to the emperor, local officials had to be bribed, and Chinese justice seemed unfair. The Chinese confined foreign traders to a small, restricted zone and forbade them to learn Chinese. On top of that, the Chinese wanted nothing from the West except silver, until the foreigners, especially the British, started offering opium.

The spread of the opium habit and the growing outflow of silver alarmed high Chinese officials as early as 1729. They issued edicts forbidding the importation of the drug, but these were not strictly enforced until 1839. Then a heroic and somewhat fanatical Imperial Commissioner, Lin Ze-Xu (Lin Tse-hsu), laid siege to the foreign factories in Canton and detained the traders until they surrendered over 20,000 chests of the drug, almost a year's worth of trade. The foreigners also signed bonds promising to desist from dealing with it forever, upon threat of death. The opium was destroyed.

The traders did not find Lin's inflexible manner the least bit amusing. The resulting tension led to the Opium Wars and a succession of unequal treaties forced by superior British firepower. The most important of these treaties required China to cede the island of Hong Kong to Britain; later, another treaty added Kowloon. Finally, in 1898, China leased the New Territories to Britain for 99 years.

British-ruled Hong Kong flourished from the start of trade, especially the trade in opium, which was not outlawed in Hong Kong until after World War II. The population grew quickly, from 4,000 in 1841 to over 23,000 in 1847, as Hong Kong attracted anyone anxious to make money or just to live without the fetters of feudalism and family.

Each convulsion on the Chinese mainland—the Taiping rebellion in the mid-1800s, the 1911 republican revolution, the war lords of the 1920s, the 1937 Japanese invasion—resulted in another group of refugees here. Then Japan invaded Hong Kong itself. The population, which was 1.4 million just before the Japanese arrived, dropped to a low of 600,000 by 1945. Many Hong Kong residents were forced to flee to Macau and the rural areas of China. The Japanese period is still remembered with bitterness by many local residents.

The largest group of Chinese refugees came as a result of the civil war in China between the Nationalists and Communists that ended with a Communist victory in 1949. Many refugees, especially the Shanghainese, brought capital and business skills. The population of Hong Kong was 1.8 million in 1947. By 1961 it stood at 3.7 million. For 25 days in 1962, when food was short in China, Chinese border guards allowed 70,000 Chinese to walk into Hong Kong. Ordinarily, it is very difficult for Chinese citizens to get permission to leave China.

With the antilandlord, anticapitalist, and antirightist campaigns in China, and especially with the Cultural Revolution (1967–1976), more and more refugees risked imprisonment and the sharks in Mirs Bay to reach Hong Kong. Inspired by the leftist fanaticism of the Red Guards in China, local sympathizers and activists in Hong Kong set off bombs, organized labor strikes, and demonstrated against the British rulers and Hong Kong's Chinese policemen. They taunted the latter by saying, "Will the British take you when they go?" But the revolutionaries did not have popular support and the disruptions lasted less than a year.

In the late 1970s half a million Chinese refugees came to Hong Kong, disillusioned with Communism and eager for a better standard of living for themselves and their families.

Until October 1980, the Hong Kong government had a curious "touch-base" policy—a critical game of "hide and seek." Any Chinese who managed to get past the barbed wire, attack dogs, and tough border patrols to the urban areas was allowed to stay and work. Manpower was needed for local industries then. At first, a similarly lenient policy was applied to the Vietnamese boat people who arrived between 1975 and 1982. More than 100,000 of these refugees were allowed to work in Hong Kong pending transfer to permanent homes abroad, and 14,000 were given permanent resident status. As the number of countries willing to take them has dwindled, Hong Kong has been detaining recently arrived refugees indefinitely in closed camps, much like prisons, in the hope that no more boat people will come.

In the early 1980s jobs became less plentiful as a result of the worldwide recession. With an ever-increasing population, the standard of services in Hong Kong began deteriorating. After consulting China, the government decreed that everyone had to carry a Hong Kong identification card.

The future of Hong Kong after the expiration of the New Territories lease on June 30, 1997 was understandably the big question hanging over the colony from the moment Britain's then prime minister, Margaret Thatcher, set foot in Beijing in September 1982, to start the talks with China's top man, Deng Xiaoping. China stated from the beginning that it wanted to repossess all of Hong Kong. Officially, Britain was willing to return only New Territories, but no one believed a Hong Kong without them would be economically viable. New Territories consists of more than 97% of the land in Hong Kong and includes most of the manufacturing facilities, the airport, and the container port.

China proposed that Hong Kong become a Special Administrative Region under the Chinese flag, with a Chinese governor. The Chinese added a 50-year guarantee of autonomy, effective July 1, 1997, labeling the deal "One country/two systems."

The negotiations between China and Britain lasted for nearly two years, with China applying pressure by announcing that if a solution were not found by September 1984, it would declare one unilaterally. An agreement was inevitable.

Hong Kong's economy didn't react well to this political uncertainty. Land prices fell. The stock market plunged by as much as 50% from late 1981 to late 1983. The Hong Kong dollar careened to almost HK$10 to the U.S. dollar in September 1983, from HK$5.7 at the end of 1981. This forced the government to intervene reluctantly by stabilizing the local unit at HK$7.80 to U.S.$1. Emigration reached record levels.

The final agreement, both signatories say, gives Hong Kong many safeguards and special freedoms that are not permitted in other regions of the People's Republic of China. After the government-backed massacre in Beijing two years ago, however, many citizens of Hong Kong and Britain are demanding that new, additional safeguards be negotiated for the Crown Colony. Today, uncertainty about Hong Kong's future as a Special Administrative Region of China continues unabated.

1 Essential Information

Before You Go

Visitor Information

Hong Kong For maps and additional information on travel to Hong Kong, contact the **Hong Kong Tourist Association (HKTA)**. There are four offices in the United States: 360 Post Street, Suite 404, San Francisco, CA 94108, tel. 415/781–4582; 333 North Michigan Avenue, Suite 2400, Chicago, IL 60601, tel. 312/782–3872; 10940 Wilshire Boulevard, Suite 1220, Los Angeles, CA 90024, tel. 213/208–4582; and 590 Fifth Avenue, Suite 590, New York, NY 10036, tel. 212/869–5008. In Great Britain: 4/F, 125 Pall Mall, London SW1Y 5EA, tel. 071/930–4775.

Macau For information on travel to Macau from North America, contact the **Macau Tourist Information Bureau (MTIB)**. There are four offices in the United States: 316, 70A Greenwich Avenue, New York, NY 10011, tel. 212/206–6828; 3133 Lake Hollywood Drive, Box 1860, Los Angeles, CA 90078, tel. 213/851–3402; Box 22188, Honolulu, HI 96922, tel. 808/538–7613; and 630 Green Bay Road, Kenilworth, IL 60043, tel. 708/251–6421. In Canada: 5059 Yonge Street, North York, Ontario M2N5P2, tel. 416/733–8768 and 1530 W. 8th Avenue, Suite 305, Vancouver, BC V6J IT5, tel. 604/736–1095. In Great Britain: 6 Sherlock Mews, Paddington Street, London W1M 3RH, tel. 071/224–3390.

Guided Tours

For a small island, Hong Kong is a big favorite with tour operators. Some 50 operators offer hundreds of packages, everything from intensive shopping and dining trips to tours pairing Hong Kong with Japan, China, Thailand, Singapore, and even India. Listed below is a select sampling of packages to give you an idea of what is available. Your travel agent or regional HKTA office can provide more details.

When considering a tour, be sure to find out (1) exactly what expenses are included (particularly tips, taxes, side trips, additional meals, and entertainment); (2) government ratings of all hotels on the itinerary and the facilities they offer; (3) cancellation policies for you and for the tour operator; and (4) the single supplement, should you be traveling alone. Most tour operators request that bookings be made through a travel agent—there is no additional charge for doing so.

General-interest Tours **Abercrombie & Kent International** (1420 Kensington Rd., Oak Brook, IL 60521, tel. 708/954–2944 or 800/323–7308) offers several deluxe tours at prices that reflect their high level of service. **InterPacific Tours International** (111 E. 15th St., New York, NY 10003, tel. 212/953–6010 or 800/221–3594) uses Hong Kong as its base of operations in the Orient and has a range of packages (and prices) as a result. Other popular operators in the area include **Pacific Delight Tours** (132 Madison Ave., New York, NY 10016, tel. 212/684–7707 or 800/221–7179) and **Japan and Orient Tours** (3131 Camino del Rio N., Suite 1080, San Diego, CA 92108, tel. 619/282–3131 or 800/877–8777).

Special-interest Tours **Shopping:** "Shop 'til you drop" is the motto of many a Hong Kong tour. **TBI Tours** (787 Seventh Ave., Suite 1101, New York, NY 10019, tel. 212/489–1919 or 800/223–0266) plunges a visitor into Hong Kong's many shops and outlets, as does **InterPacific Tours. Abercrombie & Kent** will even create a tour that combines shopping in Hong Kong with a culinary tour of Bangkok, Thailand.

Sports: InterPacific Tours has a Hong Kong/China golf package as well as jogging and bicycling trips that include a stint atop the Great Wall.

Music: Dailey-Thorp Travel (315 W. 57th St., New York, NY 10019, tel. 212/307–1555) offers deluxe opera and music tours set around special appearances by local or visiting performers.

Culture: Travel Concepts (373 Commonwealth Ave., Suite 601, Boston, MA 02115, tel. 617/266–8450) offers the splash and fun of the Hong Kong Dragon Boat Festival and International Races. *See* Festivals and Seasonal Events.

Bales Tours Ltd. (Bales House, Barrington Rd., Dorking, Surrey RH4 3EJ, tel. 0303/76881) offers several escorted journeys. A 16-day tour taking in Hong Kong, Beijing, Shanghai, and the Imperial Grand Canal is priced at £1,675 including airfare and half board. An 18-day tour that includes a cruise along the Yangtse River costs £1,998.

Kuoni Travel Ltd. (Kuoni House, Dorking, Surrey RH5, 4AZ, tel. 0306/740500) has a 10-day hotel package to Hong Kong and Bali, with an extra five nights on Bali free during certain periods. Prices per person are from £873. A 14-day package that includes Macau and Thailand as well as four nights in Hong Kong costs from £1,046. A five-night hotel package in Hong Kong ranges in price from £632 to £1,187, depending on the season. Kuoni also offers a range of half-day, full-day, and evening sightseeing tours, with prices ranging from £7 to £36.

Sovereign Holidays (Groundstar House, London Road, Crawley, West Sussex RHIO 2TB, tel. 0293/561444) offers hotel packages with prices from £547. Sovereign also has combination tours to Hong Kong, Bangkok, Singapore, and Bali (price is £1,725 for 14 nights in a first-class hotel).

Thomas Cook Faraway Holidays (Box 36, Thorpe Wood, Peterborough PE3 6SB, tel. 0733/330300) offers "The Oriental Journey," a 17-day escorted tour of Bangkok, Hong Kong, China, Singapore, and Phuket. Prices are from £1,475.

Tradwinds Faraway Holidays, (Station House, 81–83 Fulham High St., London SW6 3JP, tel. 071/731–8000) offers five or seven nights in Hong Kong with a choice of budget, first-class, or deluxe hotels. Prices (on a room-only basis, per person sharing a twin room) range from £628 to £1,044 for five nights in low season and £788 to £1,149 in high season. For seven nights the prices range from £684 to £1,347.

Contact **British Airways Pound Stretcher** (Atlantic House, Hazelwick Ave., Three Bridges, Crawley, Sussex RHIO 1NP, tel. 0293/518–060) for information about their holidays that start at £650 for five nights.

Package Deals for Independent Travelers

Japan and Orient Tours offers the "Hong Kong Travel Bargain"—with accommodations for six nights, round-trip airfare, and a sightseeing tour. **Globus-Gateway** (150 S. Los Robles

Ave., Suite 860, Pasadena, CA 91101, tel. 818/449–0919 or 800/556–5454 has a nine-day Hong Kong/Tokyo package, an 11-day Hong Kong/Singapore/Bangkok package, and others. **Cathay Pacific Airways** (tel. 800/233–2742) has a number of air/hotel packages that can include destinations other than Hong Kong. **United Airlines** (tel. 800/328–6877) offers air-inclusive hotel packages in Hong Kong as well as a five-day city package. **Gogo Tours** (69 Spring St., Ramsey, NJ 07446, tel. 201/934–3500 or 800/821–3731) serves up three- or six-night hotel packages. **American Express Vacations** (P.O. Box 5014, Atlanta, GA 30302, tel. 800/241–1700, or 800/282–0800 in Georgia) includes airfare in its eight-day "Hong Kong Express" package.

When to Go

The high tourist season, October through late-December, is popular for a reason: The weather is pleasant, with sunny days and comfortable, cool nights. January, February, and sometimes early March are not only cold but also dank, with long periods of overcast skies and rain. March and April can be either cold and miserable or beautiful and sunny. By May, the cold, damp spell has broken and the temperature is warm and comfortable. The months of June through September are the typhoon season, when the weather is hot and sticky, with lots of rain. All visitors to Hong Kong should know in advance that typhoons (called hurricanes in the Atlantic) must be treated with respect. Fortunately, Hong Kong is prepared for these blustery assaults. If a storm is approaching, the airwaves will be crackling with information, and your hotel will make certain through postings in the lobby that you know the applicable signal. In addition, public places will have postings.

When a No. 8 signal is posted, Hong Kong and Macau close down completely. Head immediately for your hotel, and stay put. This is serious business—bamboo scaffolding can come hurtling through the streets like spears, ships can be sunk in the harbor, and large areas of the colony are often flooded.

Macau's summers are slightly cooler and wetter than Hong Kong's. In the 19th century, many Hong Kong residents summered in Macau to escape the heat.

Climate The following are average daily maximum and minimum temperatures for Hong Kong.

Jan.	64F	18C	May	82F	28C	Sept.	85F	29C
	56	13		74	23		77	25
Feb.	63F	17C	June	85F	29C	Oct.	81F	27C
	55	13		78	26		73	23
Mar.	67F	19C	July	87F	31C	Nov.	74F	23C
	60	16		78	26		65	18
Apr.	75F	24C	Aug.	87F	31C	Dec.	68F	20C
	67	19		78	26		59	15

Updated hourly weather information in 750 cities around the world—450 of them in the United States—is only a phone call away. Dialing **Weather Trak** at 900/370–8725 will connect you to a computer, with which you can communicate by touch tone— at a cost of 75¢ for the first minute and 50¢ a minute thereafter. A taped message will tell you to dial the three-digit access code to any of the 750 destinations. The code is either the area code (in the United States) or the first three letters of the foreign city. For a list of all access codes send a stamped, self-addressed envelope to Cities, Box 7000, Dallas, TX 75209. For further information, phone 214/869–3035 or 800/247–3282.

Festivals and Seasonal Events

Top seasonal events in Hong Kong include Chinese New Year, in late January or February; the Hong Kong Arts Festival in January and February; the mid-June Dragon Boat Festival, probably the most colorful festival of all; the many lunar festivals celebrated throughout the year; and annual sporting events such as the Rugby Sevens in late March or early April, and the Macau Grand Prix in November. For exact dates and further details about the following events, contact the HKTA (*see* Visitor Information, above).

Jan. 1: New Year's Day is a public holiday.
Mid-Jan.–Feb.: Hong Kong Arts Festival takes place in theaters and halls throughout Hong Kong.
Late Jan.: Hong Kong Marathon is sponsored by the Hong Kong Distance Runner's Club.
Late Jan.–Feb.: Chinese New Year is a time to visit friends and relatives and wear new clothes, and a time when the city virtually comes to a standstill.
Feb. or Mar.: Spring Lantern Festival is on the last day of Chinese New Year celebrations, when streets and homes are decorated with brightly colored lanterns.
Early Mar.: Hong Kong Open Golf Championship, at the Royal Hong Kong Golf Club in Fanling.
Late Mar. or early Apr.: The Invitation Sevens, a premier event, is a rugby tournament sponsored by Cathay Pacific and the Hong Kong Bank.
Late Mar. or early Apr.: Easter holidays.
Early Apr.: Ching Ming Festival is the time when families visit the burial plots of ancestors and departed relatives.
Late Mar. or early Apr.: Hong Kong International Film Festival features films and film stars from several countries and is a busy, rewarding fortnight for film buffs.
Late Apr. or early May: Birthday of Tin Hau, goddess of the sea. Fishermen decorate their boats and converge on seaside temples to honor Tin Hau. Everyone even remotely connected with the sea happily participates, including some commuters who use the Hong Kong ferries. The busiest area is around the Tin Hau Temple in Junk Bay.
May: Birthday of Lord Buddha, when temples throughout the territory bathe the sacred Buddha's statue. The Po Lin Monastery on Lantau Island has ceremonies as elaborate as any.
May: Bun Festival on Cheung Chau Island is a three-day spirit-placating rite that culminates in a grand procession with young children taking part in tableaux. Thousands of people converge for the finale.
June: Birthday of Her Majesty the Queen is a public holiday.
May or June: Dragon Boat Festival pits dragon-head boats against each other in races to commemorate the hero, Ch'u Yuen. The long and many-oared boats are rowed to the beat of a drum. International races, sponsored by the HKTA, follow a week later.
Mid-Aug.: Seven Sisters (Maiden) Festival is a celebration for lovers and a time when young girls pray for a good husband.

Aug.: Hungry Ghosts Festival is a time when food is set out to placate roaming spirits temporarily released from hell. Offerings are made everywhere.

Sept.: Mid-Autumn and Lantern Festival brings families together. Mooncakes are eaten while the moon rises. More public and spectacular are the crowds with candle lanterns that gather in the park and other open spaces.

Late Sept. or early Oct.: Birthday of Confucius marks special remembrances of the revered philosopher.

Mid-Oct.: Chung Yeung Festival commemorates a Han Dynasty tale about a man taking his family to high ground to avoid disaster.

Late Nov.: Macau Grand Prix is unavoidable if you happen to be in Macau this weekend, as the racing is done in the streets and it's none too peaceful.

Mid-Dec.: Hong Kong Judo Championship takes place at Queen Elizabeth Stadium.

What to Pack

Whatever the time of year, it is wise to pack a folding umbrella. From May to September, lightweight short-sleeve or sleeveless clothes in cotton or linen are most suitable for the high humidity. Bring some comfortable shoes and loose-fitting cotton shorts for walking. Air-conditioning in hotels and restaurants can be glacial, so women should bring a sweater or shawl for evening use indoors. Don't forget your swimsuit and high-protection suntan lotion. Several hotels have pools, and you may want to spend some time on one of the many beaches. Dress in Hong Kong is fairly informal, but a few hotels and restaurants do insist on a jacket and tie for men in the evenings. It is best to pack a lightweight summer jacket.

In October, November, March, and April, a jacket or sweater should suffice, but during the winter months, December to February, you should bring a raincoat or a light overcoat. It never really gets cold enough to wear furs, but you will see them worn by fashion-conscious Hong Kong women as soon as the first winter breezes blow.

Taking Money Abroad

The safest way to carry money abroad is in the form of traveler's checks, which are insured by the issuing company against loss or theft. The most recognized traveler's checks are American Express, Barclays, Thomas Cook, and those issued through major commercial banks such as Citibank and Bank of America. Some banks will issue checks free to established customers, but most charge a 1% commission fee. Be sure to keep a note of the check numbers in a separate place from the checks themselves so you have a record if they are lost.

Buy some of the traveler's checks in small denominations to cash toward the end of your trip. This will save you from having to cash a large check and ending up with more foreign money than you need.

All major credit cards are widely accepted, except in some of the smaller restaurants and shops.

Although you won't get as good an exchange rate at home as abroad, it's wise to change a small amount of money into Hong

Kong dollars before you go to avoid long lines at airport currency exchange booths. Most U.S. banks will exchange your money into Hong Kong dollars. If your local bank can't provide this service, you can exchange money through Deak International. To find the office nearest you, contact them at 630 Fifth Avenue, New York, NY 10111, tel. 212/757–6915 or 800/448–6516.

Getting Money from Home

There are at least three ways to get money from home:

(1) Have it sent through a large commercial bank with a branch in Hong Kong. The only drawback is that you must have an account with the bank; if not, you'll have to go through your own bank and the process will be slower and more expensive.

2) Have it sent through American Express. If you are a cardholder, you can cash a personal check or a counter check at an American Express office for up to $1,000 ($5,000 if you have a gold card); up to $500 will be in cash and the rest in traveler's checks. There is a 1% commission on the traveler's checks. American Express has a new service that should be available in most major cities worldwide by January 1989, called American Express MoneyGram. Through this service, you can receive up to $10,000 cash. It works this way: you call home and ask someone to go to an American Express office or an American Express MoneyGram agent (located in a retail outlet) and fill out an American Express MoneyGram. It can be paid for with cash or any major credit card. The person making the payment is given a reference number and telephones you with that number. The American Express MoneyGram agent calls an 800 number and authorizes the transfer of funds to an American Express office or a participating agency in Hong Kong. In most cases, the money is available immediately on a 24-hour basis. You pick it up by showing identification and giving the reference number. Fees vary according to the amount sent. To send $300, the fee is $30; for $5,000, $195. For the American Express MoneyGram location nearest your home, and to find out where the service is available overseas, call 800/543–4080. You do not have to be a cardholder to use this service.

3) Have it sent through Western Union. The U.S. number is 800/325–6000. If you have a MasterCard or Visa, you can have money sent for any amount up to your credit limit. If not, have someone take cash or a certified cashier's check to a Western Union office. The money will be delivered in two business days to a branch of Citibank in Hong Kong (Wheelock House, Pedder St., Central, or 72 Nathan Road, Tsimshatsui, Kowloon). Fees vary with the amount of money sent: for $1,000 the fee is $69; for $500, $59.

Currency

The units of currency in Hong Kong are the Hong Kong dollar ($) and the cent. There are bills of 1,000, 500, 100, 50, 20, and 10 dollars. Coins are 5, 2, and 1 dollars and 50, 20, and 10 cents. The Hong Kong dollar is fixed at 7.8 dollars to the U.S. dollar. At press time (mid-1991), it was 6.74 to the Canadian dollar, and 13.9 to the pound sterling.

There are no currency restrictions in Hong Kong. Moneychanging facilities are available at the airport, in hotels, in banks, and at private money changers scattered through the tourist areas. You will get better rates from a bank or money changer than from a hotel. However, be aware of money changers who advertise "no selling commission" and do not mention the "buying commission" you must pay when you exchange foreign currency or traveler's checks for Hong Kong dollars.

The official currency unit in Macau is the pataca, which is divided into 100 avos. Bank notes come in five denominations: 500, 100, 50, 10, and 5 patacas; coins are 5 and 1 patacas and 50, 20, and 10 avos. The pataca is pegged to the Hong Kong dollar (within a few cents). Hong Kong currency circulates freely in Macau but not vice versa, so remember to change your patacas before you return to Hong Kong.

What It Will Cost

Hotels   Aside from a few guest houses and hostels (*see* Student and Youth Travel, below), prices start at the equivalent of U.S.$50 to U.S.$60 per night; a 10% service charge, and a 5% government service charge are added.

Food   It is still possible to go into a small Chinese restaurant and have a bowl of noodles and Chinese tea for the equivalent of about U.S.$2. Portions of dim sum, a smorgasbord of Chinese specialties served in small portions, plate by plate, can be had for as low as HK$5. You could have a splendid meal, with a couple of beers and Chinese tea, for about HK$60, or the equivalent of U.S.$7.50. Posh Western and Chinese restaurants, in contrast, are expensive. A three-course steak meal at your hotel grill could easily set you back HK$300 to HK$400 (U.S.$38–U.S.$51), plus a 10% service charge, excluding cocktails and wine.

Shopping   Clothing is high on everyone's shopping list. Foreign brands will be a big bargain if you shop in street markets such as the one in Stanley Village, less so in luxury shopping complexes such as The Landmark or the hotel arcades. That famous Hong Kong made-to-measure suit is still a very good deal. Remember that goods (with the exception of alcohol, tobacco, petroleum products, perfume, cosmetics, and soft drinks) are duty-free, everywhere in Hong Kong, not just in stores touting that they are duty-free. Also, there are no sales taxes or Value Added Taxes, except for the 5% hotel room tax and the airport departure taxes. Bargaining, particularly at street markets and at small camera and hi-fi shops, is a must.

Tipping   Hotels and major restaurants add a 10% service charge. In many of the more traditional Chinese restaurants, a waiter will bring small snacks at the beginning of the meal and charge them to you, even if you did not order them. This money is in lieu of a service charge. It is customary to leave an additional 10% tip in all restaurants, and in taxis and beauty salons.

Sample Prices   HK$14–HK$24/U.S.$1.80–U.S.$3, plus 10% (hotel coffee *Cup of Coffee*   shop).
HK$4.50/U.S.$.58 (McDonald's).

Hamburger   HK$40–HK$50/U.S.$5–U.S.$6.50 (hotel coffee shop).
HK$4/U.S.$.50 (McDonald's).

Soft Drink	HK$16–HK$25/U.S.$2–U.S.$3.20, plus 10% (hotel bar). HK$3.30/U.S.$.42 (McDonald's, medium).
Beer	HK$15–HK$30/U.S.$2–U.S.$4 (pub, hotel bar). HK$20–HK$50/U.S.$2.50–U.S.$6.40 (bar, hostess club).
Whiskey	HK$22–HK$40/U.S.$2.80–U.S.$5 (pub, hotel bar).
Taxi	HK$8/U.S.$1 first 2 km (1.25 mi).
Subway	HK$3–HK$7/U.S.$.38–U.S.$.90.
Double Room	HK$230/U.S.$29.50 (budget guest house). HK$550–HK$700/U.S.$70–U.S.$90 (moderate hotel).
Tailored Suit	HK$1,500–HK$3,500/U.S.$192–U.S.$448.70.

Passports and Visas

Americans Passports are required for entering Hong Kong. Applications for a new passport must be made in person; renewals can be obtained in person or by mail (*see* below). First-time applicants should apply well in advance of their departure date to one of the 13 U.S. Passport Agency offices. In addition, local county courthouses, many state and probate courts, and some post offices accept passport applications. Necessary documents include: (1) a completed passport application (Form DSP-11); (2) proof of citizenship (birth certificate with raised seal or naturalization papers); (3) proof of identity (unexpired driver's license, employee ID card, or any other document with your photograph and signature); (4) two recent, identical, two-inch square photographs (black-and-white or color); (5) $42 application fee for a 10-year passport (those under 18 pay $27 for a five-year passport). If you pay in cash, you must have the exact amount. No change is given. Passports are mailed to you within about 10 working days. To renew your passport by mail, you'll need a completed Form DSP-82, two recent, identical passport photographs, a recent passport less than 12 years old from the date of issue, and a check or money order for $35.

Visas are not required of U.S. citizens visiting Hong Kong for up to 30 days. For longer stays, contact the British Embassy, 3100 Massachusetts Ave., NW, Washington, DC 20008, tel. 202/462–1340.

Canadians Canadian citizens need a passport to enter Hong Kong. Send a completed application (available at any post office or passport office) to the Bureau of Passports (Suite 215, West Tower, Guy Favreau Complex, 200 René Lévesque Blvd. West, Montréal, Québec H2Z1X4). Include $25, two photographs, a guarantor, and proof of Canadian citizenship. Applications can be made in person at the regional passport offices in Calgary, Edmonton, Halifax, Montreal, Toronto, St. John's (Newfoundland), Vancouver, Victoria, or Winnipeg. Passports are valid for five years and are nonrenewable.

Visas are not required of Canadian citizens visiting Hong Kong for up to 90 days.

Britons All British citizens are required to have a passport to enter Hong Kong. Application forms are available from travel agencies and main post offices. Send the completed form to a regional passport office or apply in person at a main post office. The application must be countersigned by your bank manager, or by a solicitor, barrister, doctor, clergyman, or justice of the peace who knows you personally. In addition, you'll need two photographs and the £15 fee. The occasional tourist might opt for a British visitors passport. It is valid for one year, costs £7.50 and is nonrenewable. You'll need two passport photographs and identification. Apply at your local post office.

U.S. citizens holding valid passports may visit Hong Kong for one month without a visa, provided they have an onward or return ticket and enough money for their stay. Europeans, South Americans, most Asians, Commonwealth citizens, and nationals of non-Communist countries may visit for one to three months without a visa under the same conditions. Canadians are usually granted stays of three months. Holders of British passports issued in the United Kingdom may visit Hong Kong for six months; no visas are required. Britons will, however, need a visa if they plan a side trip to China. Apply for visas (£20) through the Chinese Embassy (31 Portland Pl., London W1N 3AH, tel. 071/636–5637) or obtain one easily in Hong Kong from China Travel Service offices (78 Connaught Rd. Central, tel. 853–3888; or 27 Nathan Rd., Kowloon, tel. 721–1331) or through travel agents. As a rule, extensions are readily granted. Questions about visas, once you're in Hong Kong, should be directed to: the Department of Immigration (Wanchai Tower, 7 Gloucester Rd., Hong Kong, tel. 824–6111).

To enter the neighboring territory of Macau, visas are not required for citizens of the United States, Canada, the United Kingdom, Australia, and most Western European and Asian countries. Nationals of countries that do not maintain diplomatic relations with Portugal may not obtain visas upon arrival, but must obtain them from Portuguese consulates overseas. Contact the Portuguese Consulate (1001–2, Tower II, Exchange Sq., 8 Connaught Pl., Hong Kong, tel. 523–1338), which is open weekdays 9–2:30.

Customs and Duties

On Arrival Except for the usual prohibitions against narcotics, explosives, firearms, and ammunition, and modest limits on alcohol, tobacco products, and perfume, you can bring anything you want into Hong Kong, including an unlimited amount of money.

Nonresident visitors may bring in, duty free, 200 cigarettes or 50 cigars or 250 grams of tobacco, and one liter of alcohol.

On Departure With the exception of narcotics, explosives, firearms, and ammunition, you can take anything you want out of Hong Kong. There are no restrictions on currency.

Americans. U.S. residents may bring home duty-free up to $400 worth of foreign goods, so long as they have been out of the country for at least 48 hours and haven't made an international trip in 30 days. Each member of the family is entitled to the same exemption, regardless of age, and exemptions can be pooled. For the next $1,000 worth of goods, a flat 10% rate is assessed; above $1,400, duties vary with the merchandise. Included for travelers 21 or older are one liter of alcohol, 100 cigars (non-Cuban), and 200 cigarettes. Only one bottle of perfume trademarked in the United States may be imported. However, there is no duty on antiques or art more than 100 years old. Anything exceeding these limits will be taxed at the port of entry and may be taxed additionally in the traveler's home state. Gifts valued at less than $50 may be mailed to friends or relatives at home duty-free, but must not exceed one package per day to any one addressee and must not include perfumes costing more than $5, tobacco, or liquor.

Canadians. Canadian residents have an exemption ranging from $20 to $300, depending on the length of stay out of the country. For the $300 exemption, you must have been out of the country for one week. For any given year, you are allowed one $300 exemption. You may also bring in duty-free: (1) up to 50 cigars, 200 cigarettes, and 2.2 pounds of tobacco; and (2) 40 ounces of liquor, provided these are declared in writing to customs on arrival and accompany the traveler in hand or checked-through baggage. Personal gifts should be mailed as "Unsolicited Gift—Value under $40." Request the Canadian Customs brochure, *I Declare*, for further details.

Britons. Returning to Britain you may bring home: (1) 200 cigarettes or 100 cigarillos or 50 cigars or 250 grams of tobacco; (2) two liters of table wine with additional allowances for (a) one liter of alcohol over 22% by volume (38.8 proof; most spirits) or (b) two liters of alcohol under 22% by volume (fortified or sparkling wine) or (c) two more liters of table wine and (3) 60 milliliters of perfume and 250 milliliters of toilet water, and (4) other goods up to a value of £32, but not more than 50 liters of beer or 25 lighters.

Traveling with Film

Don't pack your unprocessed film in your checked luggage; if your bags get X-rayed, you may be saying goodbye to your photographs. Carry the undeveloped film with you through security and ask to have it inspected by hand. It helps if you keep your film in a separate plastic bag, ready for quick inspection. Inspectors at U.S. airports are required by law to honor requests for hand inspection; abroad, you'll have to depend on the kindness of strangers. The danger is that the old airport scanning machines—still in use in some third-world countries—use heavy doses of radiation that can turn a family portrait into an early morning fog. The newer models—used in all U.S. airports—are safe for anything from five to 500 scans, depending on the speed of your film. The effects are cumulative; you can put the same roll of film through several scans without worry. After five scans, you're asking for trouble.

If your film gets fogged and you want an explanation, send it to: National Association of Photographic Manufacturers (550 Mamaroneck Ave., Harrison, NY 10528). They will try to determine what went wrong. The service is free.

Language

The official languages of Hong Kong are English and Chinese. The most commonly spoken Chinese dialect is Cantonese, but Mandarin is gaining popularity because it is the official language of China. In Macau, the languages are, officially, Portuguese and Chinese, but many people speak some English.

In hotels, major restaurants, shops, and tourist centers, almost everyone speaks fluent English. However, this is not the case with taxi drivers and workers in small shops and market stalls. In a local street café, you may not find anyone who speaks English, or an English-language menu, and you will have to resort to pointing at the food on someone else's table.

It is possible to do business for years without knowing more than a few polite phrases in Chinese and a snatch of taxi-driver's lingo. But, in an office, you must have at least one good bilingual secretary.

There may come a time when you need an official translator or an official translation of a document. The hotel business centers can be of assistance as can those outside the hotels. For specialist work in all languages, try **Translanguage Center** (1604 Tung Wah Mansion, 199 Hennessy Rd., Wanchai, Hong Kong Island, tel. 573–2728) or **Polyglot Translations** (1702 H.K. Chinese Bank Bldg., 61 Des Voeux Rd., Central, Hong Kong Island, tel. 521–5689).

Staying Healthy

There are no serious health risks associated with travel to Hong Kong, but you should remember that you are in the tropics and need to protect yourself from the fierce midday sun, from 11 AM to 3 PM. Wear a hat and try not to rush around. Drink plenty of liquids and if you feel tired, *rest*. In the summer, try to do your walking and sightseeing in the early morning and late afternoon.

The **International Association for Medical Assistance to Travelers** (IAMAT) is a worldwide association offering a list of approved doctors whose training meets very high standards. For a list of Hong Kong physicians and clinics that are part of this network, contact IAMAT (417 Center St., Lewiston, NY 14092, tel. 716/754–4883; in Canada, 40 Regal Rd., Guelph, Ont. NIK 1B5; in Europe, 57 Voirets, 1212 Grand Lancy, Geneva, Switzerland). Membership is free.

Shots and Medications Inoculations and antimalaria drugs are not needed for Hong Kong. If you have a health problem that might require purchasing prescription drugs while in Hong Kong, have your doctor write a prescription using the drug's generic name.

Water Although the Hong Kong government declares that the water is safe to drink, even locals prefer to boil it or to drink mineral water in bottles.

Insurance

Travelers may want insurance coverage in three areas: health and accident, loss of luggage, and trip cancellation. Your first step is to review your existing health and homeowner policies; some health insurance plans cover health expenses incurred while traveling, some major medical plans cover emergency transportation, and some homeowner policies cover the theft of luggage.

Health and Accident Several companies offer coverage designed to supplement existing health insurance for travelers:

Carefree Travel Insurance (Box 310, 120 Mineola Blvd., Mineola, NY 11501, tel. 516/294–0220 or 800/323–3149) provides coverage for emergency medical evacuation and accidental death and dismemberment. It also offers 24-hour medical phone advice. **International SOS Assistance** (Box 11568, Philadelphia, PA

19116, tel. 215/244–1500 or 800/523–8930), a medical assistance company, provides emergency evacuation services, worldwide medical referrals, and optional medical insurance.
Travel Guard International, underwritten by Transamerica Occidental Life Companies (1145 Clark St., Stevens Pt., WI 54481, tel. 715/345–0505 or 800/782–5151), offers reimbursement for medical expenses with no deductibles or daily limits, and emergency evacuation services.
Wallach & Co., Inc., Health Care Abroad (243 Church St. NW, Suite 100D, Vienna, VA 22180, tel. 703/281–9500 or 800/237–6615) offers comprehensive medical coverage.

For British travelers we recommend that you insure yourself against health and motoring accidents. **Europ Assistance** (252 High St., Croydon, Surrey CR0 1NF, tel. 081/680–1234) is a firm that offers this service. It is also wise to take out insurance to cover loss of luggage (though check that this isn't already covered in any existing homeowner policies you may have). Trip cancellation insurance is another wise buy. **The Association of British Insurers** (Aldermary House, Queen St., London EC4N 1TT, tel. 071/248–4477) will give comprehensive advice on all aspects of vacation insurance.

Lost Luggage Luggage loss is usually covered as part of a comprehensive travel-insurance package that includes personal accident, trip cancellation, and sometimes default and bankruptcy insurance. Several companies offer comprehensive policies, including **Access America, Inc.,** a subsidiary of Blue Cross Blue Shield (Box 11188, Richmond, VA 23230, tel. 800/334–7525 or 800/284–8300).
Near Services. (450 Prairie Ave., Suite 101, Calumet City, IL 60409, tel. 708/868–6700 or 800/654–6700).
Travel Guard International (*see* Health and Accident Insurance, above).
Tele-Trip (Box 31685, 3201 Farnam St., Omaha, NE 68131, tel. 800/228–9792), a subsidiary of Mutual of Omaha, and **The Travelers Corporation** (Ticket and Travel Dept., 1 Tower Sq., Hartford, CT 06183, tel. 203/277–0111 or 800/243–3174). Tele-Trip operates sales booths at airports and issues insurance through travel agents. It will insure checked luggage for up to 180 days; rates vary according to the length of the trip. The Travelers Corporation will insure checked or hand luggage for $500 to $2,000 valuation per person, and also for a maximum of 180 days. Rates for one to five days for $500 valuation are $10; for 180 days, $85.

Before you go, itemize the contents of each bag in case you need to file an insurance claim. If your luggage is stolen and later recovered, the airline must deliver the luggage to your home, free of charge.

Trip Cancellation Flight insurance is often included in the price of a ticket when paid for with American Express, Visa, or other major credit cards. It is usually included in combination with travel-insurance packages available from most tour operators, travel agents, and insurance agents.

Car Rentals

It is unlikely you will want to rent a car in Hong Kong. The driving conditions are difficult, traffic is constantly jammed, and parking is usually impossible. Public transportation is excellent and the taxis are inexpensive. If you do decide to rent a car, take one *with* a driver. Several operators offer such services, which can be arranged through your hotel. Charges are from HK$400 for the first three hours, and from HK$130 for each subsequent hour.

If you are determined to drive yourself, you'll need an international driver's license. Car rental companies in Hong Kong include: **Avis** (50 Po Loi St., Zung Fu Car Park, Hunghom, Kowloon, tel. 334–6007), **National Car Rental** (Tung Ming Building, Des Voeux Rd., Central, tel. 525–1365), **Fung Hing Hire Co.** (58 Village Rd., Happy Valley, Hong Kong, tel. 572–0333), and **Mutual Transport & Trading Co.** (39 Tak Wan Shopping Arcade, 1st fl., 12 Pak Kung St., Hunghom, Kowloon, tel. 363–6939).

Student and Youth Travel

Although there are few student discounts available, Hong Kong is within the budget of the student traveler once accommodations have been found. Inexpensive digs include the **Chungking Mansions** (Nathan Rd., Tsimshatsui, Kowloon), offering a rabbit warren of not-so-clean rooms for about U.S.$25 to U.S.$30. Holders of **International Youth Hostels** cards may contact Room 1408A, Watson's Estate, Watson's Road, North Point, Hong Kong, tel. 570–6222, to see if there is space in the territory's very crowded hostels. The **YMCA** (41 Salisbury Rd., Tsimshatsui, Kowloon, tel. 369–2211), across from the Peninsula Hotel, is the most popular place for inexpensive accommodations, but it is hard to get a booking.

An International Student Identity Card is of value at the **Hong Kong Student Travel Bureau** (1021 Star House, Salisbury Rd., Kowloon, tel. 730–3269). They can help you with travel discounts and sometimes with discounted lodging rates.

Traveling with Children

Publications *Family Travel Times* is an eight- to 12-page newsletter published 10 times a year by **Travel With Your Children** (TWYCH; 80 Eighth Ave., New York, NY 10011, tel. 212/206–0688). Subscription costs $35 and includes access to back issues and twice-weekly opportunities to call in for specific advice.
Hong Kong for Kids is a free brochure published by the HKTA (590 Fifth Ave., 5th floor, New York, NY 10036, tel. 212/869–5008).

Family Travel Organizations **American Institute for Foreign Study** (102 Greenwich Ave., Greenwich, CT 06830, tel. 203/869–9090) offers a family vacation program in Hong Kong and China specifically designed for parents and children.
Rascals in Paradise Family Vacation (Adventure Express, 650 Fifth Ave., Suite 505, San Francisco, CA 94107, tel. 800/443–0799) organizes tours to Hong Kong and China accompanied by a preschool teacher (depending on the age of the children) and emphasizes cultural exchange with visits to schools and lessons on such things as how to write your name in Chinese.

Hotels Almost all hotels allow children under 12 to stay in their parents' room free of charge. Some raise the age limit to 18. Most hotel restaurants offer children's plates, and English-language children's programs appear on television.

Getting There On international flights, children under two not occupying a seat pay 10% of adult fare. Various discounts apply to children two to 12 years of age.

Regulations about infant travel on airplanes are in the process of changing. Until they do, however, if you want to be sure your infant is secure and traveling in his or her own safety seat, you must buy a separate ticket and bring your own infant car seat. (Check with the airline in advance; certain seats aren't allowed.) Some airlines allow babies to travel in their own car seats at no charge if there's a spare seat available, otherwise safety seats will be stored and the child will have to be held by a parent. (For the booklet *Child/Infant Safety Seats Acceptable for Use in Aircraft*, write to the Federal Aviation Administration, APA-200, 800 Independence Ave., SW, Washington DC 20591 tel. 202/267–3479.) If you opt to hold your baby on your lap, do so with the infant outside the seatbelt so he or she won't be crushed in case of a sudden stop.

Also inquire about special children's meals or snacks. The February 1990 and 1992 issues of *Family Travel Times* include "TWYCH's Airline Guide," which contains a rundown of the children's services offered by 46 airlines.

Baby-sitting Child-care arrangements are usually easy to make through the
Services hotel concierge.

Hints for Disabled Travelers

Hong Kong is not the easiest of cities for people in wheelchairs because there are few ramps or special accesses. Progress is being made, however, and the airport, City Hall, Hong Kong Arts Centre, and the Academy for Performing Arts all have made efforts to assist people in wheelchairs. *A Guide for Physically Handicapped Visitors in Hong Kong* is available through the HKTA, and will prove invaluable. Not only does it list those rare places that have special facilities for the handicapped, but it also explains the best access to hotels, shopping centers, government offices, consulates, restaurants, and churches.

The Information Center for Individuals with Disabilities (Fort Point Place, 1st fl., 27–43 Wormwood St., Boston, MA 02210–1606, tel. 617/727–5540) offers useful problem-solving assistance, including lists of travel agents that specialize in tours for the disabled.
Moss Rehabilitation Hospital Travel Information Service (1200 West Tabor Rd., Philadelphia, PA 19141–3009, tel. 215/456–9600; TDD 215/456–9602) provides information on tourist sights, transportation, and accommodations in destinations around the world.
Mobility International USA (Box 3551, Eugene, OR 97403, tel. 503/343–1284) is an internationally affiliated organization with 500 members. For a $20 annual fee, it coordinates exchange programs for disabled people around the world and offers information on accommodations and organized study programs.
The Society for the Advancement of Travel for the Handicapped (26 Court St., Penthouse, Brooklyn, NY 11242, tel. 718/858–5483) offers access information. Annual membership costs $45, or $25 for senior travelers and students. Send $1 and a self-addressed envelope for specific information.
Travel Industry and Disabled Exchange (TIDE, 5435 Donna Ave., Tarzana, CA 91356, tel. 818/368–5648) is an industry-

based organization with a $15 per person annual membership fee. Members receive a quarterly newsletter and information on travel agencies and tours.

The Itinerary (Box 2012, Bayonne, NJ 07002, tel. 201/858–3400) is a bimonthly travel magazine for the disabled.

Hints for Older Travelers

The American Association of Retired Persons (AARP, 1909 K St. NW, Washington, DC 20049, tel. 202/662–4850) has two programs for independent travelers: (1) *The Purchase Privilege Program*, which offers discounts on hotels, airfare, car rentals, and sightseeing; and (2) the *AARP Motoring Plan*, provided by Amoco, which offers emergency aid and trip routing information for an annual fee of $33.95 per couple. The AARP also arranges group tours through **American Express Vacations** (Box 5014, Atlanta, GA 30302, tel. 800/241–1700 or, in GA, 800/637–6200).

When using an AARP or other identification card, ask for a reduced hotel rate at the time you make your reservation, not when you check out. At participating restaurants, show your card to the maitre d' before you're seated, since discounts may be limited to certain set menus, days, or hours. When renting a car, be sure to ask about special promotional rates, which may offer greater savings than the available discount.

Elderhostel (75 Federal St., 3rd floor, Boston, MA 02210, tel. 617/426–7788) is an innovative educational program for people 60 and older. Participants live in dorms on some 1,200 campuses around the world. Mornings are devoted to lectures and seminars; afternoons, to sightseeing and field trips. The all-inclusive fee for two to three week trips, including room, board, tuition, and round-trip transportation, ranges from $1,800 to $4,500.

National Council of Senior Citizens (925 15th St. NW, Washington, DC 20005, tel. 202/347–8800) is a nonprofit advocacy group with some 5,000 local clubs across the country. Annual membership is $12 per person or per couple. Members receive a monthly newspaper with travel information and an ID card for reduced-rate hotels and car rentals.

Mature Outlook (6001 N. Clark St., Chicago, IL 60660, tel. 800/336–6330), a subsidiary of Sears Roebuck & Co., is a travel club for people over 50, with discounts at Holiday Inns (including those in Hong Kong) and a bimonthly newsletter. Annual membership for U.S. residents only is $9.95 per couple. Instant membership is available at participating Holiday Inns.

Further Reading

James Clavell's *Taipan* and *Noble House* are blockbuster novels covering the early history of the British colony and the multifaceted life found there around the 1950s. Both books provide insights, sometimes sensationalized, sometimes accurate. Robert S. Elegant's *Dynasty* is another epic novel tracing the development of a powerful Eurasian family. It has some simplified history, but it does reveal a lot about the way that locals think. Another bestseller set in Hong Kong is John LeCarre's *The Honorable Schoolboy*, a superb spy thriller. On a smaller scale is Han Suyin's *A Many Splendoured Thing*. Another classic novel is Richard Mason's *The World of Suzie Wong*, which covers an American's adventures with a young woman in the Wanchai bar area. Austin Coates's *Myself a Mandarin* is a lively and humorous account of a European magistrate handling Chinese society, and his *City of Broken Promises* is a rags-to-riches biography of an 18th-century woman from Macau.

Maurice Collis's beautifully written classic, *Foreign Mud*, covers the early opium trade and China wars. G.B. Endicott's *History of Hong Kong* traces Hong Kong from its beginnings to the riot-wracked 1960s. Trea Wiltshire's *Hong Kong: Improbable Journey* focuses exclusively on recent times. Richard Hughes's *Borrowed Time, Borrowed Place* looks at Hong Kong immediately before the signing of the 1984 Sino-British Agreement that will give Hong Kong back to the People's Republic of China in 1997. David Bonavia's *Hong Kong 1997: The Final Settlement* provides history and analysis of the agreement.

There are many specialist publications available for the businessperson. *The Wall Street Journal Guides for Business Travelers-Asia* provides thorough coverage of Hong Kong, including ratings of hotels and restaurants. Most of the banks and major realty companies publish economic newsletters for their customers. The Hong Kong Trade Development Council publishes eight product magazines that are on sale in Hong Kong or free to qualified companies. The Asian Sources series has 11 product magazines and one newsletter. Business International has newsletters and studies on China and Asia. Asia Letter also has a series of newsletters on Asia and specific countries. The American Chamber of Commerce publishes books on Hong Kong and China, including *Living in Hong Kong*, *Doing Business in Hong Kong*, and *Establishing an Office in Hong Kong*, which are available to members and nonmembers. The *Far Eastern Economic Review Yearbook* and the Hong Kong Government *Yearbook* are required reference books; the *Monthly Digest* from the government's Census & Statistics Department may also be useful. *Hong Kong Tax Planning*, as the name implies, is a useful book to cut through all the legalese of Hong Kong's tax codes. The China Phone Book Co. publishes a slew of useful publications on China in addition to their telephone and telex directories.

Arriving and Departing

From North America by Plane

Airport Efficiency is the word at the Hong Kong International Airport. Except for peak periods, you should locate your luggage and clear customs and immigration in less than 45 minutes.

There are free carts in the baggage area that you can wheel straight through to the exits marked Groups, Hotel Cars, Greeting Area, and Transportation Terminal (for taxis and buses into town). There are also airport porters available to help you, for HK$2 per piece of luggage.

The HKTA has an **Information Counter** just outside the customs hall where you can pick up free visitor publications and make inquiries. The **Hong Kong Hotels Association (HKHA)** runs a reservations service there, too. Both desks are open daily from 8 AM to 10:30 PM. Banks and currency exchange counters are also in this area.

At the airport, the departure tax is HK$150 (free for children under 11). This is collected at the airline check-in counters, though some travel agents will collect it when you buy your tickets. No flight-boarding announcements are made, so check developments on the arrivals and departures boards.

Luggage Storage   There is a place to store your luggage in the departure hall. The charge is HK$15 per piece per day for the first four days, and HK $25 per day thereafter.

Phone Calls   Overseas phone calls can be made from the **Cable and Wireless** (C&W) office in the departure or transit halls.

The Airlines   **United Airlines** (tel. 800/241–6522) flies daily out of New York and Chicago, with stops on the West Coast and in Tokyo. It also flies out of Los Angeles, with stops in Honolulu and Tokyo, and has nonstop flights from Seattle and San Francisco. **Northwest** (tel. 800/225–2525) has departures from New York and Chicago that go via the West Coast and Tokyo. It also has flights from Seattle, San Francisco, and Los Angeles via Tokyo. **Cathay Pacific Airways** (tel. 800/233–2742 in the USA; in Canada 800/663–1338) has daily nonstop service out of Vancouver and four nonstop flights a week from Los Angeles. **Canadian Airlines International** (tel. 800/426–7000 in CA) flies six times a week out of Vancouver, all flights direct to Hong Kong. **Singapore Airlines** (tel. 800/742–3333) flies daily out of San Francisco and three times a week from Los Angeles, all via Honolulu.

Flying Times   From New York, via Tokyo, 20 hours, via Seattle or San Francisco (and then nonstop to Hong Kong), also 20 hours—but you avoid crowded conditions and probable delays at Tokyo's Narita Airport; from Chicago, via Tokyo, 20 hours; from Los Angeles, via Honolulu, 17 hours; and from San Francisco or Los Angeles, direct, 13 hours.

Luggage Regulations
Carry-on Luggage   If you are flying to and from Hong Kong directly, you will be able to take two bags. The heaviest cannot weigh more than 70 pounds. The total dimensions cannot exceed 107" (length + width + height), and the largest bag cannot be more than 62 inches. You are allowed one carry-on piece of luggage, plus a handbag. If you stop en route, you can only check luggage totaling 44 pounds if you are flying economy class, 66 pounds if flying business or first class. You will be allowed one piece of carry-on luggage in addition to a handbag, duty-free shopping bag, or camera case. Leaving Hong Kong, the carry-on piece must be able to fit inside a 22" × 14" × 9" box, unless it is a garment bag. If you can't meet these regulations, ask an airline supervisor for an exemption. You can usually get one, but don't count on it.

Checked Luggage   U.S. airlines allow passengers to check in two or three suitcases whose total dimensions (length + width + height) do not exceed 62" and whose weight does not exceed 70 pounds per piece.

Rules governing foreign airlines vary from airline to airline, so check with your travel agent or the airline itself before you go. All the airlines allow passengers to check in two bags. In general, expect the weight restriction on the two bags to be not more than 70 pounds each, and the size restriction of each bag to be 62" total dimensions.

Labeling Luggage   Be sure to put your business address on each piece of luggage, including hand luggage.

Enjoying   The key to successful, long-haul flying is comfort. Loose-fitting
the Flight   casual clothes are a must unless business formality requires otherwise. Your carry-on luggage should have enough toiletries to help you freshen up before arrival and to hold you over in an airport. Feet swell at high altitudes, so consider taking off your shoes. Jet lag will be eased by going easy on food and alcohol. It's important, though, to drink plenty of nonalcoholic liquids. For sleeping, there are those who swear by an aisle seat for legroom, and others who prefer window seats for something to lean against. Middle seats are to be avoided. Pipes and cigars are forbidden on all flights. Nonsmokers should ask for seats as far away from the smoking section as possible. U.S. airlines are required by law to find nonsmoking seats for all passengers on the day of the flight, provided they meet check-in time restrictions.

Between the   There is often a long line for taxis, so if you're staying at a ho-
Airport and   tel, it's best to follow the signs to the area where the hotel lim-
Center City   ousines wait. If you do take a taxi, expect to pay HK$20 to
By Taxi   HK$30 for a Kowloon destination and up to HK$70 for a Hong Kong Island destination, inclusive of a HK$20 fee for the Cross-Harbour Tunnel.

By Airbus   A fast and efficient way to get to and from the airport is to use the **Airbus** (tel. 745–4466), which runs every 15 minutes from 7 AM to midnight. Route A1 (HK$8) runs through the Kowloon tourist area, serving the Ambassador, Empress, Grand, Holiday Inn Golden Mile, Hyatt Regency, Imperial, International, Kowloon, Miramar, New World, Park, Peninsula, Regent, Shangri-La, and Sheraton hotels, plus the YMCA, Chungking Mansions, and the Star Ferry. Routes A2 and A3 (HK$12) go to Hong Kong Island. A2 serves the Harbour View International House, Furama, Hilton, Mandarin, and Victoria hotels. A3 serves the Causeway Bay hotels—Caravelle, Excelsior, Lee Gardens, and Park Lane Radisson. The new A4 (HK$8) route goes to the China terminal (for ferries to Macau and China) via hotels in Yaumati and Mongkok.

By Hotel Car   To get to the airport, you can order a hotel car in advance. A hotel car costs HK$200 to HK$300 from Hong Kong Island, and HK$50 to HK$195 from Kowloon.

From North America by Ship

Royal Viking (750 Battery St., San Francisco, CA 94111, tel. 415/398–8000 or 800/634–8000) sails from Vancouver and San Francisco. Ask your travel agent for details. Other cruise lines that include Hong Kong as a port of call are **Cunard, Princess,** and **Holland America.** Ask your travel agent for a complete list.

From the U.K. by Plane

Cathay Pacific Airways (tel. 071/930–7878) and **British Airways** (tel. 081/897–4000) have daily flights from London to Hong Kong. Various Asian national airlines fly to Hong Kong via their capital cities, usually at reasonable rates. There are some direct flights on Cathay Pacific and British Airways. The flying time is usually 16 to 17 hours with a stopover, or 12 to 13 hours nonstop.

From the U.K. by Ship

Hong Kong is a major port of call for around-the-world cruises. Fabulous floating palaces, such as **Cunard's** *Queen Elizabeth II* and **P&O's** *Canberra* still pull away from Southampton regularly, and dock in Hong Kong for a day or two. *Cunard Line, 30A Pall Mall, London SW1Y 5LS, tel. 071/491–3930. P&O, 77 New Oxford St., London WCIA 1PP, tel. 071/831–1234.*

Area Travel

Hong Kong is a hub for travel in the area. In fact, it takes longer to drive to Kai Tak Airport and proceed through the facilities than it does to fly to Manila and Taipei. The most crowded times to travel in and out of the colony are Chinese New Year, the Easter/Ching Ming holidays, especially when they fall together, and the year-end. "Crowded" takes on meanings in Hong Kong you would never contemplate elsewhere. Imagine 25%–30% of the colony on the move to China or Macau, and you will get the picture.

Staying in Hong Kong

Important Addresses and Numbers

Tourist Information
: **Information centers** are just beyond customs at the Hong Kong International Airport; on the Star Ferry Concourse in Kowloon, at Shop G2, Royal Garden Hotel (69 Mody Rd., Tsimshatsui East, Kowloon), and in the basement of Jardine House on Hong Kong Island. These centers stock in-depth fact sheets on specific areas, and a free shopping guide. They also have a monthly official guidebook for HK$10, which is available for free at the hotels.

Trade Information
: **Hong Kong Trade Development Council** (38/F, Office Tower Convention Plaza, 1 Harbour Rd., Hong Kong Isl., tel. 833–4333, telex: 73595 CONHK HX, cable: CONOTRAD HONGKONG). The TDC has 23 overseas offices, including four in the United States and one in the United Kingdom.

Trade Department (Ocean Centre, ground, 1st, 13th, 14th, and 15th floors, 5 Canton Rd., Kowloon, tel. 722–2333, telex: 8845126 CNDI, fax: 735–6135).

Industry Department (Ocean Centre, 14th fl., 5 Canton Rd., Kowloon, tel. 737–2573, fax: 730–4633).

Chambers of Commerce
: **Hong Kong General Chamber of Commerce** (United Centre, 22nd fl., Queensway, Hong Kong Island, tel. 529–9229, telex: 83535 HX, cable: CHAMBERCOM HONGKONG, fax: 527–9843).

American Chamber of Commerce in Hong Kong (1030 Swire House, Connaught Rd., Hong Kong Island, tel. 526–0165, telex: 83664 AMCC HX, cable: AMCHAM HONGKONG, fax: 810–1289).

Federation of H.K. Industries (408 Hankow Centre, 5–15 Hankow Rd., Kowloon, tel. 723–0818, telex: 30101 FHKI HX, cable: FEDINDUSTR HONGKONG, fax: 721–3494).

Chinese Manufacturers Association (Chinese Manufacturers Assoc. Bldg., 64–66 Connaught Rd., Hong Kong Island, tel. 545–6166, fax: 541–4541, cable: MAFTS' HK).

Hong Kong Productivity Council (World Commerce Centre, 12th and 13th fls., 11 Canton Rd., Kowloon, tel. 735–1656, telex: 32842 HX, cable: PROCENTRE).

The Indian Chamber of Commerce Hong Kong (Hoseinee House, 2nd fl., 69 Wyndham St., Hong Kong Island, tel. 523–3877, telex: 64993 HX, cable: INDCHAMBER HONGKONG, fax: 845–0300).

The Hong Kong Japanese Chamber of Commerce and Industry (Hennessy Centre, 38th fl., 500 Hennessy Rd., Hong Kong Island, tel. 577–6129, fax: 577–0525).

British Chamber of Commerce (Shui On Centre, 17/F, 8 Harbour Rd., Wanchai, Hong Kong Island, tel. 824–2211, telex: 82759 BRIT HX, fax: 824–1333).

Swedish Chamber of Commerce (Shun Ho Tower, 24–30 Ice House St., Central, Hong Kong Island, tel 525–0349, telex: 68350 KAMVI HX, fax: 868–5344).

Consulates and Commissions

U.S. Consulate (26 Garden Rd., Hong Kong Island, tel. 845–3877).

U.K. Commission (Overseas Visa Section, Hong Kong Immigration Dept., Wanchai Tower, 7 Gloucester Rd., Hong Kong, tel 824–6111).

Canadian Commission (Tower 1, Exchange Sq., 11th–14th Floors, Connaught Pl., Hong Kong Island, tel. 810–4321).

Emergencies

Police, fire, or **ambulance** (tel. 999).

Royal Hong Kong Police Visitor Hot Line (tel. 527–7177). English-speaking police wear a red shoulder tab.

Doctors Hotels have a list of accredited doctors and can arrange for a doctor to visit your hotel room. Otherwise, consult the nearest government hospital. Check the Government section of the Business telephone directory under Medical and Health Department for a list. The main ones are the **Queen Mary Hospital,** the **Queen Elizabeth Hospital,** the **British Military Hospital,** the **Tang Shiu Kin Hospital,** and the **Princess Margaret Hospital.** The fee for an office consultation can run from HK$120 to HK$350.

Special Phone Numbers

General Post Office (tel. 523–1071).

Taxi Complaints (tel. 577–6866).

Time and Weather (tel. 1852).

Getting Around

There are probably more kinds of transportation in Hong Kong than anywhere else in the world. Hong Kong is a series of interlinked islands, plus a chunk of the Chinese mainland. Ferries, a subway system, and tunnels connect Hong Kong Island with the Kowloon peninsula and the Outer Islands. There are also excellent bus services throughout Hong Kong Island, Kowloon, and New Territories, and a number of routes linking the two sides of the harbor. On Hong Kong Island, there are two kinds of trams, a street-level tram running across the north shore of the island, and the Peak Tram, which is a funicular railway traveling up Victoria Peak, the mountain that dominates the central part of the island. Helpful in using this system effectively is the leaflet *Places of Public Interest by Public Transport*, published by the HKTA.

Walking is the easiest and most rewarding way to explore the built-up districts of Hong Kong Island and Kowloon. For trips around the island, into New Territories, and to the smaller, more remote islands you will need to travel by a combination of taxi, bus, tram, underground Mass Transit Railway (MTR), and various ferries. The harbor, that living, breathing focus of Hong Kong's energies, can be fully appreciated only by boat—on the Star Ferry, by organized tour on a junk, or aboard a two-masted brigantine.

By Subway The **Mass Transit Railway** (MTR) is a splendid, air-conditioned subway that links Hong Kong Island to the shopping area of Tsimshatsui and outward to parts of New Territories. Trains are frequent, safe, and easy to use (there are only three lines). Station entrances are marked with a simple line symbol resembling a man with arms and legs outstretched. There are clearly marked ticket machines inside the station that accept exact change. Change is available at the HK$1 and HK$2 machines or at the Hang Seng Bank counters, also inside the stations. The ticket machines issue plastic tickets with a magnetic strip through them. Tickets are the size of credit cards and give you access to the system through an electronic gate. Fares range from HK$3 to HK$7 and there is a special **Tourist Ticket** for HK$25, which can save you money.

By Taxi Taxis are easy to spot in Hong Kong because they are usually red and have a roof-sign saying "TAXI" that lights up when the taxi is available. They are obliged by law to have working meters. Fares in the urban areas start at HK$8 and go up by HK$.90 per 0.25 kilometer. There is a surcharge of HK$2 per large piece of baggage and a HK$20 surcharge for crossing the harbor through Cross-Harbour Tunnel. The Aberdeen Tunnel carries a surcharge of HK$5; the Lion Rock Tunnel toll is HK$6. These surcharges are shown on a small sign on the dashboard. Most people give a small tip, either by leaving the odd change or from HK$0.50 to HK$1 for a large fare. Taxis are usually reliable in Hong Kong, but if you have a complaint—about overcharging, for example—there is a special hot line (tel. 577–6866). Be sure to have the taxi license number, which is usually displayed somewhere on the dashboard.

It is difficult to find taxis from 3:30 to 6 PM. Apart from these times, and on rainy days, there is seldom a shortage of taxis. If a taxi does not stop for you, check to see if you're in a no-stopping zone, identified by a yellow line along the curb of the main road. Most taxi drivers speak some English, but to avoid problems, get someone at your hotel to write out your destination in Chinese.

Outside the urban areas, in New Territories, taxis are mainly green and white. They cost less than urban red taxis, with fares starting at HK$7 for the first two kilometers (1.2 mi), then HK$.80 for every quarter kilometer (roughly .2 mi). The boundary areas dividing urban taxis from rural taxis are near the New Clearwater Bay Road; Sekkong north of the Chinese University; Shum Cheng; and the "10-mile" stone on Castle

Peak Road. Urban taxis may travel into rural zones, but rural taxis must not cross into the urban zones. There are no interchange facilities for these taxis, so you are advised not to try to reach the urban area using a green taxi.

Many taxis are radio-controlled. When you call for one, you should expect to pay both for your ride and for the pick-up.

By Minibus   These 14- to 16-seat yellow vehicles with single red stripes rush all over Hong Kong. They are quicker and slightly more expensive than ordinary buses, and stop almost anywhere on request. Their destination is written on the front, but the English-language characters are small. Wave the minibus down when you see the one you want. Since fares are adjusted throughout the journey, you could pay as little as HK$2 or as much as HK$6, according to time and place. Visitors who want to travel from Central to Causeway Bay for shopping should look for the minibus marked "Daimaru," the name of a big store in Causeway Bay.

By Maxicab   These are the same as minibuses but have single green stripes and run fixed routes. They go from beside the car park at the Star Ferry, Hong Kong side, to Mid-levels and Ocean Park; and from HMS Tamar (just beyond City Hall at Star Ferry) they run to Victoria Peak. Fares begin at HK$3. The most popular route goes from Star Ferry Kowloon to Tsimshatsui East for HK$1.60–HK$2.

By Tram   All visitors should take a street tram at least once. Take your camera and head for the upper deck. The trams run along Hong Kong Island's north shore from Kennedy Town in the west, all the way through Central, Wanchai, Causeway Bay, North Point, and Quarry Bay, ending in the former fishing village of Shaukiwan. There is also a branch line that turns off in Wanchai toward Happy Valley, where horse races are held during the season. The destination is marked on the front and the fare is only HK$1 (HK$.50 children). Avoid rush hours.

By Peak Tram   This funicular railway dates back to 1888 and rises from ground level to **Victoria Peak** (1,305 feet), offering a panoramic view of Hong Kong. Both residents and tourists use the tram, which has five stations. The fare is HK$8 one way or HK$14 roundtrip. There is a restaurant at the top. The tram runs daily from 7 AM to midnight, every 10-15 minutes. There is a free shuttle bus to and from the Star Ferry.

By Rickshaw   Rickshaws are operated by a few old men who take tourists on a token ride and pose for pictures (for which they charge heavily). The scale of charges is supposed to be around HK$50 for a five-minute ride, but the rickshaw men are merciless. A posed snapshot costs from HK$10 to HK$20. Make sure the price is agreed upon before you take the photo, otherwise unpleasant scenes may follow.

By Train   The **Kowloon-Canton Railway** (KCR) has 12-commuter stops on its 22-mile (34-km) journey through urban Kowloon and the new cities of Shatin and Taipo, on its way to the Chinese border. The main station is at Hunghom, Kowloon, where you can catch the express trains to China. Adult fares range from HK$2.50 to HK$23.50. The crossover point with the MTR is at Kowloon Tong Station (tel. 606–9606).

By Ferry   The **Star Ferry** is one of Hong Kong's most famous landmarks. These double-bowed, green-and-white vessels cross the harbor between Central on Hong Kong Island and Tsimshatsui in Kowloon. The ferries cross every few minutes, hundreds of times daily, from 6:30 AM to 11:30 PM. The cost for the seven-minute ride is HK$1.20, upper deck, and HK$1, lower deck (children HK$.80). The Star Ferry also runs a service to Hunghom between 7 AM and 7:20 PM at 10- to 20-minute intervals for HK$1.20–HK$1.50 (HK$.80–HK$1.20 children).

The ferries of the **Hong Kong Ferry Company (HKF)** go to Hong Kong's beautiful outer islands. There are two- and three-deck ferries; the ones with three decks have an air-conditioned first-class section on the top deck, with access to the outside deck for magnificent views. The ferries go regularly to Lantau, Lamma, Cheung Chau, and Peng Chau. The HKF ferries leave from the Outlying Islands Pier, about a 10-minute walk west of the Star Ferry Pier on Hong Kong Island. Telephone for exact timetables (tel. 542–3081), or get ferry schedules from the HKTA. Return fares vary from HK$12 to HK$36. Most trips take about an hour and are very scenic. The ferries are extremely crowded and noisy on weekends. If you have to go to the more distant parts of Hong Kong, you may find that a linking ferry service will enable you to beat the traffic. For example, there are **hover-ferries** from Central to Tsuen Wan and Tsimshatsui East. The fares are HK$3.50–HK$6 during peak hours, HK$2.50–HK$5 off-peak. These trips take about 20 minutes per section, which is much faster than the trip by road.

By Helicopter Hong Kong's only helicopter service offers tours around Hong Kong Island, Kowloon Peninsula, and New Territories (*see* Guided Tours, below). It also has helicopter pads in Lantau, at Ngong Ping by the Po Lin Monastery, by Discovery Bay, Shek Pik, and by the popular beach of Cheung Sha. Fee for the charter sightseeing service is HK$3,705 for 30 minutes. Contact **Heliservices** (tel. 520–2200). The helipad is on Fenwick Pier Street, Hong Kong Island.

By Limousine Most of the best hotels have their own limousines. The Mandarin and The Peninsula hotels have chauffeur-driven Rolls-Royces for rent. You can also rent cars (*see* Car Rentals in Before You Go, above), but only a masochist would do so in Hong Kong. Cars with drivers can be arranged through your hotel.

On Foot If you're not defeated by the heat, it is pleasant to stroll around parts of Hong Kong. On Hong Kong Island, for example, you can enjoy a walk through the very traditional Western district where life has not changed much over the years. If you are a very keen walker, you can go for a long stroll in New Territories or on Lantau Island. Contact the HKTA for maps.

Telephones

Local Calls Local calls are free. For pay phones, use a HK$1 coin.

Although there are a growing number of pay phones, the tradition is to pop into any store and ask to use the telephone. Many small stores keep their telephone on the counter facing the street, no doubt hoping your eyes will browse while your ear and mouth are occupied.

Local Information Dial 108 for directory assistance. The operators usually speak English, but be prepared to spell out names. If a number is constantly busy and you think it might be out of order, call 109 and the operator will check the line.

International Many hotels offer direct dial, as do many business centers, but always with a hefty surcharge. Call 013 for international inquiries and for assistance with direct dialing. Call 010 for operator-assisted calls to most countries, including the United States, Canada, and the United Kingdom. Dial 011 for international conference calls or outgoing collect calls. Long-distance (person-to-person, station-to-station, or direct dial) calls can also be made from C&W. AT&T's "USA Direct" service allows you to make direct calls to the United States from coin-operated phones by using their access code from Hong Kong (tel. 008–1111).

Mail

Postal Rates Postcards and letters under 10 grams for North America or Europe cost HK$2.30 and HK$1.10 for each additional gram. Aerograms are HK$1.80.

Receiving Mail The General Post Office is speedy and efficient, with deliveries twice daily, six days a week, and overnight delivery in the main business areas.

Travelers can receive mail at the **American Express** office (16–18 Queen's Rd. Central, First Floor, New World Tower, Central, tel. 801–7714) Monday through Friday 9 AM–5:30 PM.

Newspapers

Newspapers and magazines from all over the world are readily available in Hong Kong. Both the *Asian Wall Street Journal* and the *International Herald Tribune* print international editions in Hong Kong to supplement the two English-language daily newspapers, *The South China Morning Post* and the *Hongkong Standard*, both of which carry international news. The *Far Eastern Economic Review* leads the pack in business publications. *Time* and *Newsweek* both print in Hong Kong and the newsweekly *Asiaweek* is also here.

Opening and Closing Times

Most banks are open 9 AM to 4:30 PM, but some open in the evening and even on Sundays for special purposes; there is 24-hour automated banking in many branches. Office hours are more or less the same as in the West, 9 AM–5 or 6 PM, but the shops usually open about 10 AM and stay open until late at night, especially in the tourist and residential areas.

Business Services

Convention Center The **Hong Kong Convention and Exhibition Centre** is a state-of-the-art, completely integrated, 4.4 million-square-foot complex on the Wanchai waterfront. There are two exhibition halls of 97,000 square feet each, with a main convention hall capable of seating 2,600. The complex, Asia's largest, houses two hotels, a 600-room Grand Hyatt and a 900-room New World, an apartment block, and a 54-story trade-mart/office building. *Hong Kong Convention and Exhibition Centre, Harbour Rd., Wanchai, Hong Kong Island, tel. 864–8888.*

Business Centers In a mercantile community such as Hong Kong, you'd expect business centers outside the hostelries, and there are many. Some are considerably cheaper than those in hotels. Others cost about the same but offer private desks (from HK$1200 to HK$5,000 weekly for private offices and meeting facilities).

Other amenities include a private address and personal answering and forwarding services. Many service centers are tied in with accountants and lawyers for those who want to register a company quickly. Some will even process visas and wrap gifts for you.

One hotel business center, equipped like those normally found outside the hostelries, is the **China Traders Centre** in the Regal Airport Hotel. A short walk across a footbridge from the passenger terminal, it has offices and conference rooms. It is popular with transient businesspersons who need only the daylight hours to transact business before winging their way out again. Their club, the China Traders Circle, which has free membership, offers discounts on offices that can be rented by the hour, day, week, or month.

The **American Chamber of Commerce** (1030 Swire House, Central, Hong Kong Isl., tel. 526–0165, telex: 83664 AMCC HX, fax: 810–1289, cable: AMCHAM) not only offers short-term rental conference space, but also has a splendid and succinct Business Briefing Program (U.S.$200 members/U.S.$300 nonmembers). The chamber also has a library and a *China Trade Services* section.

Other organizations of note:

Asia Business Centre (3rd fl., The Centremark, 287–299 Queen's Rd., Central, tel. 544–8773, telex: 80577 WINGP HX, fax: 854–0203).

Margaret Sullivan Secretarial Services (13 Duddell St., Central, Hong Kong Island, tel. 526–5946, telex: 63210 ALAYE HX, fax: 845–0989) also provides personnel for the import-export trade.

Pacific Centre (Bank of Tokyo Building, 10th fl., 1 Kowloon Park Dr. tel. 721–0880, telex: 56443 WATC HX, fax: 723–9005).

Telex Most hotels have telexes and will send messages for guests. All the business centers have them, too. However, if you want to avoid the hotel surcharge or your business is closed, the public telex for sending is through **Cable & Wireless (C&W)**. There are many offices throughout the territory, but the two 24-hour ones are Exchange Square in Central, Hong Kong Island, and Hermès House, Middle Rd. (across the street from the Sheraton), Tsimshatsui, Kowloon. The public C&W facility at the airport is open from 8 AM to 11 PM.

Facsimile In Hong Kong, facsimile (fax, telecopying) has grown by leaps and bounds because local calls, hence local faxes, are free. The Chinese language, which cannot be used on telex, lends itself to the pictorial. For a public fax service, the Post Office and C&W offer a joint service called "Postfax." Check the **General Post Office** (tel. 523–1071) to find out which post offices have the service in addition to the main ones. At C&W it is only available at their two main 24-hour offices.

Photocopying All hotels and business centers have photocopy machines, as do many stores, particularly stationery stores, scattered throughout the territory. However, for some heavy-duty copying, including oversize pages (architectural drawings) or color reproduction, **Rank Xerox** has Copy Service Centres operating during office hours (New Henry House, 10 Ice House St. and Chung Hing Commercial Bldg., 62–63 Connaught Rd., both in Central District, and Wah Kwong Bldg., 48–66 Hennessy Rd., Wanchai, all on Hong Kong Island). In Kowloon, there is one at 4 Canton Road in Tsimshatsui and another in the Peninsula Centre, Tsimshatsui East.

Couriers The Post Office runs a **Speedpost** service akin to the overnight
International express service run by the U.S. Postal Service. Large international couriers, including **DHL, Federal Express, TNT Skypak,** and **Purolator,** all have large operations here.

Local Messengers In the posher hotels, deliveries can be arranged through the concierge. Most business centers offer a service, too. However, there is a good chance that both of them will contact **DHL's** local courier service, run simultaneously with their international one. They have numerous **Express Centres** located in major buildings and various Mass Transit Railway Stations. For the one nearest you, call 765–8111. They will also pick up from your hotel. The minimum charge is HK$50 for under one kilogram, but of course weight and distance determine price. If the timing is right at the Express Centre, you should be able to get same-day delivery.

Dry Cleaning Hotels have dry cleaning services, but if you spill something on your shirt at lunch and want it in pristine condition for your 3 PM appointment, head for **Martinizing Dry Cleaning** and its one-hour service. The main plant is at 7 Glenealy Road, Central. The other pick-up offices are at Bank of America Tower and World Wide House, both in Central; Causeway Centre, Harbour Road, in Wanchai; and in Harbour City, Canton Road, Tsimshatsui, Kowloon. There are also dry-cleaning outlets inside many of the MTR stations.

Guided Tours

It is possible to travel the length and breadth of Hong Kong Island, Kowloon, New Territories, and the Outlying Islands using public transportation, and perhaps a taxi or two. Those whose time is limited, or who prefer to relax and leave the organization to professionals, can choose from a wide variety of tours. Unless otherwise stated, the tours listed here can be booked at major hotels.

Orientation Tours **Hong Kong Island.** The standard is a three- to four-hour tour of the island that departs from all the major hotels daily in the mornings and afternoons. Cost by coach runs about HK$120; by private car, with a maximum of four passengers, HK$600–HK$700. Although routes vary, the following areas are generally covered: Victoria Peak, Wanchai, Aw Boon Haw Gardens, Repulse Bay and Deep Water Bay, Aberdeen, the University of Hong Kong, and Western and Central districts.

Kowloon and New Territories. This tour usually takes in sights as varied as Kwai Chung Container Terminal, the Castle Peak fishing village, a Taoist temple, the town of Yuen Long, the Chinese border at Lokmachau, and the Royal Hong Kong Golf Club at Fanling. The tour has morning and afternoon departures from all major hotels, lasts three to four hours, and costs

HK$120 to HK$140 by coach and HK$600 to HK$700 by car. A slight variation is "The Land Between Tour," which lasts six hours and costs HK$250 (HK$200 children). It offers a glimpse of rural Hong Kong and takes in Tai Mo Shan, Hong Kong's tallest mountain; the fish breeding ponds; chicken farms; the Luen Wo Market in Fanling; and the Chinese border at Luk Keng. The return route passes Plover Cover Reservoir, Tolo Harbour (where you'll lunch on a terrace), and the racetrack at Shatin.

Harbor and Islands, Watertours of Hong Kong Ltd., and the **Seaview Harbour Tour Co. Ltd.** operate a variety of tours by junks and cruisers within the harbor, and to some of Hong Kong's 235 islands, including Lamma, Lantau, and Cheung Chau. Some of the tours offer a land-and-sea combination. They vary from a two-hour "Harbour Afternoon" tour (HK$130) to a 6-hour "Grand Tour" combining a harbor cruise with Aberdeen and the islands, with Chinese lunch (HK$320). A "Sunset Cruise" lasts four hours and costs HK$225.

General-interest Tours

Sung Dynasty Village. This is a replica of a 1,000-year-old southern Chinese village, where you can wander through old shops to sample the wares, witness a traditional Chinese wedding ceremony, and have your fortune told. The tour takes about three hours and includes lunch, dinner, or a snack. Prices range from HK$170 to HK$250. Departures are staggered throughout the day, beginning at 9 AM.

Ocean Park. Tours to this marineland, amusement park, and aviary cost from HK$165 to HK$250 (HK$130 children) and include all rides. You can purchase a **Citibus Tour** (tel. 736–3888) ticket from any MTR Station for HK$156 (HK$76 children). The ticket includes round-trip transportation in an open-top double-decker bus from the MTR Admiralty Station in Central. The same bus serves Middle Kingdom and Water World, Ocean Park's additional attractions.

Special-interest Tours

Culture

The Cultural Centre and HKTA have introduced a "Cultural Diversions Tour," which includes a guided tour of the center, a Chinese cultural show, and dinner. The tours begin at 5:45 PM every Monday and Thursday (except January 1, Chinese New Year, and Easter), costs HK$290 (HK$240 for children), and can be booked through HKTA offices.

Heritage

Every Wednesday and Saturday morning the **HKTA** offers a four-hour "Heritage Tour" that takes in the Lei Cheng Uk tomb, Sam Tunk Uk Folk Museum, Tai Fu Tai mansion, and Man Shek Tong ancestral hall. Tickets (HK$250) are available from HKTA.

Helicopter

Heliservices Hong Kong Limited (St. George's Bldg., 22nd Fl., Hong Kong Island, tel. 520–2200) offers a choice of flight paths around the colony during daylight hours in an Aerospatiale Squirrel, which seats five passengers. The least expensive charter is a 30-minute tour around Hong Kong Island, Kowloon Peninsula, and New Territories for HK$3,705 for four passengers. The heliport is on Fenwick Pier Street, Central.

Horse Racing

The **HKTA** (tel. 801–7177) runs a tour to both Shatin and Happy Valley tracks during the September through May season that includes hotel pickups and a meal. The cost is about HK$350. You must bring your passport because this tour is for nonresidents only.

Nightlife Most night tours take you out on the water for a glimpse of reflected neon. They include the "Hong Kong Night Tour," which offers a choice of Chinese or Western dinner at either the **Jumbo** floating restaurant in Aberdeen or the **Revolving 66 Restaurant.** Dinner is followed by a visit to a Chinese night market. Costs vary from HK$230–HK$430.

Sports The HKTA provides hotel pickups, a Western meal, and admission to the **Clearwater Bay Golf & Country Club,** where you can play golf, squash, or tennis, and enjoy the saunas and Jacuzzis. The price is HK$260, plus individual charges for sports activities.

Sailing The **Hilton Hotel** (tel. 523–3111, ext. 2009) operates pleasure cruises on its brigantine, *Wan Fu,* which can also be rented for private parties. Cruise costs vary from HK$250–HK$435 per person, and include a box lunch or barbecue dinner. Fees for renting the brigantine for private parties is HK$1,300 per hour excluding food and drink, with a minimum of two hours.

Trams **Tourist Enterprises** (tel. 368–0647) has a tour that features an hour's clanking on one of Hong Kong Island's private trams each evening from 6 PM. The tour also includes a stop at the Poor Man's Nightclub street market, and a grand dinner cruise or dinner in a leading hotel of your choice. Prices start at HK$390.

Tram Dim Sum Tours (tel. 366–7024) are two-hour rides on board replica antique trams, with dim sum snacks and unlimited drinks. With four departures daily, the tour runs HK$97 (HK$80 children).

Tourist Tram. The antique trams can be boarded anywhere along the regular tram route between Western District and Causeway Bay at a fare of HK$10.

2 Portraits of Hong Kong

Doing Business in Hong Kong

by Saul Lockhart

An American based in Hong Kong since 1967, Saul Lockhart is the author or co-author of six guidebooks on Asia. He has written numerous articles over the years for a variety of American, Asian, and European publications.

Made in Hong Kong. That familiar phrase—seen on everything from designer fashions and computers to toys, radios, and the proverbial left-handed widget—is the clue to the territory's export-oriented, manufacturing economy. The spirit of Hong Kong is the spirit of entrepreneurship; with people as its only natural resource, this tiny island is the world's 13th largest trading entity outside OPEC and COMECON.

Hong Kong is one of the rare places on earth that plays the free-trade game according to the classical rules, with only one or two peculiarities arising out of its colonial past. It is a free port—that is, there are no import duties or export levies, although there are domestic excises on alcohol (therefore on alcoholic beverages and perfumes), tobacco and tobacco products, petroleum products, and soft drinks. Some articles, such as firearms, ammunition, certain toxic drugs and, of course, narcotics, are controlled. There are limited controls on banking and finance, and on stock, futures, and commodities exchanges. But, by and large, these are minimal and usually implemented only after some calamitous, often illegal, event. The territory's bankers practice confidentiality, though it is not codified, as in Switzerland. The Independent Commission Against Corruption has the power to force banks to disclose all accounts and transactions.

With a few historical exceptions, you cannot own land in Hong Kong; it all belongs to the Crown (the government), but long- and short-term leases are auctioned off to all comers. With the signing of the 1984 Sino-British Agreement, which will return sovereignty to the People's Republic of China at the end of June 1997, land leases and mortgages are to extend past the magic 1997 mark as if it were not there. Otherwise, there are no business ownership limitations. A national of any country may do business or set up business, although nationals of countries that, for the time being, are not politically friendly with either Great Britain or China may be refused entry, working visas, or residence permits.

In such a multinational community, Cantonese may be the chief language but hotels, western-style entertainments, and international communications are all conducted multilingually, and translators and bilingual secretaries can easily be hired to help you do business.

Economist Milton Friedman called Hong Kong's the "last *laissez-faire* economy," which must have been music to the ears of the local government. Hong Kong is living proof that Rudyard Kipling's statement about East and West—"ne'er the twain shall meet"—was wrong. Not only do East and West meet in Hong Kong, but each side also generally makes a profit on the relationship.

And profit-making starts at the top. Only in the most adverse of times has the Hong Kong government's budget gone into the red. Annual surpluses are planned and expected; deficit spending is anathema. In fact, an intentional game is played each year at budget time, when the economic performance for that year is always underestimated; 8.5% was the growth-rate prediction for 1990, while at the year's end, the figure stood at 28%. This phenomenon seems to be changing, however, with the approach of 1997.

This mercantile community is the world's largest exporter of clothing, furs, toys and games, watches and clocks, imitation jewelry, metal watchbands, electrical hair-dressing apparatus, artificial flowers, flashlights, and electric lamps. After light industry and manufacturing, on-shore and off-shore financial and business services fill out the rest of the economic equation.

Hong Kong Island is where the big-time commerce is: the bank HQs, the big company HQs, the lawyers, accountants, public relations, and advertising people, and so forth. Central District, as the name implies, is where the giants live.

Kowloon is where the industry is, and also the main tourist activity. In any case, you can get to and from the Island and Kowloon by road or subway (through two undersea tunnels) in 10 to 30 minutes, or by passenger ferry (the famous Star Ferry) in 10 minutes, except during rush hours.

In New Territories there are seven new towns being built, with new factories, offices, dwellings, schools, hospitals, hotels, and other facilities. Finally, a number of the outlying islands are also developing fast, with new incomes and market possibilities. Visit at least one (and also Macau which, after many decades of sleepy stagnation, is embracing rapid development; you can get there in about an hour by jetfoil).

A healthy percentage of Hong Kong's 5.9 million annual visitors come to do business. As a result, its hotels cater specially to business travelers, with plenty of meeting rooms, business services, and "business class" concierge floors. When you book your hotel room, make it known in advance that you are a businessperson; in Hong Kong, which thrives on commerce, that makes you a VIP.

Business in Hong Kong is cosmopolitan and formal. Despite the summer heat, a suit is advisable when calling on people. When you have become a familiar face, then more casual attire is suitable for daytime factory visits. Meetings with

Chinese businesspersons can become very formal and very alcoholic. Be sure to have bilingual business cards printed—hundreds of them. Many in the West may laugh at the Asian penchant for whipping out their cards, but it is the preferred way of keeping track of people in Hong Kong.

Because Hong Kong is very much a club town, visitors quite often feel left out, particularly at lunchtime or on weekends. Quite obviously, you will not be able to join a social or sporting club just for your few days here, but there still may be a way to partake by checking on your own memberships before you depart. Most of Hong Kong's private social and sporting clubs have reciprocal arrangements with clubs overseas. For example, membership in the Club Corporation of America, with its more than 200 clubs in the United States, can gain you entrance to the Pacific Club in Central or the Tower Club in Kowloon for a bit of weekend recreation. The American Club has reciprocal rights with other American Clubs in Asia, the World Trade Centre Club has sister clubs in the United States, and Foreign Correspondents' Club members can use about two dozen press clubs around the world. Many country clubs, private clubs, eating clubs, and cricket, golf, and sailing clubs have reciprocal rights.

Recent arrivals are stunned by the pace of Hong Kong, and staggered by cocktail chitchat from perfect strangers who want to know, after a two-minute acquaintance, how much rent you pay, how much you make, how much your car costs, and so forth. Natives are direct in situations in which Westerners are more circumspect. But that is because everyone in Hong Kong is in a rush to make his or her pile. The mentality is probably due to the historical uncertainty of Hong Kong's status—everyone knew that one day China would deal in her own way and in her own time with what she always considered an internal matter. That is precisely what happened, much to the chagrin of former prime minister Thatcher, who had her own ideas about Britain staying on to run the place when she initiated the September 1982 negotiations that led to the Sino-British agreement two years later.

Even before the political crackdown in China in 1989, there was considerable uncertainty in Hong Kong about life after 1997. Today, it seems nothing can be taken for granted. As the 1984 agreement stands now, however, Hong Kong will be allowed to exist as a Special Administrative Region (SAR) of the People's Republic, with separate laws and a high degree of autonomy in domestic affairs. The SAR will be vested with executive, legislative, and independent judicial powers, including the authority of final adjudication. The laws currently in force will remain basically unchanged.

Rights and freedoms, including those of person, speech, press, assembly, association, travel, movement, correspondence, strike, occupation, inheritance, and religion, will be ensured, as will the right of academic research. Private property and foreign investment will be protected. Hong Kong will retain its status as a free port with its own shipping registry, a separate customs authority, and an international financial center. Foreign exchange, gold, securities, and futures markets will continue. The Hong Kong dollar will continue to circulate as a separate, freely convertible currency, distinct from China's *renminbi;* there will be no exchange controls. Hong Kong will manage its own finances and China will not levy any taxes on the SAR.

Hong Kong will be allowed to maintain and develop independent economic and cultural relations and to conclude agreements with foreign countries and trade organizations, such as the GATT and MFA, and air and tax agreements.

China will hold sway over foreign and defense matters, and Chinese troops will replace the British garrison. A Chinese-appointed governor, who may or may not be Hong Kong Chinese, will be responsible to Beijing, much as the current governor is responsible to London.

Novelist Han Suyin summed up Hong Kong's way of coping with such uncertainties in a 1959 *Life* magazine article. Hong Kong, she said, "works splendidly on borrowed time in a borrowed place." Add to the mixture a bit of the refugee syndrome—more than half of the 5.7 million people have fled the Middle Kingdom, the Motherland, at one time or another since 1949—and Hong Kong's business (and social) pace is more understandable.

Impacts and Images

by *Jan Morris*

Jan Morris is the author of more than 20 books, including such best sellers as Journeys, Destinations, *and* Manhattan '45. *In this excerpt from her book,* Hong Kong, *Morris describes the ever-changing face of the city and its intrinsically Chinese character.*

Hong Kong is in China, if not entirely of it, and after nearly 150 years of British rule the background to all its wonders remains its Chineseness—98 percent if you reckon it by population, hardly less if you are thinking metaphysically.

It may not look like it from the deck of an arriving ship, or swooping into town on a jet, but geographically most of the territory is rural China still. The empty hills that form the mass of the New Territories, the precipitous islets and rocks, even some of the bare slopes of Hong Kong Island itself, rising directly above the tumultuous harbor, are much as they were in the days of the Manchus, the Mings or the neolithic Yaos. The last of the leopards has indeed been shot (1931), the last of the tigers spotted (1967, it is claimed), but that recondite newt flourishes still as *Paramesotriton hongkongensis*, there are still civets, pythons, barking deer and porcupines about and the marshlands abound with seabirds. The predominant country colors are Chinese colors, browns, grays, tawny colors. The generally opaque light is just the light one expects of China, and gives the whole territory the required suggestion of blur, surprise and uncertainty. The very smells are Chinese smells—oily, laced with duck-mess and gasoline.

Thousands of Hong Kong people still live on board junks, cooking their meals in the hiss and flicker of pressure lamps among the riggings and the nets. Thousands more inhabit shantytowns, made of sticks, canvas and corrugated iron but bustling with the native vivacity. People are still growing fruit, breeding fish, running duck farms, tending oyster beds; a few still grow rice and a very few still plow their fields with water buffalo. Village life remains resiliently ancestral. The Tangs and the Pangs are influential. The geomancers are busy still. Half-moon graves speckle the high ground wherever *feng shui* decrees, sometimes attended still by the tall brown urns that contain family ashes. Temples to Tin Hau, the Queen of Heaven, or Hung Shing, God of the Southern Seas, still stand incense-swirled upon foreshores.

But the vast majority of Hong Kong's Chinese citizens live in towns, jam-packed on the flatter ground. They are mostly squeezed in gigantic tower-blocks, and they have surrounded themselves with all the standard manifestations of modern non-Communist chinoiserie: the garish merry signs, the clamorous shop-fronts, the thickets of TV aerials, the banners, the rows of shiny hanging ducks, the washing on its poles, the wavering bicycles, the potted plants massed on balconies, the canvas-canopied stalls sell-

ing herbs, or kitchenware, or antiques, or fruit, the bub-
bling caldrons of crab-claw soup boiling at eating stalls, the
fantastic crimson-and-gold façades of restaurants, the
flickering television screens in shop windows, the trays of
sticky cakes in confectionery stores, the profusion of masts,
poles and placards protruding from the fronts of buildings,
the dragons carved or gilded, the huge elaborate posters,
the tea shops with their gleaming pots, the smells of cooking, spice, incense, oil, the racket of radio music and ampli-
fied voices, the half-shouted conversation that is peculiar to
Chinese meeting one another in the street, the ceaseless
clatter of spoons, coins, mah-jongg counters, abaci, hammers and electric drills.

I t can appear exotic to visitors, but it is fundamentally a
plain and practical style. Just as the Chinese consider a
satisfactory year to be a year in which nothing much
happens, so their genius seems to me fundamentally of a
workaday kind, providing a stout and reliable foundation,
mat and bamboo, so to speak, on which to build the structures of astonishment.

What the West has provided, originally through the medi-
um of the British Empire, later by the agency of international finance, is a city-state in its own image, overlaying
that resilient and homely Chinese style with an aesthetic
far more aggressive. The capitalists of Hong Kong have
been terrific builders, and have made of the great port, its
hills and its harbors, one of the most thrilling of all metro-
politan prospects—for my own tastes, the finest sight in
Asia. More than 5.5 million people, nearly twice the population of New Zealand, live here in less than four hundred
square miles of land, at least half of which is rough mountain country. They are necessarily packed tight, in urban
forms as startling in the luminous light of Hong Kong as the
upper-works of the clippers must have been when they first
appeared along its waterways.

The Tangs and the Lius may still be in their villages, but
they are invested on all sides by massive New Towns,
started from scratch in starkly modernist manner. All over
the mainland New Territories, wherever the hills allow,
busy roads sweep here and there, clumps of tower-blocks
punctuate the skyline, suburban estates develop and blue-
tiled brick wilts before the advance of concrete. Even on
the outlying islands, as Hong Kong calls the rest of the ar-
chipelago, apartment buildings and power stations rise
above the moors. Flatland in most parts of Hong Kong being so hard to find, this dynamic urbanism has been created
largely in linear patterns, weaving along shorelines, clam-
bering up gullies or through narrow passes, and frequently
compressed into almost inconceivable congestion. Some 80
percent of the people live in 8 percent of the land, and parts
of Kowloon, with more than a quarter of a million people
per square mile, are probably the most crowded places in all

human history. An amazing tangle of streets complicates the topography; the architect I. M. Pei, commissioned to design a new Hong Kong office block in the 1980s, said it took nine months just to figure out access to the site.

There is not much shape to all this, except the shape of the place itself. Twin cities of the harbor are the vortex of all Hong Kong, and all that many strangers ever see of it. On the north, the mainland shore, the dense complex of districts called Kowloon presses away into the hills, projecting its force clean through them indeed by tunnel into the New Territories beyond. The southern shore, on the island of Hong Kong proper, is the site of the original British settlement, officially called Victoria but now usually known simply as Central; it is in effect the capital of Hong Kong, and contains most of its chief institutions, but it straggles inchoately all along the island's northern edge, following the track worn by the junk crews when, before the British came at all, adverse winds obliged them to drag their vessels through this strait. Around the two conglomerates the territory's being revolves: one talks of Kowloon-side or Hong Kong–side, and on an average day more than 115,000 vehicles pass through the underwater tunnel from one to the other.

Once the colony had a formal urban center. Sit with me now in the Botanical Gardens, those inescapable amenities of the British Empire that have defied progress even here, and still provide shady boulevards, flower beds and a no more than usually nasty little zoo almost in the heart of Central. From this belvedere, fifty years ago, we could have looked down upon a ceremonial plaza of some dignity, Statue Square. It opened directly upon the harbor, rather like the Piazza d'Italia in Trieste, and to the west ran a waterfront esplanade, called the Praya after its Macao original. The steep green island hills rose directly behind the square, and it was surrounded by structures of consequence—Government House, where the Governor lived; Head Quarter House, where the General lived; a nobly classical City Hall; the Anglican cathedral; the Supreme Court; the Hongkong and Shanghai Bank. The effect was sealed by the spectacle of the ships passing to and fro at the north end of the square, and by the presence of four emblematically imperial prerequisites: a dockyard of the Royal Navy, a cricket field, the Hong Kong Club and a statue of Queen Victoria.

It has all been thrown away. Today Statue Square is blocked altogether out of our sight by office buildings, and anyway only the specter of a plaza remains down there, loomed over, fragmented by commercialism. Even the waterfront has been pushed back by land reclamation. The surviving promenade is all bits and pieces of piers, and a three-story car park obstructs the harbor view. The cricket ground has been prettified into a municipal garden, with turtles in a pond. Government House and the cathedral are hardly visible through the skyscrapers, the Hong Kong Club occupies four floors of a twenty-four-story office block. Queen Victoria has gone.

This is the way of urban Hong Kong. It is cramped by the force of nature, but it is irresistibly restless by instinct. Except for the harbor, it possesses no real center now. The territory as a whole has lately become a stupendous exercise in social design, but no master plan for the harbor cities has ever succeeded—Sir Patrick Abercrombie offered one in the heyday of British town planning after the Second World War, but like so many of his schemes it never came to anything. Proposals to extend that promenade were repeatedly frustrated down the years, notably by the military, who would not get their barracks and dockyards out of the way; all that is left of the idea is the howling expressway that runs on stilts along the foreshore.

Today beyond Statue Square, all along the shoreline, across the harbor, far up the mountain slopes, tall concrete buildings extend without evident pattern or logic. There seems to be no perspective to them either, so that when we shift our viewpoint one building does not move with any grace against another—just a clump here, a splodge there, sometimes a solitary pillar of glass or concrete. Across the water they loom monotonously behind the Kowloon waterfront, square and Stalinesque; they are limited to a height of twelve stories there, because the airport is nearby. On the sides of distant mountains you may see them protruding from declining ridges like sudden outcrops of white chalk. Many are still meshed in bamboo scaffolding, many more are doomed to imminent demolition. If we look down the hill again, behind the poor governor's palace immolated in its gardens, we may see the encampment of blue-and-white awnings, interspersed with bulldozers and scattered with the laboring straw-hatted figures of construction workers, which shows where the foundations of yet another skyscraper, still bigger, more splendid and more extravagant no doubt than the one before, are even now being laid.

The fundamentals, then, are plain and practical, the design is inchoate, the architecture of a somewhat mixed character; yet Hong Kong is astonishingly beautiful. It is made so partly by its setting, land and sea so exquisitely interacting, but chiefly by its impression of irresistible activity. It is like a caldron, seething, hissing, hooting, arguing, enmeshed in a labyrinth of tunnels and overpasses, with those skyscrapers erupting everywhere into view, with ferries churning and hovercraft splashing and great jets flying in, with fleets of ships lying always offshore, with double-decker buses and clanging tramcars, with a car it seems for every square foot of roadway, with a pedestrian for every square inch of sidewalk, and funicular trains crawling up and down the mountainside, and small scrubbed-faced policemen scudding about on motorbikes—all in all, with a pace of life so unremitting, a sense of movement and enterprise so challenging, that one's senses are overwhelmed by the sheer glory of human animation.

Food and Drink in Hong Kong and Macau

by Barry Girling

A food, travel, and entertainment columnist, Barry Girling has lived in Hong Kong since 1977.

I f you are coming to Hong Kong for the first time, there are certain misconceptions that you must leave at home. First, Hong Kong doesn't just have some of the better Chinese food in the world; it has the best.

Such a statement may not find immediate recognition in Taiwan or the People's Republic of China, but the proof of the pudding is in the eating, as they say in the West, and those Taiwanese and mainland Chinese who can afford it come to Hong Kong to eat. It is historical fact that chefs were brought from Canton to Peking to serve in the Chinese emperors' kitchens, and that for many centuries the Cantonese were acknowledged as the Middle Kingdom's finest cooks.

There is an old Chinese maxim that tells listeners where to find the prettiest girls, where to get married, where to die, where to eat, and so forth; the answer to "where to eat" is Canton (now called Guangzhou in the approved official romanization of Chinese names that also changes Peking to Beijing).

Hong Kong's 5.7 million-plus population is 98% Chinese, and the vast majority of that number are Cantonese (that includes a significant group of Chiu Chow people, whose families originated around the port city of Swatow). Food is a subject of overriding importance to the Cantonese, and it can be claimed of them as it is of the French, that they live to eat rather than eat to live. Find out how true that statement is on a culinary tour of Hong Kong.

There's no such thing as a fortune cookie in a Hong Kong restaurant; it was the overseas Chinese who came up with that novelty. Chop suey was invented overseas, too. The exact origin is disputed: Some people say it began on the California gold fields; others give credit (or blame) to Australian gold miners.

The Cantonese made an art out of a necessity, and, during times of hardship, used every part of an animal, fish, or vegetable. Some dishes on a typical Hong Kong menu will sound strange, even unappetizing—goose webs, for example, or cockerels' testicles, cows' innards, snakes (in season), pigs' shanks, and other things that may not be served at McDonald's. But why not succumb to new taste experiences? Who scorns the French for eating snails and frogs, or the Japanese for eating raw fish, or the Scots for stuffing a sheep's stomach lining?

Visit a daytime dim-sum palace. Served from before dawn to around 5 or 6 PM, the Cantonese daytime snacks of dim sum are miniature works of art. There are about 2,000 types in the Cantonese repertoire. Most dim-sum restaurants prepare 100 varieties daily. Generally served steaming in bamboo baskets, the buns, crepes, and cakes are among the world's finest hors d'oeuvres. Many are works of culinary engineering—such as a soup with prawns served in a translucent rice pastry shell, or a thousand-layer cake, or the ubiquitous spring roll.

There are hundreds of dim-sum restaurants. The Hong Kong Tourist Association (HKTA) publishes a comprehensive listing of some of the better ones that welcome tourists. The publication also provides color illustrations of the main dim-sum favorites. Many of the top-rated Chinese restaurants in hotels, and some of the better restaurants, provide (somewhat incongruously) elegant settings for lunchtime dim sum—with bilingual check sheets, waiter service, and private tables. Such class costs about HK$8 or more per basket. History-minded snackers will prefer, preferably in the company of Cantonese colleagues, to visit the culinary shrine of the **Luk Yu Teahouse** in Central (24 Stanley St.).

Luk Yu is more than a restaurant. It is one of Hong Kong's few historical monuments. It's fitting that a restaurant should be an unofficially preserved monument in this culinary capital of the world. It opened in the early 20th century as a wood-beamed, black-fanned, brass-edged place for Chinese gentlemen to partake of tea, dim sum, and gossip. When it was forced to relocate over a decade ago, everything was kept intact—marble-back chairs, floor spitoons, kettle warmers, brass coat hooks, lock-up liquor cabinets for regular patrons, and a Sikh doorman. Despite the modern air-conditioning, fans still decorate a plain ceiling that looks down on elaborately framed scrolls, carved-wood booth partitions, and colored glass panels. The ancient wood staircase still creaks as Hong Kong's gentlemen ascend to the upper floors to discuss the territory's government and business.

Modernity has brought the English language, bilingual menus (but not for the individually served dim sum items), and some good manners to Luk Yu. And so the adventurous tourist will seek out daytime dim-sum palaces where such modern affectations do not exist—as in the authentic teahouses of Mongkok, where local customers still "walk the bird" at dawn (the Chinese tradition—considered very "masculine"—of taking one's caged bird out for a morning stroll with its friends).

Birds are also to be eaten, of course. As far as the Cantonese are concerned, anything that "keeps its back to heaven" is fit for cooking. Only cannibals won't be satisfied in Hong Kong. Bird-tasting experiences in Hong Kong should include a feast of quails; smooth, salted chicken; sweet roasted chicken in lemon sauce; and minced pigeon served in lettuce leaf "bowls" (that are rolled up with a plum sauce "adhesive"). Pigeons in dozens of different forms can best be enjoyed in New Territories, around the new city of Shatin.

Fish can be enjoyed anywhere. Hong Kong is a major port with numerous fishing communities—something easily forgotten by the city-centered visitor. Go to the islands, to **Lamma** especially, for fine seafood feasts. Or take the bus and ferry trip to **Leiyuemun,** where you can choose your dinner from the massive fish tanks, haggle over its price, and take it into any restaurant for cooking and an al fresco feast.

At **Causeway Bay,** a small fleet of sampans turns dining out into a memorable experience. Your private floating restaurant table bobs past other craft selling shellfish, fresh fruit and vegetables, beer and spirits. There is even a floating Cantonese Opera minitroupe that can be hired to serenade your open-air floating meal.

The prime floating experience is, of course, the **Jumbo restaurant** at Aberdeen. It is moored to another floating home of seafood and gaudy multicolored carvings and murals that are a sight worth seeing. The Jumbo, a 2,000-seat three-decker, is a marvel of outrageous ostentatiousness.

It's time to note that there is no such thing as "Chinese" cooking in China. Every good "Chinese" cook has his (or sometimes her) own repertoire that will reflect his clan's origin. Most Hong Kong restaurants are Cantonese. Others concentrate on Pekingese or northern styles, Shanghai specialties, or the other regional styles of Szechuan or Chiu Chow cooking. There are a few spots that offer Hakka-style food, some Mongolian specialty restaurants (featuring hot pots), a Hunanese restaurant, and even a Taiwanese café on Food Street.

Food Street, in Causeway Bay, is a good place for a first-timer to start discovering the variety of food available in Hong Kong. There are now two covered and fountained arcades of relatively well-managed restaurants to suit most tastes and budgets. All around them, in an area that's generally named after the "Daimaru" department store, are literally hundreds of other cafés and restaurants.

Other favored eating places are found in **Wanchai,** once the fictional home for "Suzie Wong" and now a struggling nightlife area that has run out of sailors. Restaurants have appeared instead, alongside the topless bars, hostess-filled nightclubs, and dance halls that are expensive ways to get a drink in Hong Kong.

In "old" **Tsimshatsui,** on both sides of Nathan Road, from the Peninsula Hotel up to the Jordan Road junction; there is another batch of good, long-established restaurants. And Tsimshatsui East has skyscrapers bursting with a wide variety of eating spots—from grand Cantonese restaurants to cheerful little cafés. There, as everywhere, you'll find not only Cantonese fare but Korean barbecues, Singaporean satays, Peking duck, Shanghainese breads and eel dishes, fine Western cuisine—and junk food, of course.

The **Harbour City** complex, along Canton Road, has many fine spots tucked into shopping arcades or courtyards. **Central,** once morguelike at night, is now a bustling dining district with a warren of trendy bistros and good Indian restaurants up the hillside lanes, on and off Wyndham Street and Lan Kwai Fong. All are much favored by resident expatriates.

Then there are the hotels, culinary competitors full of stylish salons—so stylish it's now hard to find a simple, old-fashioned coffee shop. Travel away from downtown districts and you find more temptations. Every housing estate and community center now boasts at least one brass-and-chrome home of good Cantonese cuisine, often as chic as it is wholesome.

Deciding what and where to eat can be a headache in Hong Kong. There is an embarrassment of riches. This guidebook's restaurant listings will help. Once in Hong Kong, buy the HKTA's *Visitor's Guide to Chinese Food in Hong Kong.* It costs HK$10 and is a useful introduction to Chinese regional cuisines, chopstick wielding, dim-sum selecting, and other topics that can confuse a novice.

Foodwise, it helps to think of China as a Europe with a difference. As in Europe, there are obvious culinary variations between the cold-wintered northern regions (the Pekingese/Mongolian cuisine) and the temperate or semitropical southern climes (where Szechuan's chilied spiciness seems natural). The difference is that the various Chinese regions have been practicing cooking as a fine art for quite a few centuries longer than their European counterparts.

In simple terms, the Northern or Peking cuisine is designed to fill and warm—noodles, dumplings, and breads of various types are more evident than rice. Mongolian or Manchurian hot pots (a sort of fondue-cum-barbecue) are specialties, and firm flavors (garlic, ginger, leek, etc.) are popular. Desserts, of little interest to Cantonese, are heavy and sweet. Feasts have long been favored in the north, and not just by emperors composing week-long banquets with elaborate centerpieces such as Peking duck (a three-course marvel of skin slices, sautéed meat, a rich soup of duck bones, and Tien Tsin cabbage). Beggar's chicken, about which you'll hear varying legendary origins, is another culinary ceremony, in which a stuffed, seasoned, lotus-leaf-wrapped, and clay-baked bird releases heavenly aromas when its clay is cracked open.

Farther south, the Shanghai region (including Hangzhou) developed tastes similar to Peking's but with an oilier, sweeter style that favored preserved meats, fish, and vegetables. In Hong Kong, the Shanghainese cafés are generally just that—unostentatious cafés with massive "buffet" displays of preserved or fresh snacks that are popular with late-nighters.

The phenomenal development of a middle class in Hong Kong in recent years has prompted the appearance of grander, glitzier restaurants, for Shanghainese and all other major regional cuisines. Those run by the Maxim's group are always reliable, moderately priced, and welcoming to visitors.

The territory's Chiu Chow restaurants also come alive late at night—especially in the Chiu Chow-populated areas of the Western District (on Hong Kong Island) or in parts of western Kowloon. As with Shanghainese and Cantonese cuisine, the Chiu Chow repertoire emphasizes its homeland's marine traditions, especially for shellfish. The exotic-sounding "bird's nest" is the great Chiu Chow delicacy. It's the refined, congealed saliva of nest-building swallows (mainly gathered from Gulf of Siam cliff-face nests). Although it may sound terrible, it is often exquisitely flavored. The dish is also deemed to be an aphrodisiac, as are many of China's most expensive luxury food items. That's why a visit to a Chinese department store should include a shocked glance at the "medicine" counter's natural foods. The prices of top-grade bird's nest, shark's fins, deer horns, ginseng roots, and other time-tested fortifications are staggering. The laws of supply and demand are very apparent on the price tags.

The roughest, simplest fare can appear to be that of the Szechuan region. At first tasting, the fiery peppercorned dishes, akin to both Thai and Indian cuisines, can be tongue-searing. After a while, when the taste buds have blossomed again, the subtleties of Szechuan spices will be apparent—particularly in the classic smoked duck specialty, where camphor wood chips and red tea leaves add magical tinges to a finely seasoned, day-long-marinated duck.

Other regional variations (such as those of Hunan or the Hakka people) are not as distinctive as the major regional cuisines and are rarely found in Hong Kong. But there are a host of alternates for any visitor who wants a taste of adventure.

Chinese-influenced Asian cuisines are well represented. Even before the exodus of ethnic Chinese from Vietnam, that nation's exciting blend of native, French, and Chinese cooking styles was popular in Hong Kong. Now there are many cafés and a few smart restaurants specializing in prawns on sugar cane, mint-leaved meals, Vietnamese-style (labeled "VN") salamis, omelets, and fondues. Look, too, for Burmese restaurants.

The most ubiquitous Asian cuisine is the multiethnic "Malaysian," a budget diner's culinary United Nations that includes native Malay, Indian, and Straits Chinese dishes, as well as "European" meals and the Sino-Malay culinary cross-culture of the *nonya* cooking (developed by Malay wives to satisfy Chinese spouses).

Indian restaurants are also popular, and not just with Hong Kong's population of immigrants from the subcontinent. Usually the Indian kitchens concentrate on the northern Moghul styles of cooking, with reliable tandoori dishes. Vegetarians also find pleasures at Indian cafés. Thailand has not been forgotten, and the territory sports more than 24 spicy Thai restaurants.

Northeast Asia is also well represented. Some observers claim that Hong Kong has some of the world's finest Japanese restaurants, which thrive on local seafood catches and still tempt big spenders with their imports of the highly prized Kobe or Matsukaya beef (marbled slices of fine flavor produced by beer-massaged and pampered steers). Smaller spenders welcome the many local Korean cafés, whose inexpensive *bulgogi* (barbecues) provide that country's distinctive, garlicky, marinated meats and the mini-buffet of preserved kimchee selections.

Then there's Indonesia, which has given Hong Kong another host of inexpensive, nourishing cafés. From Europe, there is a culinary wonderland of fine French restaurants (mostly in the top hotels), British pubs, German wining-and-dining havens, deli delights, and a sprinkling of delightfully offbeat eating experiences—from Dutch-Flemish to Austrian, Spanish-Filipino, and Californian.

Although the Cantonese are the world's finest cooks, they are among the least polite waiters and waitresses in the world. The Cantonese are proud, some say arrogant, and their dialect has a belligerent tone and abruptness that translates poorly in English. Don't expect smiles or obsequiousness: Hong Kong isn't Bangkok or Manila. It's friendly in its own abrupt way, and it's certainly efficient, and if you meet smiles as well, count yourself lucky. And give the extra percentage on the tip that the pleasant waiter deserves.

Don't tip at local corner cafés or the few remaining roadside food stalls, since it's not expected. And wherever you eat, at the top or lower ends of the culinary scale, always check prices beforehand, especially for fresh fish, which is now a luxury in Hong Kong. "Seasonal" prices apply to many dishes and can be steep. And note that there are various categories of prized Chinese delicacies on menus—shark's fin, abalone, bird's nest, and bamboo fungus, for example—which can cost an emperor's ransom. Although few Hong Kong restaurants set out to rip off tourists (certainly not those that are sign-bearing members of the HKTA), waiters will of course try to "sell up."

Also, don't settle for the safe standbys for tourists. Sweet and sour pork, chop suey, and fried rice can be marvelous in Hong Kong. But the best dishes are off the menu, on table cards, written in Chinese, advertising seasonal specialties. Ask for translations, ask for interesting recommendations, try new items—show that you are adventurous and the captains will respond, giving you the respect and fine dishes you deserve.

A Shopper's Paradise

by Patricia Davis

Whatever your reason for coming to Hong Kong, and whether or not you are a shopper by nature, it is very unlikely that you will leave the place without having bought *something*. Indeed, there's a roaring trade in bargain-priced luggage because so many visitors run out of space in the suitcases they arrived with. Even nonshoppers get tempted to part with their money—and some have admitted to actually enjoying the experience.

Although the thought of crowded streets, mind-boggling choices, and endless haggling can be daunting, there is no place more conducive to big-time spending than Hong Kong! The variety of goods is astonishing: everything from international designer products to intriguing treasures and handicrafts from all over Asia. Just as astonishing is the fantastic choice of places to shop, which range from sophisticated boutique-lined malls to open-air markets and shadowy alleyways.

There are several good reasons why Hong Kong is such an extraordinary shopping mecca. The first is its status as a free port, whereby everything, other than alcohol, tobacco, perfumes, cosmetics, cars, and some petroleum products, comes in without import duty. The second is the fact that Hong Kong has a skilled and still relatively inexpensive labor force. Goods made here are considerably cheaper than they will be by the time they reach shop shelves anywhere else in the world. The third factor is the highly competitive nature of the retail business—the result of a local policy of free trade, which encourages everyone to try to undercut his neighbor. To this end, many shops, with the exception of those in the Western and Central districts, stay open until 10 PM. Shops are also humming on Sundays and on all holidays apart from Chinese New Year, which falls either in the last two weeks of January or during the first two of February, when everything closes for at least three days.

There's a saying among expatriate residents that nothing in Hong Kong is as you expect it, and it is certainly true where shopping is concerned! Hong Kong cannot be compared to any other international shopping center—Paris, Milan, London, or New York—and you will be disappointed if you try. The only practical comparisons worth making are those on your calculator.

So what's so different about Hong Kong? For a start, consider the geography of the place. It is very small, and very heavily populated. It has had to grow upward and downward rather than outward, which means that there are shops and small businesses in all sorts of unexpected places. You'll find a trendy fashion designer tucked away on the third floor of a scruffy alleyway building, a picture framer operating out of the basement of a lighting shop, a tailor snipping and stitching in the back room of a shoe shop. Many of the buildings will appear dingy and dirty, and you will be convinced that no self-respecting business can be carried on there. But it can and it is. And these are the places where Hong Kong residents do much of their shopping. Also disconcerting for people who come expecting to find the streets lined with bargains, is the discovery that prices for the same goods vary from sky-high to rock-bottom within a 100-yard stretch of shops. But this is the land of free trade. And it is why shopping around and sticking to reputable establishments are prerequisites to any successful purchase, particularly if it is an expensive one.

By reputable establishments we mean ones that have been recommended by a friend who lives or shops regularly in Hong Kong, by this guide, or by the Hong Kong Tourist Association via its invaluable booklet *The Official Guide to Shopping, Eating Out and Services in Hong Kong*, or their leaflets on fur and *Factory Outlets in Hong Kong (Ready-to-Wear & Jewelry)*. You have a better chance of getting a good buy if you are a friend of a valued customer, or if there is the risk of a complaint being lodged with the HKTA.

All shops bearing the HKTA's red junk logo in their window are supposed to provide good value for money, accurate representation of products sold, and prompt rectification of justified complaints, but if you have problems, call the HKTA (tel. 801–7177). For complaints about non-HKTA shops, call the Consumer Council (tel. 736–3636).

The law of the jungle is alive and well in Hong Kong, so be prepared for lots of shoving and pushing on the sidewalks, little respect for taxi lines, a limited amount in the way of gallantry, and an overwhelming urge on the part of sales staff to sell you something, no matter what!

Contrary to popular belief, not everyone speaks English. In the main tourist shopping areas you can probably count on most shop staff speaking some English—but do not assume that they understand all you say, even if they nod their heads confidently. Don't get irritated if communications get muddled. Displays of anger and raised voices do not impress the Chinese. In their eyes you will have lost respect and they will probably become less, rather than more, helpful.

Many of the taxi drivers' English is limited, too, and so it can make life easier if you get your destination written down in Chinese by the hotel concierge before you set off. Most taxis now carry a radio microphone that lets you speak to their headquarters where your instructions will be translated.

Once on the right road, however, shopping around and bargaining are your golden rules. The pressure from sales staff can sometimes be exasperating. If you are just browsing, make it very clear that is what you are doing. Don't be pushed into a big purchase. Make a note of the details of the item(s) and prices on the shop's business card so you know where to return. Always ask about discounts—sizable ones for multiple purchases. You should be able to get a discount just about everywhere except in Japanese department stores, the China product stores, and some of the larger boutiques, which sell on a fixed-price basis. When other shops try to convince you that everything is fixed price, don't believe them. You should get at least 10%, and more likely 40%, from jewelers and furriers.

Equally, do not necessarily believe a salesman when he assures you that his price is his "very best" unless you have done enough shopping around to know that he is offering you a good deal. Never be bashful to ask for a discount. It is the accepted and expected way of conducting business all over Asia.

Your success in negotiating may be greater if the shop is not full. A salesman or woman is less likely to be beaten down if there is a large audience of other shoppers.

After checking out the prices in several different shops, you should get a good idea of what you should have to pay. Don't imagine that you will get the very best price (you won't know what it is, anyway); these are generally given only to local Chinese customers. Your best bet is to compare the price with what you might have to pay for such an item back home.

If you are planning to shop in markets, alleys, or market stalls, it's best not to go very dressed up, or to carry only large denomination notes or big-figure traveler's checks. This will not help your bargaining position, and will just serve to highlight the fact that you are a rich tourist able to pay at least three times the fair price!

When you are shopping in these places make sure you inspect the goods you buy very carefully. Many of them are "imperfects" that didn't make it through quality control; in other words, they are seconds. Look closely at lengths of fabric; they may have faults. When you buy clothing, inspect the actual item handed to you. You may have chosen it on the strength of a sample hanging up, but what you are given could be different. It may not be the same size, it could have more serious faults.

At the other end of the scale, if you are intending to shop for something important like jewelry or a fur coat, it can work in your favor to dress smartly. It is amazing how much more seriously you are taken if you look the part.

If you do not know much about the commodity you are buying, do not hesitate to ask the salesperson to explain or show you the difference between, say, a HK$30,000 diamond and a HK$10,000 one of the same size, or the difference between the two mink coats that look similar to you but carry vastly different price tags. Any reputable dealer in these specialist items should be happy to show you what you are getting for the extra money, and how it compares to the less expensive item. The understanding of such factors can go a long way to helping you to make up your mind about which is really the better buy.

Having satisfied yourself that you really want the item and have struck the right price for it, it is time for the exchange of money. (Although credit cards and traveler's checks are widely accepted, best prices are offered for cash purchases.) An appropriate guarantee and a fully itemized receipt should be forthcoming from the shop for any major purchase. Such details as the model number and serial number of manufactured goods like cameras, audiovisual or electronic equipment, or the description of gems and precious metal content in jewelry and watches, should be noted.

Check that your purchase is covered by the right kind of guarantee; local guarantees that are valid for 12 months in Hong Kong only, or local retailer guarantees, will not be much good to overseas visitors on a short shopping spree. Make sure you get a worldwide/international guarantee that carries the name or logo of the relevant sole agent in Hong Kong and that there is a service center in your home town or country. And if you are having something shipped home for you (many shops are geared up for this) make sure that the insurance covers not only loss, but also damage, in transit.

So much for the nuts and bolts. But forewarned is forearmed, which, we hope, will make the whole experience of shopping in Hong Kong all the more fun. Because fun it certainly is. Whether you are drifting about in the comfort of the air-conditioned shopping malls, exploring the factory outlets of Hung Hom, or poking about in the alleys and back streets, you are getting a look at the life and guts of Hong Kong. It's as much a cultural experience as a shopping expedition. In a way, that can be the most unexpected bargain of your whole trip.

3 Exploring Hong Kong

Orientation

Hong Kong is one of the world's most compact, intense travel experiences. The population density in the city is almost overwhelming, and the atmosphere everywhere is vibrant with life, energy, and the frantic quest for money and personal achievement. Here is the very essence of Western capitalism, yet the heart of the place is truly Oriental. This blend *and* contrast are what make Hong Kong so fascinating.

There is so much to see and do here that it's easy to be lured away from a hectic business schedule or a rigid sightseeing routine and instead head down alleyways lined with shops selling everything from fine jewelry to sportswear and filled with the aroma of food stalls and some of the world's best Chinese restaurants. You won't find much ancient history here because Hong Kong has existed as a city for little more than 100 years. But there's a feeling of old China here, more so than in mainland China. The Chinese have been flocking to Hong Kong for decades, bringing with them their traditions as well as their energy and entrepreneurial spirit. Hong Kong has given full scope to that spirit, leaving it unhindered by political or social limitations.

The feeling of Hong Kong, what it is and why it exists, can be discovered only from the harbor. That body of water, chosen centuries ago by fishermen from China as a perfect shelter from the raging *tai'foos* ("big winds," the origin of the word "typhoon"), is still the territory's centerpiece.

In the 1970s the Cross-Harbour Tunnel was built, linking Hong Kong Island, the financial, business, and government center of the colony, with the mainland. The MTR opened in the early 1980s, helping to link the far-flung parts of the territory to each other and to Hong Kong Island. Before that, the populace depended on passenger and vehicular ferries, the latter painfully slow, with great line-ups at either end. Furthermore, Hong Kong was run as a dual economy, with branches of offices, delivery fleets, and other businesses on one side of the harbor duplicating facilities on the other side. There were even separate laws and charges covering buses, taxes, and electricity.

The sense of separation still remains, even though it now takes only a few minutes to drive through the tunnel (excluding the often long waiting times on either side to get into the tunnel), or less than 30 minutes to get from Hong Kong Central to the farthest point in the territory on the MTR. The Hong Kong business world long ago gave up the dual-economy system and streamlined operations. But in the minds of many people, going from one section of the territory to another still seems akin to traveling for hours instead of minutes.

"Let's have dinner in Kowloon," says a Kowloon-side resident to his Hong Kong friend, and the first thought in the Hong Konger's mind is, "All the way to Kowloon!" The reverse is also true. Invite your colleague to dinner at your home on the south side of the island, in Repulse Bay or Shouson Hill, and, despite the Aberdeen Tunnel that cuts traveling time to mere minutes, the first response is likely to be, "So far?" And so it is for Hong Kongers or Kowloonians to venture to New Territories, or for mainliners to visit the islands.

Hong Kong Island   Until 1841, the island that is now modern Hong Kong was home to a few fishermen and their families. Hong Kong, 30 square miles (78 sq km) in size, did not have a single natural water source, its vegetation was sparse, and its center was mountainous. Except for the natural harbor, all its geographical, historical, and demographic factors should have guaranteed Hong Kong permanent obscurity.

Hong Kong was officially ceded to Great Britain in 1841 at the end of the First Opium War with China. At that time it was hardly considered a valuable prize. The British military acknowledged its usefulness as an operational base or transshipping port, but was angry that it wasn't offered a port on the mainland of China. The British foreign minister called Hong Kong "that barren island," and Queen Victoria's consort, Prince Albert, publicly laughed at this "jewel" in the British Crown.

Hardly an auspicious beginning for the island that author Han Su-Yin was to describe a century later as the "deep roaring bustling eternal market . . . in which life and love and souls and blood and all things made and grown under the sun are bought and sold and smuggled and squandered."

Han's description is the impression one gets now when arriving on the island for the first time by Star Ferry. (One of the unfortunate results of progress is that many visitors now get their initial view of Hong Kong Island as they emerge from the cavernous Cross-Harbour Tunnel or from the steps of the MTR, rather than from the legendary Star Ferry.)

It was only blocks away from the Star Ferry terminal that Captain Charles Elliott of Britain's Royal Navy first set foot on what he called "this barren rock." Today, "this barren rock" contains some of the world's most expensive real estate and a skyline to rival that of any of the world's major cities.

Exploring Hong Kong Island

Many of the British who set up their trading warehouses on Hong Kong Island were of Scottish ancestry. They were among the most nationalistic (or homesick) in the Victorian world, and so almost everything of importance was named after Queen Victoria. The central section was named Victoria City, the mountain peak was Victoria Peak, the military barracks, Victoria Barracks, and the prison, Victoria Prison. Later came Victoria College and Victoria Park.

Central Hong Kong is still officially named Victoria City, but today everyone calls it **Central.** The buildings here are both modern and ornate. They gleam in gold, silver, ivory, and ebony, reflecting a jewel-like iridescence from the harbor. No one can fail to be overwhelmed by this first view of Hong Kong.

Central District is in the center of the north side of the island, and, because the island is small, the truly energetic could walk its circumference in a day. The extreme western end of the island is **Western District.** To the east of Central lie **Wanchai,** famed at one time for its nightlife, and **Causeway Bay,** which was once a middle-class Chinese community but is now primarily a business and tourist area filled with offices, hotels, restaurants, and shops.

Farther east is **Quarry Bay,** once solely a factory and tenement section and now also a middle-class housing area. Shaukiwan and Chai Wan, at the eastern end of Quarry Bay, were once very poor, but are now undergoing rapid urban development.

In the center of the island is the **Mid-Levels** area, which is almost entirely residential. It is worth a visit because it has some of the few remaining examples of Victorian apartment architecture left in Hong Kong. Here, too, is **Hong Kong University** and the **Botanical Gardens.**

High above Mid-Level is **Victoria Peak,** known simply as The Peak, jutting up 1,805 feet above sea level. Residents here take special pride in the positions to which they have, quite literally, risen. It is the most exclusive residential area on the island.

Aberdeen, on the southwest side of the island, has a busy fisherman's harbor and is where you will find the "floating garden" restaurants; **Ocean Park,** which has Asia's largest oceanarium and the new Middle Kingdom; and **Water World.** Aberdeen also contains a factory area, Wong Chuk Hang, and the highway interchange for the Aberdeen Tunnel, which slices through the mountains and comes out at the **Happy Valley Race Track.**

Leaving Aberdeen and heading east on a winding ocean-front highway, you will come to scenic **Deep Water Bay.** Farther east is **Repulse Bay,** another of Hong Kong's prestigious residential areas, and a very popular beach. Still following the winding road, you will come upon the tiny village of **Stanley,** with its open-air market; then **Big Wave Bay,** one of the territory's few surfing beaches; and then the pleasant village of **Shek O,** another old settlement that today is a mix of village houses and baronial mansions.

Central and Western Districts

Numbers in the margin correspond with points of interest on the Central and Western Districts map.

❶ **Star Ferry** is the logical place to start your tour of Central District. Since 1898, the ferry terminal has been the gateway to the island for visitors and commuters crossing the harbor from Kowloon. Crossing the harbor on the Star Ferry and riding around Hong Kong Island on the two-decker tram are two musts for first-time visitors. The charge is minimal: the Star Ferry charges HK$1.20 first class, HK$1 second class; and the tram from Central to Causeway Bay and beyond is HK$1. In front of the terminal you will usually see a few red rickshaws. Once numbering in the thousands, these two-wheel, man-powered "taxis" are all but gone. Also in front of the terminal is one of the *Tote* (off-track betting offices). To the right, as you face

❷ inland, are the main **Post Office** and the towering **Jardine House,** which is easy to spot with its many round windows. Jardine House, formerly Connaught Centre, was completed in 1973 and was one of Central's first skyscrapers.

❸ Farther to your right is the futuristic **Exchange Square,** with its gold- and silver-striped glass towers. This complex is home to the Hong Kong Stock Exchange, and contains some of the

❹ most expensive rental space on the island. In front is **Blake**

Central and Western Districts

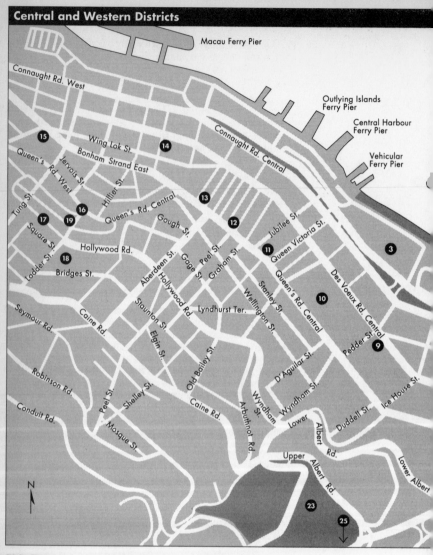

Macau Ferry Pier

Outlying Islands
Ferry Pier

Central Harbour
Ferry Pier

Vehicular
Ferry Pier

Connaught Rd. West

Wing Lok St.

Connaught Rd. Central

Bonham Strand East

Queen's Rd. West

Jervois St.

Hillier St.

Queen's Rd. Central

Gough St.

Jubilee St.

Queen Victoria St.

Tung St.

Square St.

Ladder St.

Hollywood Rd.

Bridges St.

Aberdeen St.

Gage St.

Peel St.

Graham St.

Hollywood Rd.

Stanley St.

Wellington St.

Queen's Rd. Central

Des Voeux Rd. Central

Pedder St.

Seymour Rd.

Caine Rd.

Staunton St.

Elgin St.

Lyndhurst Ter.

D'Aguilar St.

Wyndham St.

Duddell St.

Ice House St.

Robinson Rd.

Peel St.

Shelley St.

Old Bailey St.

Caine Rd.

Arbuthnot Rd.

Wyndham St.

Lower Albert Rd.

Conduit Rd.

Mosque St.

Upper Albert Rd.

Lower Albert

N

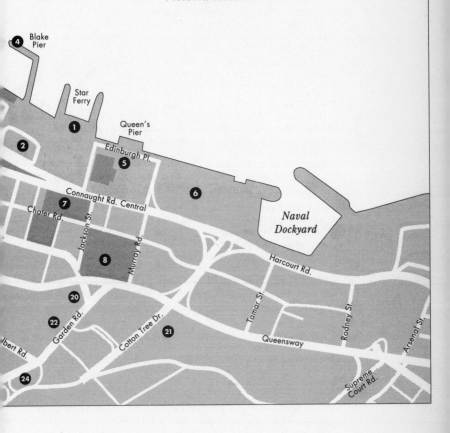

Victoria Harbour

Blake Pier

Star Ferry

Queen's Pier

Edinburgh Pl.

Connaught Rd. Central

Chater Rd.

Jackson St.

Murray Rd.

Naval Dockyard

Harcourt Rd.

Garden Rd.

Cotton Tree Dr.

Tamar St.

Queensway

Rodney St.

Arsenal St.

Supreme Court Rd.

lbert Rd.

Pier. The open-air café at the far end is one of the best and least expensive spots from which to enjoy the panoramic view of the harbor while eating or drinking.

⑤ The **City Hall complex** (Central, between Edinburgh Pl. and Connaught Rd.) faces out over Queen's Pier and the harbor. In addition to municipal offices, it contains a theater, concert hall, museum, exhibition and art galleries, and a library. Many of the events in the annual International Arts and Film Festival are held here.

A popular attraction in the City Hall complex is the **Hong Kong Museum of Art,** which contains a large collection of Chinese antiquities, including ceramics, bronzes, lacquerware, jade, and embroideries. The art collection includes thousands of paintings and works of calligraphy from the 17th century to the present. The museum has a gift shop. *City Hall complex, tel. 522–4127. Admission free. Open Mon.–Wed. and Fri.–Sat. 10–6, Sun. and holidays 1–6; closed Thurs.*

⑥ **HMS *Tamar,*** next to the City Hall Complex, is not a ship but the 28-story headquarters of the British Army and Royal Navy. The area gets its name from a ship once anchored in the harbor. The building and a small harbor are all that remain of the old naval dockyard that occupied the entire shore area, as far as Wanchai. Today, visiting warships often anchor offshore here, their crews coming ashore for nightlife and shopping, as sailors have always done in Hong Kong.

⑦ **Statue Square** is a small oasis of green between Connaught Road Central and Chater Road. Filled with shaded walks and fountains, it is popular with office workers during lunch time. It is also a favorite gathering spot on weekends for hundreds of housemaids from the Philippines. The square is surrounded by some of the most important buildings in Hong Kong, and is above the **Central MTR Station,** one of the busiest subway stations in the world, handling almost 2 million passengers daily.

A modern building bordering the square houses the **Hong Kong Club,** one of the last social bastions of the fading British colonial system. The club, as attractive as an ice-rink cafeteria, will accept anyone today, but even now there is only 10% Chinese membership. Next door is the **Legislative Council** building, with its domes and colonnades. It formerly housed the Supreme Court and is one of the few remaining grand Victorian buildings left in this area. Right now the Council has a largely consultative role, without any real power. How important this body will be once the British hand over power to China in 1997 remains to be seen. In front of the Council building is the **Cenotaph** monument to all who lost their lives in the two world wars.

The modern glass-and-steel-structure at the end of the square is the headquarters of the **Hongkong and Shanghai Bank.** Known simply as The Bank, this is the largest and most powerful financial institution in Hong Kong. It still issues local bank notes and has enormous influence in every field of investment. The building was designed to make a positive statement about the future of Hong Kong and its capitalistic system. To the left of the bank is the even taller headquarters of the **Bank of China,** designed to rival its neighbor in both aesthetic and financial force. Perhaps this is an indication that China plans to challenge capitalism on its own terms after 1997.

Between these two giant bank towers is the **Hilton Hotel** (2 Queen's Rd., Central), one of the earliest of the post-war luxury hotels and still one of the best in town. As is the custom with many Hong Kong hotels, the lobby is several stories above ground level, to allow space for the all-important shopping arcades.

❽ In front of the Hilton is a small park, **Chater Garden** (Chater and Jackson Rds.), former home of the Hong Kong Cricket Club. A favorite local pastime was watching the cricket players enjoying the game at a leisurely pace, oblivious to the traffic noise and bustle. The club has now moved to new grounds outside the city center, chased away by the high price of real estate. Conservationists won their battle against developers to preserve the park, to the delight of all who come to sit and relax in this small, green oasis.

On the west side of Statue Square is the **Mandarin Oriental Hotel** (5 Connaught Rd.), one of the finest hotels in the world. The mezzanine coffee lounge is a pleasant place to stop for a drink.

Head west and follow the tracks of the rattling old trams that pass in front of the Hongkong Bank. This will take you along **Des Voeux Road,** which is lined with elegant shops and tall office buildings.

❾ **The Landmark** (Des Voeux Rd. and Pedder St.) is an impressive shopping complex, with atrium, cafés, and hundreds of top-name shops equal in quality to anything New York or London has to offer. Concerts, cultural shows, and other events are presented here free of charge—one of the few experiences in Hong Kong without a price tag on it.

Follow Pedder Street, beside The Landmark, and turn west on **Queen's Road Central,** one of the main shopping arteries. Narrow lanes on either side are filled with tiny shops and stalls filled with goods.

❿ **Li Yuen Street East and West,** for example, are bargain alleys for clothing, shoes, costume jewelry, woolens, and handbags.

⓫ **Central Market** (Queen's Rd. Central and Queen Victoria St.) is the city's largest public food market. More than 300 stalls offer every type of food—fish on the first floor, meat on the second, fruits and vegetables on the third. Opposite the market is a **Chinese Merchandise** department store, which offers reasonably priced Chinese goods, from household items to antiques, handicrafts, luggage, and souvenirs. Next to Central Market is **Jubilee Street,** filled with food stalls offering bowls of noodles, rice dishes, and a wide variety of snacks.

⓬ **Wing On Street** (off Queen's Rd. Central) a small side street, better known as **Cloth Alley,** is worth exploring because of its stalls overflowing with fabrics and sewing accessories. If you buy here, bargain like mad, as you would in any open-air market area in Hong Kong.

⓭ On **Wing Sing Street** (off Queen's Rd. Central) you will find every type of egg on sale—tiny quail eggs, large goose eggs, and preserved eggs, known as 1,000-year-old eggs, which are actually only a few months old and treated with a pungent mixture of lime, wood-ash, and tea leaves. Eggs preserved in salt are also sold here, their shells black from a charcoal coating. The next alley to the west is **Wing Lok Street,** lined with many traditional Chinese shops selling everything from rattan goods to medicines.

Queen's Road Central now forks to the left, but you should continue straight ahead to Bonham Strand East. **Man Wa Lane** is a tiny street (off Bonham Strand East) where you'll find carvers of *chops* (engraved seals). You can have your initials engraved in roman letters or Chinese characters on plastic, ivory, or jade. It takes about an hour to engrave a chop, which you can pick up later or on the following day.

⑮ Bonham Strand East and West is an area left relatively untouched by the modern world. The streets are lined with traditional shops, many open-fronted. Among the most interesting ones are those selling live snakes, both for food and medicinal use. The snakes, from pythons to cobras, are imported from China and kept in cages outside the shops. Here you can sample a bowl of snake soup or an invigorating snake-gallbladder wine. The main season for the snake trade is October through February.

Bonham Strand West is famous for traditional Chinese medicines and herbal remedies. Many of the old shops have their original facades and are lined with shelves of jars and drawers containing hundreds of strange-smelling ingredients, such as wood barks and insects, all meant to be dried and ground up, infused in hot water or tea, or taken as powders or pills. Some of the more innocuous remedies are made from ginseng, said to be good for virility and prolonging life.

At the western end of Bonham Strand West is **Des Voeux Road West**—you'll recognize it by the tram tracks. On the left side of the street as you continue west, you will find all kinds of shops selling preserved foods such as dried and salted fish, black mushrooms, and vegetables. This is a good area for lunchtime *dim sum* (hot snacks).

If you want to see street barbers at work, turn left and walk up **Sutherland Street.**

⑯ Queen's Road West is filled with embroidery shops selling richly brocaded wedding clothes and all types of embroidered linens, clothing, and household goods. Also along this street are shops where colorful items are made and sold for burning at Chinese funerals. Houses, cars, furniture, and TV sets—all made of paper and bamboo—are among the items necessary to ensure the departed a good life in the hereafter.

⑰ Funerals are also the theme for some shops along **Hollywood Road.** Here you will find traditional Chinese coffins and more of the elaborate ceremonial items needed for a funeral. Farther along you will find shops selling different grades of rice, displayed in brass-banded wood tubs. The rice is sold by the *catty* (about 1¼ lb). Look to the left for a sign saying "Possession Street." This was the place where Captain Charles Elliott of the British Royal Navy stepped ashore in 1841 and claimed Hong Kong for the British Empire. It is interesting to note how far today's harbor is from this area, which was once on the water's edge—the result of a century of massive land reclamation.

Farther east along Hollywood Road are many antiques, curio, and junk shops, as well as shops selling every type of Asian art and handicraft. Some items are genuinely old, but most are made to look old and passed off as antiques. Porcelain, embroidered robes, paintings, screens, snuff bottles, and wood and ivory carvings are among the many items that can be found here in profusion. Bargain hard if you want a good price.

18 **Man Mo Temple** is also on Hollywood Road, in the midst of the antiques and curio shops. It is one of Hong Kong's oldest and most important temples and is dedicated to Man, the god of literature, and Mo, the god of war. The statue of Man is dressed in green and holds a writing brush. Mo is dressed in red and holds a sword. To their left is a shrine to Pao Kung, god of justice, whose face is painted black. To the right is Shing Wong, god of the city. Coils of incense hang from the roof beams, filling the air with a heavy fragrance. The temple bell, cast in Canton in 1847, and the drum next to it are sounded to attract the attention of the gods when a prayer is being offered. If you want to check your fortune, stand in front of the altar, take one of the small bamboo cylinders available there, and shake it until one of the sticks falls out. The number on the stick corresponds to a particular fortune. But there's a catch—the English translation is in a book on sale in the temple.

19 To reach **Upper Lascar Row/Cat Street** from the temple, walk down the steps of **Ladder Street.** In the days before wheeled traffic, most of the steep, small lanes on the hillside were filled with steps. **Cat Street** (actually Upper Lascar Row) is a vast flea market. You won't find Ming vases here or anything else of real monetary value, but perhaps you'll come across an old Mao badge or an old teakettle or pot.

More worthwhile for the antiques collector is the section of shops and stalls known as **Cat Street Galleries,** adjacent to the flea market. The complex has four stories of galleries offering every type of art and handicraft, some old, most new. *38 Lok Ku Rd., tel. 543–1609. Open Mon.–Sat. 9–6, Sun. 11–5.*

Continue downhill and you will return to **Queen's Road Central.** Along this section are shops selling many different kinds of tea and traditional Chinese art supplies, including writing brushes, paper, and ink. Here, too, you can buy fans or have a calligrapher write a good luck message for you on an item you purchase.

Heading back along Queen's Road Central, toward Central Market, you will see a number of street markets in the stepped lanes to your right. On the left is the ornate facade of the **Eu Yan Sang Medical Hall** where traditional Chinese medicines are sold. You can browse for hours throughout this area, past market stalls and shops selling strange and wonderful goods, streets filled with the aroma of exotic foods, and lined with ornate old buildings that seem to be begging to be explored.

From Central to the Peak

20 The **Hilton Hotel** (2 Queen's Rd. Central) is where you start this tour, which will eventually take you to the Peak, towering above the harbor and the city. But don't worry, you don't have to walk all the way.

Queen's Road Central was once the seafront, and site of the old military parade grounds. Most of the important colonial buildings of the Victorian era were within easy reach of this area. Walking around this part of Central is a bit tricky because of a series of elevated motorways. However, there are pedestrian tunnels and overpasses. With a little patience and a good map, you should not have too much trouble finding your way about on foot.

㉑ **The Museum of Tea Ware** in Flagstaff House is easy to reach by walking through the tunnel under Cotton Tree Drive (located in the new Hong Kong Park, *see* Parks). Built in 1845, Flagstaff House is the city's oldest colonial building and was once the official residence of the commander of the British forces. Since 1984 it has housed the Museum of Tea Ware. The museum displays include everything connected with the art of serving tea, from the 7th century onward. *Cotton Tree Dr., tel. 869–0690. Admission free. Open 10–5. Closed Wed.*

㉒ **St. John's Cathedral,** completed in 1849 and a good example of Victorian-Gothic architecture, is the official Anglican cathedral. *Garden Rd., just above the Hilton. Open daily 10–8.*

Government House, a handsome white building up the hill from the cathedral, is the official residence of the governor. It was built in 1891 (Upper Albert Rd.).

㉓ A visit to **The Zoological and Botanical Gardens** is a delightful way to escape the city's traffic and crowds. In the early morning, people come here to practice t'ai chi ch'uan (the ancient art of shadow-boxing). The quiet pathways are lined with semi-tropical trees, shrubs, and flowers. The collection of animals in the zoo is small, although there are some exotic ones, such as leopards and jaguars. There is also an aviary with more than 300 species of birds, including flocks of cranes and pink-and-white flamingos. *Upper Albert Rd., opposite Government House. Admission free. Open daily 6:30–7.*

㉔ Lower Peak Tram Terminus is where you will find **The Peak Tram,** the steepest funicular railway in the world. It passes five intermediate stations en route to the upper terminal, 1,805 feet above sea level, and was opened in 1880 to transport people to the top of Victoria Peak, which is the highest hill overlooking Hong Kong Harbour. Before the tram, the only way to get to the top was to walk or take a bumpy ride up the steep steps in a sedan chair. The tram has two 72-seat cars that are hauled up the hill by cables attached to electric motors. *Between Garden Rd. and Cotton Tree Dr. Fare: HK$6 one way, HK$10 roundtrip. Open daily 7 AM–midnight. Trams run every 10–15 min.*

㉕ The Chinese name for **Victoria Peak** is *Tai Ping Shan* (Mountain of Great Peace). It might also be called Mountain of Great Views, for the panorama is breathtaking. On a clear day you can see across the islands to the People's Republic of China. The area is a popular picnic spot and filled with beautiful walking paths that circle the peak.

The **Peak Tower Building,** completed in 1972, contains a restaurant, coffee shop, gift shops, and a post office. Just below the summit is a lookout pavilion which was once part of a former governor's residence. The original gardens and country walks remain and are open to the public.

As an alternative to taking the Peak Tram down the hillside, you can catch a no. 15 bus or a cab to Central. This will take you on a trip as exciting and beautiful as the one on the tram through the steep roads of the residential areas of Mid-Levels.

Wanchai

Those who expect to discover the raunchy world of the old Wanchai may be disappointed. Wanchai still has its nocturnal charms (*see* Chapter 8), but the "Wanch" of Richard Mason's novel, *The World of Suzie Wong*, seems a bit faded now. Wanchai has always been a magnet for sailors on shore leave, and was especially popular with military men on leave during the Vietnam War. Today it's a bit more touristy and expensive, but you can still find topless bars, sailors from all nations, and military patrols (MPs) on the streets when a fleet is in town.

The old Luk Kwok Hotel, better known as the Suzie Wong Hotel, has been replaced with a large modern hotel, but you can still wander about **Lockhart Road** made famous by the novel. It's filled with seedy bars and plenty of restaurants, British pubs, and tailors' shops.

Wanchai was once one of the five "wan," or areas that the British set aside for Chinese residences. Today, in addition to the old section with its bars and massage parlors, it is a mixture of office buildings, restaurants, apartment buildings, and shops. A good point to start a circular walking tour is at the junction of Queensway and Queen's Road East. This is a 10-minute ride from Central by tram or on the no. 5 bus. Get off just past the Marriott Hotel.

Numbers in the margin correspond with points of interest on the Wanchai, Causeway Bay, Happy Valley, and North Point map.

❶ **Queen's Road East** is a busy shopping street. Heading east you pass rice and food shops and stores selling rattan and traditional furniture, paper lanterns, and materials for Chinese calligraphy. Farther along, on the right, is the **Tai Wong Temple.** You can see its altar from the street and smell the scent of smoldering *joss* (Chinese idol) sticks.

❷ **Hopewell Centre** (Queen's Rd. East and Amoy St.) is 66 stories high and was Hong Kong's tallest structure until the Bank of China building was completed. There is a revolving restaurant at the top, with superb views. Even if you don't plan to eat here, it's worth a visit just to ride the exterior "glass-bullet" elevator. Continuing along Queen's Road East, you will find, on your right, the **Wanchai Post Office,** one of Hong Kong's very few protected historical landmark buildings, with wonderful old, carved-wood counters. Turn left on **Wanchai Road,** a busy market area selling a variety of foods as well as clothing and household goods. It's a good place for browsing, especially along the narrow side alleyways. To the left are several small lanes leading to **Johnston Road,** where you'll see the tram lines again. There are a number of traditional shops here, including some selling household pets. Turn left on Johnston Road, and follow the edge of **Southorn Playground,** a popular meeting place, especially for those looking for a game of cards or Chinese checkers.

Luard Road, with its cross streets—Hennessy, Lockhart, and Jaffe roads—is in the heart of Old Wanchai. At night this area is alive with multicolored neon signs and a lively trade at the bars, pubs, massage parlors, and restaurants. Hennessy Road, which roughly follows the line of the original harbor frontage, is one of the better shopping streets and another good place for

Wanchai, Causeway Bay, Happy Valley, and North Point

0   330 yards

0   300 meters

Wanchai
Ferry Pier

Hung Hing Rd.

⑦

Seafront Rd.

Wanchai
Stadium

⑥

Harbour Rd.

④

③

⑤

Harbour Dr.

Gloucester Rd.

Jaffe Rd.

Fenwick St.

Luard Rd.

O'Brien Rd.

Fleming Rd.

Stewart Rd.

Tonnochy Rd.

Marsh Rd.

Bowrinton Rd.

Canal Rd. West

Lockhart Rd.

Hennessey Rd.

Wanchai Rd.

Thomson Rd.

①

Queen's Rd. East

Johnston Rd.

Morrison
Hill

Spring Garden Ln.

Cross St.

Wanchai Rd.

②

Queen's Rd. East

Academy for
Performing Arts, **5**

Arts Centre, **4**

Aw Boon Haw (Tiger
Balm) Gardens, **14**

Cargo Handling
Basin, **7**

Causeway Bay
Typhoon Shelter, **9**

Causeway Centre, **3**

Excelsior Hotel, **8**

Food Street, **10**

Hong Kong
Convention Centre, **6**

Hopewell Centre, **2**

Kwun Yum Temple, **13**

Queen's Road East, **1**

Tin Hau Temple, **12**

Victoria Park, **11**

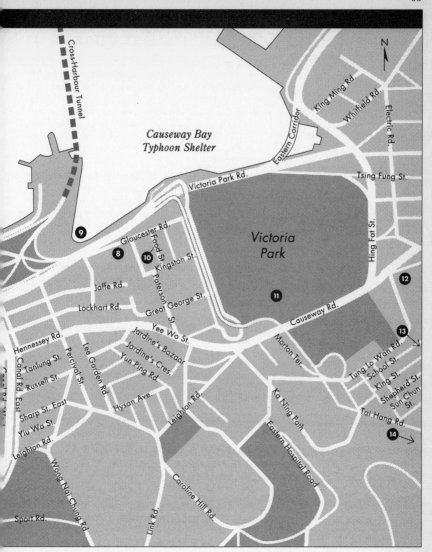

Cross-Harbour Tunnel

Causeway Bay
Typhoon Shelter

N

King Ming Rd.

Whitfield Rd.

Electric Rd.

Tsing Fung St.

Victoria Park Rd.

Eastern Corridor

Hing Fat St.

Victoria
Park

9

Gloucester Rd.

8

Food St.

10

Kingston St.

12

Jaffe Rd.

Paterson St.

Great George St.

11

Lockhart Rd.

Yee Wo St.

Causeway Rd.

13

Hennessey Rd.

Jardine's Bazaar

Morton Ter.

Tung Lo Wan Rd.

School St.

King St.

Canal Rd. East

Tanlung St.

Jardine's Cres.

Lee Garden Rd.

Yun Ping Rd.

Shepherd St.

Sun Chun St.

Russell St.

Percival St.

Hysan Ave.

Leighton Rd.

Ka Ning Path

Tat Hang Rd.

14

Sharp St. East

Yiu Wa St.

Leighton Rd.

Eastern Hospital Road

Wong Nai Chung Rd.

Link Rd.

Caroline Hill Rd.

Sport Rd.

browsing. For more good shopping, walk east on Hennessy Road to Fleming Road. Turn north, crossing Harbour Road, to the **China Arts and Crafts** department store (26 Harbour Rd.).

❸ The nearby **Causeway Centre** building houses the **Museum of Chinese Historical Relics.** The collection covers 1,000 years of Chinese history and culture, with all types of art and crafts on display. You can rent a cassette for your own guided tour, and purchase replicas of some of the objects on exhibit. *28 Harbor Rd., tel. 574–2692 or 831–8831. Admission free. Open weekdays 9:30–5, Sat. 9:30–1. Closed Jan. 1, Chinese New Year, Oct. 1 (Chinese National Day), and during the setting up of new exhibitions.*

To the east of Causeway Centre is the **Wanchai Sports Grounds** (Harbour and Tonnochy roads), opened in 1979 to provide world-class facilities for competitive sports. It has a soccer field, running track, swimming pool, and an indoor games hall. Walking back (west) along Harbour Road, you will pass the new **Hong Kong Convention and Exhibition Centre,** the largest complex of its kind in Asia.

❹ ❺ The **Arts Centre** and the **Academy for Performing Arts** are two separate buildings adjacent to each other and at the heart of Hong Kong's cultural activities. They have excellent facilities for both exhibitions and the performing arts. Throughout the year there is a busy program of activities, details of which you can obtain from the local press or at the ticket reservations office. The Academy for Performing Arts was financed with money donated by the Royal Hong Kong Jockey Club out of its profits from horse racing. One of the interesting galleries in the Arts Centre is the **Pao Galleries,** which has no permanent collection but hosts international and local exhibitions throughout the year. The Arts Centre also has an excellent restaurant. *2 Harbour Rd. Academy, tel. 823–1500; Pao, 4th–5th floors, Arts Centre Bldg., tel. 823–0200. Admission free. Open daily 10–8.*

❻ Walk east on Harbour Road to 1 Harbour Road, a huge block containing the **Hong Kong Convention Centre,** venue for many international and regional meetings and exhibitions. The Grand Hyatt and New World Harbour View hotels are on either side of the complex.

❼ From here you can taxi back to your hotel, catch the MTR at Admiralty Station, or continue walking along the harborfront to Wanchai Ferry Pier for a ferry back to Kowloon. East of the pier is the **Cargo Handling Basin** (Hung Hing Rd. near Wanchai Stadium), where you can watch the unloading of boats bringing cargo ashore from ships anchored in the harbor.

Causeway Bay, Happy Valley, and North Point

Causeway Bay is one of Hong Kong's best shopping areas. It also has a wide range of restaurants and a few sightseeing attractions. Much of the district can be easily reached from Central by the tram, which runs along Hennessy Road, or by the MTR to Causeway Bay Station. If you come by taxi, a good starting point is the Excelsior Hotel, which overlooks the harbor.

The **Excelsior Hotel** and **Noonday Gun** are a fun part of any tour of Causeway Bay. ". . . In Hong Kong they strike a gong and fire off a noonday gun," wrote Noel Coward in his song, "Mad Dogs and Englishmen." They still fire that gun, exactly at noon each day, in a small enclosure overlooking the Yacht Club Basin and Typhoon Shelter, opposite the Excelsior Hotel and the World Trade Centre. The tradition was started by Jardine Matheson and Co., the great *hong* (trading company) that gave James Clavell inspiration for his novels *Taipan* and *Noble House.* Jardines would fire a salute each time one of its ships arrived safely in the harbor. It is said that this angered the local governor, who ordered the company to use a gun instead of a cannon, and as a noon-time signal. The gun itself, with brass-work polished bright, is a three-pounder Hotchkiss, dating from 1901.

8 On weekends, from spring through fall, it is pleasant to have coffee or lunch in the first-floor coffee shop of the **Excelsior Hotel** (281 Gloucester Rd., Causeway), which overlooks the Yacht Club, and watch the yachts racing in the harbor. The South China Sea Race to Manila, in the Philippines, is held every two years at Easter. The Royal Hong Kong Yacht Club (tel. 832–2817) organizes ferry charters to view the racers start. The next race takes place in Spring 1992.

9 At the western end of **The Causeway Bay Typhoon Shelter** is a mass of tightly packed *sampans*, living quarters for a community of people who work in the harbor.

10 For a choice of meals, explore the 25 or so restaurants on **Food Street** (between Gloucester Rd. and Kingston St.). This is a small covered alley near the Excelsior Hotel, where virtually every type of cuisine is available, both Asian and Western. Most restaurants here are reasonably priced, with waiters who speak English.

11 **Victoria Park,** reached by passing under the elevated highway at the end of Gloucester Road, offers a delightful escape from the crowds and traffic, and the concrete canyons of the city. Beautifully landscaped with trees, shrubs, flowers, and lawns, it offers recreational facilities for swimming, lawn bowling, tennis, and roller skating. There is even a go-cart track. The Lantern Carnival is held here in mid-autumn, with the trees a mass of colored lights. Just before Chinese New Year, the park features a huge flower market. In the early morning, the park is filled with people practicing t'ai chi, which is fascinating to watch. At other times, the park can be a pleasant place to sit in the sun, to stroll, or to jog.

After relaxing in Victoria Park, you may be ready for more shopping. If so, you'll find plenty to keep you busy in Causeway Bay. The large Japanese department stores, **Sogo, Daimaru, Mitsukoshi,** and **Matsuzakaya,** all have branches on or near **Great George Street,** off Hennessy Road. This is a good area for buying photographic or electronic equipment—provided you bargain hard. Off Yee Woo Street is **Jardine's Crescent,** an area packed with clothing stalls.

12 Tin Hau and Kwun Yum Temples are two small Chinese temples on the far (southeast) side of Victoria Park. **Tin Hau Temple** is on a street of the same name off Causeway Road, behind Park Cinema. It is one of several temples in Hong Kong dedicated to the goddess of the sea, and is notable for its decorative roof and old stone walls. Walk south along Tung Lo Wan Road, a busy street of commercial shops, to where the road turns west,

and you will find Lin Fa Kung Street West. Turn left here and
⑬ you will come to the **Kwun Yum Temple,** dedicated to the goddess of mercy. A temple has stood on this site for 200 years, but
this one is in a heavily renovated building and is mostly new,
dating from 1986. Constructed on top of a huge boulder, it has a
high ceiling and gallery. The temple is very popular with local
devotees and is open daily 7–6.

Left of Tung Lo Wan Road is **Jones Street,** which has some fine
old traditional Chinese houses. From here continue uphill on
Tai Hang Road (a 15-minute walk or a brief taxi or No. 11 bus
⑭ ride) to **Aw Boon Haw (Tiger Balm) Gardens.** Built in 1935 with
profits from sales of a popular menthol balm, the gardens were
the pet project of two Chinese brothers, who also built their
mansion here. Eight acres of hillside are covered with grottoes
and pavilions filled with garishly painted statues and models of
Chinese gods, mythical animals, and scenes depicting fables
and moralistic stories. It's a sort of Oriental Disneyland, and
great fun to explore, especially for children. But be forewarned, some of the scenes of Taoist and Buddhist mythology
are decidedly gruesome. There is also an ornate pagoda, seven
stories high, containing Buddhist relics and the ashes of monks
and nuns. *Tai Hang Rd., Happy Valley. Admission: free. Open
daily 10–4.*

The area east of Victoria Park offers very little for the first-
time visitor. **North Point** and **Quarry Bay** are both undeniably
the "real" Hong Kong. But this means tenements and factories.
From Causeway Bay you can take the tram for a couple of miles
through this area, which is perhaps the best way to get the flavor of the environment. **Shaukiwan** has two noteworthy sights.
One is the ferry service to Kowloon's **Lei Yue Mun Village,** with
its fishing restaurants. The other is **Taikoo Shing,** a massive
city-within-a-city. Some years ago this was barren, reclaimed
land. Today, it's a middle-class housing estate. The shopping
center, **Cityplaza,** has an ice-skating and a roller-skating rink,
gardens, a theme park with children's games, restaurants, and
hundreds of shops. The village is virtually self-sufficient in
everything except home-grown food.

The South Side

*Numbers in the margin correspond with points of interest on
the South Side of Hong Kong Island map.*

The easiest way to tour the south is on an organized bus tour,
lasting about four hours, but this will show you only a few highlights. If you have time, take a city bus or taxi from Central,
and stop at the following points of interest along the way.

Starting in Central and passing through Western, the first ma-
❶ jor point of interest will be **Hong Kong University.** Established
in 1911, it has about 6,000 undergraduate and 1,700 post-grad-
uate students. Most of its buildings are spread along Bonham
Road. In this area you will also find the **Fung Ping Shan Museum,** founded in 1953. It contains an excellent collection of Chinese antiquities, especially ceramics and bronzes dating from
3,000 BC. There are also some fine paintings, lacquerware, and
carvings in jade, stone, and wood. *94 Bonham Rd. Admission
free. Open Mon.–Sat. 9:30–6.*

Continuing around the western end of the island, you come to **Pok Fu Lam** and **Wah Fu Estate** overlooking **Lamma Island.** These are two huge housing developments, complete with shops, recreational facilities, and banks. They are typical of Hong Kong's approach to mass housing. From here you ride downhill to Aberdeen, an area deserving exploration.

② **Aberdeen,** named after an English lord, not the Scottish city, got its start as a refuge for pirates some 200 years ago. After World War II, Aberdeen became fairly commercial as the *Tanka* (boat people) attracted tourists to their floating restaurants. Today, these people continue to live on houseboats and are as picturesque to the occasional visitor as their economic conditions are depressing. Some visitors regret the fact that many of these boat people are turning to factory work, but drab as that work may be, it's a definite improvement over their old way of life. The government is offering the young boat people an education geared to the needs of a fishing community.

You can still see much of traditional Aberdeen, such as the **Aberdeen Cemetery** (Aberdeen Main Rd.), with its enormous gravestones and its glorious view. Along Aberdeen's side streets you can find outdoor barbers at work and many dim sum restaurants. In the harbor, along with the floating restaurants, are some 3,000 junks and sampans. You will undoubtedly be asked to board one of these boats for a ride through the harbor. Use one of the licensed operators, which depart on 20-minute tours from the main Aberdeen sea wall opposite Aberdeen Centre. *Cost: HK$40 adult, HK$30 children. Open daily 8–6.*

Also in Aberdeen is the **Tin Hau Temple,** which has an ancient bell and drum that are still used to open and close the temple. Although rather shabby, this one of several shrines to the goddess of the sea is very colorful during the Tin Hau Festival in April and May when hundreds of boats converge along the shore.

Aberdeen's most interesting section is **Apleichau Island,** which can be reached by bridge or sampan. The island has a boat-building yard where junks are constructed, as well as some yachts and sampans. Almost all the boats are built without formal plans. From the bridge you can get a superb view of the harbor and its countless number of junks (you'll have to walk back to take a photo, since vehicles are not allowed to stop on the bridge).

③ East of Aberdeen are **Ocean Park, Water World,** and **Middle Kingdom,** parks which were built by the Royal Hong Kong Jockey Club. Ocean Park is on 170 acres of land overlooking the sea and is one of the world's largest oceanariums, attracting thousands of visitors daily. On the "lowland" site are gardens, parks, and a children's zoo. A cable car, providing spectacular views of the entire south coast, takes you to the "headland" side and to Ocean Theatre, the world's largest marine mammal theater, with seats for 4,000 people. Here, too, is one of the world's largest roller coasters and various other rides. The adjacent, 65-acre Water World is an aquatic fun park with slides, rapids, pools, and a wave cove. The park's newest attraction is Middle Kingdom, a project depicting the architecture, arts, crafts, and industries through 3,000 years of Chinese history. There are also cultural shows, souvenir shops, and restaurants. *Wong Chuk Hang Rd., tel. 532-2244 or 555-0947. Ocean Park admis-*

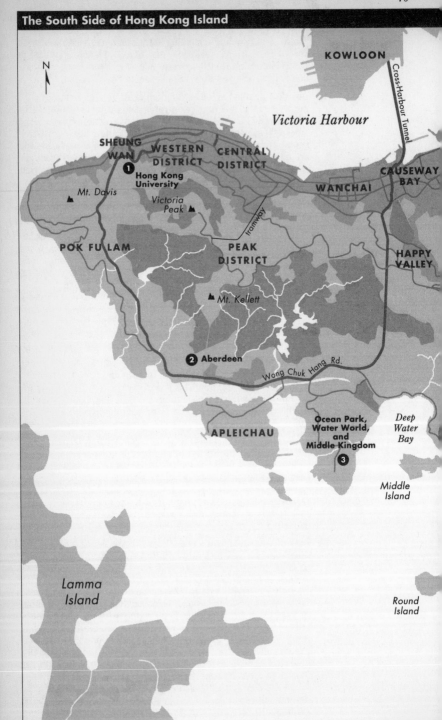

KOWLOON

Cross-Harbour Tunnel

N

Victoria Harbour

SHEUNG WAN

WESTERN DISTRICT

CENTRAL DISTRICT

CAUSEWAY BAY

① Hong Kong University

WANCHAI

▲ Mt. Davis

Victoria Peak ▲▲

Tramway

HAPPY VALLEY

POK FU LAM

PEAK DISTRICT

▲ Mt. Kellett

② Aberdeen

Wong Chuk Hang Rd.

APLEICHAU

Ocean Park, Water World, and Middle Kingdom ③

Deep Water Bay

Middle Island

Lamma Island

Round Island

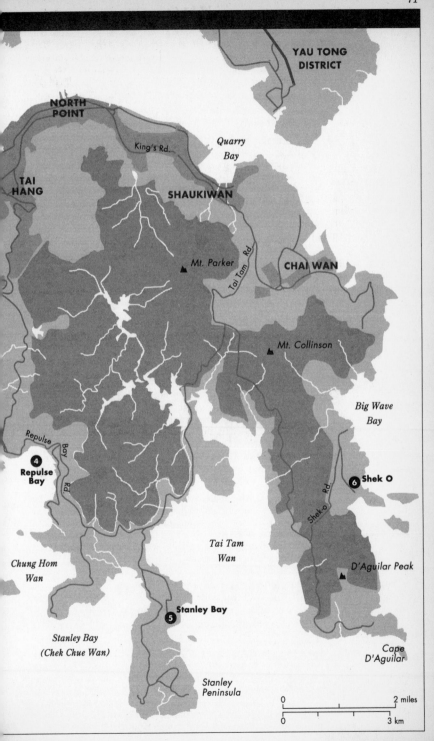

YAU TONG
DISTRICT

NORTH
POINT

King's Rd.

Quarry
Bay

TAI
HANG

SHAUKIWAN

Mt. Parker

CHAI WAN

Tai Tam Rd.

Mt. Collinson

Big Wave
Bay

Repulse Bay

4
Repulse
Bay

Repulse Bay Rd.

6 Shek O

Shek O Rd.

Chung Hom
Wan

Tai Tam
Wan

D'Aguilar Peak

5 **Stanley Bay**

Stanley Bay
(Chek Chue Wan)

Cape
D'Aguilar

Stanley
Peninsula

0		2 miles
0		3 km

sion (all inclusive): HK$140 adults, HK$70 (2 children 12 free). Open daily. Water World: tel. 555–6055. Admission: HK$60 adults, HK$40 children. Open May–Oct., daily Middle Kingdom: tel. 870–0268. Admission: HK $140 adults, HK$70 children or free with Ocean Park ticket. Open daily 10 AM–6 PM.

Deep Water Bay (Island Rd.) is just to the east of the theme parks. This was the site of the film *Love Is a Many-Splendored Thing*. Its beauty and deep coves are still many-splendored.

❹ The waterside road continues to **Repulse Bay,** named after the British warship HMS *Repulse* (not, as some local wags say, after the pollution of its waters). The famed Repulse Bay Hotel was demolished in 1982, but the **Repulse Bay Verandah Restaurant and Bamboo Bar,** replicas of the restaurant and bar in the old hotel, were opened in 1986 and are run by the same people who operated the original hotel. The hotel gained notoriety in December 1941 when invading Japanese clambered over the hills behind it and entered its gardens, which were being used as headquarters by the British. After a brief battle, the British surrendered. Today, the hillside behind the hotel features a huge development of luxury apartments.

❺ Another reminder of World War II is **Stanley Bay** (Wong Ma Kak Rd.). It became notorious as the home of the largest Hong Kong prisoner-of-war camps run by the Japanese. Today, Stanley is known for its picturesque beaches and its market, where designer fashions are sold at wholesale prices. Hong Kong has dozens of shops offering similar bargains, but it's more fun shopping for them in the countrified atmosphere around Stanley. You can also find ceramics, paintings, and books.

❻ **Shek O,** the easternmost village on the south side of the island, is filled with old houses, great mansions, a superb golf course and club, a few simple restaurants, a pretty beach, and fine views. Leave the little town square and take the curving path across a footbridge to the "island" of **Tai Tau Chau,** which is really a great rock with a lookout for scanning the South China Sea. Little more than a century ago, this open water was ruled by pirates.

From Shek O, the round-island route continues back to the north, to the housing and industrial estate of **Chai Wan** (Chai Wan Rd.). From here you have a choice of a fast journey back to Central on the MTR, or a slow ride to Central on the two-decker tram that crosses the entire north side of the island, via Quarry Bay, North Point, and Causeway Bay.

Exploring Kowloon

Numbers in the margin correspond with points of interest on the Kowloon Peninsula map.

Kowloon is a peninsula on mainland China, directly across Victoria Harbour from Central. Legend has it that Kowloon was named by a Chinese emperor who fled here during the Sung Dynasty (960–1279). He counted eight hills on the peninsula and called them the Eight Dragons—so the account goes—but a servant reminded him that an emperor is also considered a dragon, and so the emperor called the region *Gau-lung* (nine dragons), which became Kow-loon in English.

Kowloon is where most of Hong Kong's hotels are located. In the Old Tsimshatsui district is the Victorian-era clock tower of the old Kowloon-Canton Railway station, the new Hong Kong Cultural Centre, the Peninsula Hotel, and the bustling Nathan Road area. The New Tsimshatsui East district is on land reclaimed from the harbor and contains many luxury hotels and shopping centers, the Space Museum, and a waterfront esplanade. It is here that you will find the new railroad station.

In Victorian times, people would take the Star Ferry from Hong Kong Island to Kowloon and stay overnight at the still-elegant Peninsula Hotel, which was located next door to the railroad station. The next morning they boarded the Kowloon-Canton Railway trains for Peking, Moscow, London, and other Western cities.

Today visitors can take a taxi through the Cross-Harbour Tunnel from Causeway Bay or Central to Kowloon, or ride the MTR from Central to Kowloon in minutes. The Star Ferry, however, is still unquestionably the most exciting way to cross the harbor.

❶ **Star Ferry Pier** is a convenient starting place for any tour of Kowloon. Here you will also find the bus terminal, with traffic going to all parts of Kowloon and New Territories. On your left, as you face the bus station, is **Ocean Terminal**, where luxury cruise ships berth. Inside this terminal and in the adjacent **Harbour City** are miles of air-conditioned shopping arcades filled with hundreds of shops.

To the right of the Star Ferry is the **Victoria Clock Tower**, all that is left of the Kowloon-Canton Railway Station, which once stood on this site. The new station, for travel within China, is a mile (1.6 km) to the east.

Head east along **Salisbury Road,** and immediately on your left is **Star House,** where you'll find one of the best branches of the **China Arts and Crafts** department stores. Crossing Canton Road, you'll see a tree-covered hill to your left, headquarters of the **Marine Police** (Canton and Salisbury Rds.). On the far corner (Salisbury Rd. and Kowloon Park Dr.) is a branch of **Welfare Handicrafts,** which sells souvenir goods made in Hong Kong prisons. Taking the underpass across Kowloon Park Drive, you will come to the **YMCA** (41 Salisbury Rd.).

❷ The next block on the left contains the superb **Peninsula Hotel** (Salisbury Rd.). Outside are its fleet of Rolls-Royce taxis, and doormen in white uniforms. Be certain to enter the ornate lobby and enjoy an afternoon tea here at some point during your stay. Return to the Clock Tower and follow Salisbury Road past

❸ the **Hong Kong Cultural Centre,** an architecturally controversial building with tiled walls inside and out, sloped roofs, and no windows. It houses a superb concert hall and two theaters.

❹ The dome-shaped **Space Museum** houses one of the most advanced planetariums in Asia. It contains a **Hall of Solar Science, Exhibition Halls,** and a **Space Theatre** with Omnimax shows on space travel, sports, and natural wonders. *10 Salisbury Rd., tel. 721-2361. Space Theater: Admission HK$20 adults, HK$13 children. Open Mon. and Wed.–Sun.; 7 shows daily, weekdays beginning at 2:30; 8 shows Sat., beginning at 1:30; 10 shows Sun., beginning at 11:30. Closed Tues. Exhibition Hall and Hall of Solar Science: Admission free. Open*

Bird Market, **13**
Hong Kong Cultural
Centre, **3**
Kansu Street Jade
Market, **10**
Kowloon Park, **8**
Nathan Road, **7**
Peninsula Hotel, **2**
Regent Hotel, **5**
Space Museum, **4**
Star Ferry Pier, **1**
Sung Dynasty
Village, **14**
Temple Street, **9**
Tin Hau Temple, **11**
Tsimshatsui East, **6**
Yaumatei Typhoon
Shelter, **12**

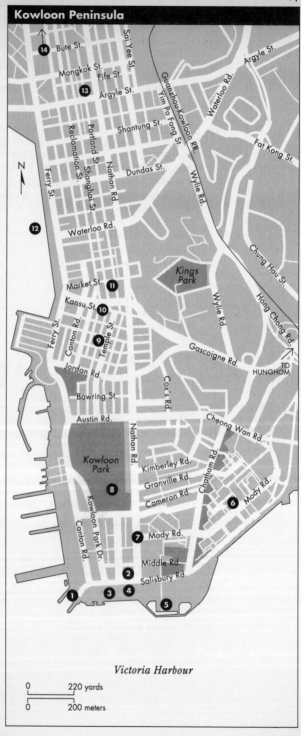

Kowloon Peninsula

Bute St.

Mongkok St.

Sai Yee St.

Fife St.

Argyle St.

Guanzhou-Kowloon RR.

Argyle St.

Waterloo Rd.

Fat Kong St.

Shantung St.

Portland St.

Reclamation St.

Shanghai St.

Nathan Rd.

Yim Po Fong St.

Wylie Rd.

Dundas St.

Ferry St.

Waterloo Rd.

Chung Hau St.

Kings
Park

Market St.

Kansu St.

Ferry St.

Canton Rd.

Temple St.

Wylie Rd.

Hong Chong Rd.

Jordan Rd.

Gascoigne Rd.

TO
HUNGHOM

Bowring St.

Austin Rd.

Cox's Rd.

Cheong Wan Rd.

Kowloon
Park

Nathan Rd.

Kimberley Rd.

Granville Rd.

Cameron Rd.

Chatham Rd.

Mody Rd.

Kowloon Park Dr.

Mody Rd.

Canton Rd.

Middle Rd.

Salisbury Rd.

N

Victoria Harbour

0   220 yards

0   200 meters

Mon. and Wed.–Fri. 2–9:30, Sat. 1–9:30, Sun. and holidays 10:30–9:30. Closed Tues.

⑤ Among Hong Kong's finest luxury hotels is the **Regent** (Salisbury Rd.). Its lobby has windows offering panoramic views of the harbor—a good place for a drink at sunset.

⑥ **Tsimshatsui East** is part of the land reclamation that has transformed the entire district into a galaxy of luxury hotels, restaurants, and entertainment and shopping complexes.

⑦ **Nathan Road,** the "Golden Mile," runs north for several miles and is filled with hotels and shops of every description. To the left and right are mazes of narrow streets lined with additional shops crammed with every possible type of merchandise.

⑧ Just off Nathan Road is **Kowloon Park.** The former site of Whitfield Military Barracks is today a restful, green oasis featuring a **Chinese Garden** with lotus pond, streams, a lake, and an aviary with a colorful selection of rare birds. On the south end of the park, near Haiphong Road entrance, is the **Jamia Masjid and Islamic Centre.** This is Hong Kong's main mosque, built in 1984. It has four minarets, decorative arches, and a marble dome.

The **Hong Kong Museum of History** is located in a renovated building in the park. Its collection covers local history, archaeology, ethnography, and natural history, with both permanent and changing exhibitions. The museum's photographs of old Hong Kong are of particular interest. *Haiphong Rd., tel. 367-1124. Admission free. Open Sat.–Thurs. 10–6, Sun. 1–6. Closed Fri.*

Continue north on Nathan Road three blocks to Jordan Road, make a left and a right onto Temple Street. The tiny streets to your right are ideal for wandering and people-watching. There is too much here to be described in detail, but the highlight of

⑨ this shopping area is **Temple Street,** which becomes an **open-air market** in the evening filled with street doctors offering cures for almost any complaint, fortune tellers, and, on most nights, Chinese opera. The best time to visit is 8–11 PM.

Shanghai Street and **Canton Road** are also worth a visit for their colorful shops and stalls selling everything from herbal remedies to jade and ivory. **Ning Po Street** specializes in shops selling paper kites and colorful paper and bamboo models of worldly possessions that are burned at Chinese funerals.

⑩ North of this maze of streets is the **Kansu Street Jade Market.** You'll get there by following Temple Street to Kansu Street and turning left. The daily jade market carries everything from ordinary pendants to precious carvings. If you don't know much about jade, take along someone who does, or you may well pay a lot more than you should. The best time to visit is from 10 to noon.

⑪ **Tin Hau Temple** (Market St., one block north of Kansu St.) is a colorful sight, with its curved tile roofs designed to deter evil spirits. One of Kowloon's oldest temples, it is filled with incense and crowds of worshipers. You'll probably be encouraged to have a try with the fortune sticks.

⑫ **The Yaumatei Typhoon Shelter,** opposite Ferry Street, is home to a colorful floating community living on the packed sampans and fishing junks. It is best explored by one of the small boats

that ply the harbor. The fishermen and their families still follow their traditional way of life, departing from here each day
and returning to unload their catch at local markets.

⑬ Return to Nathan Road, walk north eight blocks to Argyle
Street, and turn left. You can hear the **Bird Market** (Hong Lok
St., behind Mongkok MTR Station) long before you see it.
Though the area is only two blocks long, it is packed with hun-
dreds of caged birds for sale, all singing and chirping at one
time. Song birds have always been prized by the Chinese.

⑭ To go back in history hundreds of years, visit the **Sung Dynasty
Village,** northwest of Kowloon city. Take the MTR at Mongkok
station and go five stops north to Mei Foo station. From here it
is a short walk along Lai Wan and Mei Lai roads. The village
recreates the life of a Sung village 1,000 years ago. There are
faithful replicas of the houses, shops, restaurants, and temples
of the period. You can watch men work at ancient crafts, and
see people dressed in costumes of the time. The easiest way to
see the village is to take an organized tour, which can be arranged through your hotel tour desk. You can also visit on your
own. *Laichikok Amusement Park, tel. 741–5111. Admission:
weekdays HK$110 adults, HK$60 children; weekends HK$75
adults, HK$30 children. Open weekdays 10 AM–8 PM, weekends
12:30–5.*

Exploring New Territories

The visitor who has taken the trouble to explore Hong Kong
and Kowloon should go one step farther and spend at least a day
in **New Territories.** Here you will not only look across the border
into the People's Republic of China, you will also be able to enjoy panoramas of forested mountainsides and visit some of the
ancient temples and clan houses of the area.

Only about 15 miles (25 km) separate Kowloon's waterfront
from the People's Republic of China. New Territories is often
referred to as "the land between," because it is the area between Kowloon and the Chinese border. It is called New Territories because it was the last area of land claimed by the British
in extending their Hong Kong colony. A day's touring around
New Territories will show you yet another face of Hong Kong, a
rural one, with small villages, and peasants working in their
rice fields and market gardens. You will be surprised at how remote and undeveloped some parts of New Territories are, at
the miles of land without a single building, at the forests, and at
the hilltops free of high-rise, or even low-rise, buildings. The
easiest way to see the region is by taking a six-hour "Land Between" tour organized by the HKTA. *Tel. 801–7177. Departs
Queen's Pier, Central, at 8:30 AM, Holiday Inn Golden Mile at
9 AM, and Holiday Inn Harbour View at 9:10 AM. Cost: HK$250
adults, HK$200 children. Weekdays only.*

You can also rent a self-drive car or a chauffeur-driven car for a
day, or take the Kowloon-Canton Railway from Kowloon to the
Lo Wu Station on the Chinese border. There are nine stations
en route, and you can get off at any one of them. The Kowloon-
Canton Railway Corporation provides a leaflet outlining main
attractions in the areas near the railroad stations. You can pick
one up at the railroad station or any HKTA office. *For informa-*

tion, tel. 606-9333. First-class fare to Sheung Shui, the stop before the border: HK$12.

Below is a brief description of the highlights of a New Territories tour, circling clockwise out of Kowloon.

Numbers in the margin correspond with points of interest on the New Territories and the Outer Islands map.

❶ **Chuk Lam Sim** is one of Hong Kong's most impressive monasteries. The name means "The Bamboo Forest Monastery." It has three large statues of Buddha; on festival days it is packed with worshipers. Visitors going to the monastery may want to join "The Land Between Tour" organized by the Hong Kong Tourist Association (*see* Before You Go in Chapter 1).

❷ **Ching Chung Koon Taoist Temple** is located near the town of Tuen Mun. This huge temple has room after room of altars, all filled with the heady scent of incense burning in bronze holders. On one side of the main entrance is a cast-iron bell with a circumference of about five feet. All large monasteries in ancient China had such bells, which were rung at daybreak to wake the monks and nuns who would go out into the rice fields and work all day. On the opposite side of the entrance is a huge drum that was used to call the workers back in the evenings. Inside are rooms with walls of small pictures of the departed. Their relatives pay the temple to have these photos displayed, so they can see them as they pray. The temple also includes a retirement home, built from donations, which provides a quiet and serene atmosphere for the elderly. The grounds are beautiful, with plants and flowers, hundreds of dwarf shrubs, ornamental fish ponds, and pagodas.

❸ **Tuen Mun** has a population of 332,000 and is one of Hong Kong's "new towns"—independent, small cities created to take the spillover of population from the crowded areas of Kowloon and Hong Kong Island. They provide both industrial areas and living accommodations for the workers and their families. Other new towns are Tsuen Wan, Yuen Long, Shatin, Taipo, Fanling, and Junk Bay. By 1995 the seven towns are expected to house three million people, or 41% of Hong Kong's projected population of 7.3 million.

❹ **Miu Fat Buddhist Monastery,** located on Castle Peak Road near Tuen Mun, is a popular place for a vegetarian lunch. The monastery itself is ornate, with large, carved-stone animals guarding the front. Farther on is Yuen Long, completely redeveloped as an industrial and residential complex.

❺ **Lau Fau Shan** is a village famous for its fish market. Here you will find people selling freshly caught fish and shellfish, as well as dried fish and salted fish. Select what you want, pay for it, take it to one of the many restaurants, and have it cooked to order. This is the oyster capital of Hong Kong, but don't eat them raw.

❻ **Kam Tin Walled Village,** a regular stop on most tours, was built in the 1600s as a fortified village belonging to the Tang clan.

❼ There are actually six walled villages around Kam Tin, but **Kat Hing Wai** is the most popular. The original walls are intact, with guardhouses on the four corners and arrow slits for fighting off attackers. The image of antiquity is somewhat spoiled now by the modern homes and their TV antennas looming over the ancient fortifications. Directly inside the main gate is a nar-

0   2 miles

0   3 km

PEOPLES REPUBLIC OF CHINA

Deep Bay

Lok Ma Chau 8

Lo Wu

San Tin

Luen Mark

Mai Po

Lau Fau Shan 5

Kat Hing Wai

Yuen Long

6   7

Ha Tsuen

Kam Tin Walled Village

Tai Mo Shan

Miu Fat Buddhist Monastery

Ching Chung Koon Taoist Temple
2   4

3

Shek Kok Tsui

Tuen Mun

Tai Lamn Chung Reservoir

Chuk Lam Sim
1

Tsing Yi

Lai Am

Chek Lap Kok

Tung Chung
23

Trappist Monastery 27

Peng Chau 34

Mui Wo 22

Ngong Ping 26

Lantau 19

Tai O 24

25

Silvermine Bay 20

Hei Ling Chau

Precious Lotus Monastery

21

Cheung Sha

30

Praya Promenade 32   33 **Tung Wan**

31 **Cheung Chau**

Shek Kwu Chau

Soko Islands

South China Sea

N

Crooked Island

Sheung
Shut

10 **9** **Fanling**
n Wo
arket

Wu Kau
Lang

Grass
island

*Plover Cove
Reservoir*

Tolo Channel

Taipo
11
Kam Shan

Pan
Chung

13 **Tolo Harbour**

Chinese University **12**

N E W   T E R R I T O R I E S

Chek
Keng

o
an
18

Amah Rock **17**

Temple of Ten
Thousand Buddhas

15

Sai Kung

16 **Shatin**

Tsuen Wan

Sai Kung
Peninsula **14**

*Kau Sai
Chau*

High Island

Lai Chi Kok
Amusement
Park

Sung Dynasty Village

Ho Chung

Port Shelter

*Basalt
Island*

K O W L O O N

*Kowloon
Bay*

Yau Tong

Victoria

*Victoria
Harbour*

Junk Bay

Tai Wan
Tau

H O N G   K O N G

Tei Tong
Tsui

*Tung Lung
Chau*

30
Yung Shue Wan

Stanley

29 **Sok Kwu Wan**

28 **Lamma**
Island

*Stanley
Peninsula*

*Po Toi
Islands*

row street lined with shops selling souvenirs and mass-produced oil paintings.

8 Next stop is the town of **Lok Ma Chau,** where the big attraction is the view. You can stand on a hill and look down on vast fields and the Sham Chun River winding through them. Across the river, barely a mile (1.6 km) away, is the People's Republic of China. Unless you plan a tour into China, this is as close as you will get. Elderly "models" here demand HK$1 before you can photograph them.

9 **Fanling** is a town that combines the serene atmosphere of the Royal Hong Kong Golf Club with the chaos of rapid growth.
10 The nearby **Luen Wo Market** is a traditional Chinese market, well worth visiting.

11 **Taipo** means shopping place in Chinese and every visitor here discovers that the town more than lives up to its name. Located in the heart of the region's breadbasket, Taipo has long been a trading and meeting place for local farmers and fishermen. It is now being developed, with new housing and highways everywhere you look.

12 South of Taipo is the **Chinese University.** The **Art Gallery,** located in the university's **Institute of Chinese Studies** building, is well worth a visit. It has large exhibits of paintings and calligraphy from the Ming period to modern times. There are also important collections of bronze seals, carved jade flowers, and ceramics from South China. *Tel. 695–2218. Admission free. Open Mon.–Sat. 10–4:30, Sun. and holidays 12:30–4:30. Closed between exhibitions and on major holidays.*

Across from the campus is the popular **Yucca de Lac Restaurant,** which has outdoor dining facilities. About a 15-minute walk from the University is the starting point for a ferry tour of
13 **14** **Tolo Harbour** and the **Sai Kung Peninsula.** *Call the Hong Kong Ferry Co. for ferry schedule, tel. 542–3081.*

The **Sai Kung Peninsula** consists mostly of park land. Clearwater Bay Road, past Kai Tak Airport, will take you into forested areas and land that is only partially developed, with Spanish-style villas overlooking the sea.

15 Whether you enter **Shatin** by road or rail, you will be amazed to find this metropolis in the middle of New Territories. Another of the "new towns," Shatin underwent a population explosion that took it from a town of 30,000 to one of more than 461,000 in 10 years. It is home to the **Shatin Racecourse,** Hong Kong's largest. Nearby is the huge **Jubilee Sports Centre,** a vast complex of tracks and training fields designed to give Hong Kong's athletes space to train under professional, full-time coaches for international competition. Shatin is also home of **New Town Plaza,** the most extensive shopping complex in New Territories.

16 You'll need to climb some 500 steps to reach the **Temple of Ten Thousand Buddhas,** nestled among the foothills of Shatin, but a visit is worth every step. Inside the main temple are nearly 13,000 gilded clay statues of Buddha, all virtually identical. They were made by Shanghai craftsmen and donated by wor-
17 shipers. From this perch you can see the famous **Amah Rock.** Amah means "nurse" in Chinese, and the rock, which resembles a woman with a child on her back, is popular with female

⑱ worshipers. To the west of the temple is **Tai Mo Shan,** Hong Kong's highest peak, rising 3,230 feet above sea level.

Exploring the Outer Islands

Looking out the airplane window on the approach to Kai Tak Airport on a fine day, you will see clusters of small islands dotting the South China Sea. Fishing fleets trawl slowly through the blue waters. Tiny *sampans* (flat-bottom boats) scamper from one outcrop to another, ignoring the junks, ocean liners, and cargo ships steaming in and out of Hong Kong Harbour. Look closer and you will see sandy coves, long strands of fine yellow sand massaged by gentle surf, and countless tiny village settlements clinging to rocky bays and small sand bars.

These outer islands are the "Other Hong Kong," that unspoiled natural beauty that is as much a part of Hong Kong as Kowloon's crowded tenements or Hong Kong Island's concrete canyons. But most visitors miss the opportunity to see this side of the territory.

In addition to Hong Kong Island and the mainland sections of Kowloon and New Territories, there are 235 islands under the control of the British—at least until 1997. The largest, Lantau, is bigger than Hong Kong Island; the smallest is just a few square feet of rock. Most of them are uninhabited. Others are gradually being developed, but at nowhere near the density of the main urban areas.

Visiting the outer islands is a wonderfully escapist experience after the people, noise, traffic, and frantic activity of the city. Try to go on a weekday; on weekends, Hong Kongers flock to them and pack the ferries.

You can reach the islands by scheduled ferry services operated by the Hong Kong Ferry Company (HKF). The ferries are easy to recognize by the large HKF letters painted on their funnels. *Leave from the Outlying Districts Services Pier, Central. Tel. 542–3081 for schedule. Round-trip fare: HK$13–$36 depending on day and class.*

⑲ The biggest of the islands, **Lantau,** covers 55 square miles and is almost twice the size of Hong Kong Island. However, Lantau's population is less than 17,000, compared with Hong Kong Island's 1.5 million. Lantau is well worth a full day's visit, even

⑳ two. The ferry will take you to **Silvermine Bay,** which is being developed as a commuter's suburb of Hong Kong Island.

㉑ Safe, sandy beaches, such as those of **Cheung Sha,** stretch along southern Lantau's shoreline. The island's private bus services ㉒ ㉓ link the main ferry town, **Mui Wo** in Silvermine Bay, with **Tung** ㉔ **Chung,** which has a Sung Dynasty fort, and **Tai O,** the capital of Lantau. Tai O, once an ancient fishing village, is divided into two parts connected by a rope-drawn ferry. To the north is Chek Lap Kok, site of the proposed multi-billion dollar airport. In the mountainous interior of the island you will find a tea plantation with a horseback riding camp, and a Buddhist mon- ㉕ astery. The monastery, **Precious Lotus Monastery,** is near ㉖ **Ngong Ping** and has the world's tallest outdoor bronze statue of Buddha. The statue is more than 100 feet high and weighs 275½ tons. The monastery, gaudy and exuberantly commercial, is famous for its vegetarian meals served in the temple refectory, as well as for the giant Buddha.

The visitor with historical interests will find many surprises on Lantau. The imperial hold on the islands of the South China Sea was tenuous, but at one time Lantau was the temporary home for an emperor of the Sung Dynasty. That was in 1277, when 10-year-old Emperor Ti Cheng and his small retinue set up camp just behind modern Silvermine Bay's beaches. They were fleeing the Mongol forces of Kublai Khan. The young emperor died on Lantau. The Sung Dynasty was crushed the following year, leaving no traces of the island's brief moment of imperial glory.

There are traces, however, of Sung Dynasty communities of the 13th century, including their kilns and burial sites. Many excavations on the island show evidence of even earlier settlements, some dating back to Neolithic times.

㉗ For quiet and solitude, visit the **Trappist Monastery** on Eastern Lantau, and drink the fresh milk produced by a small dairy herd owned by the monks. You can spend the night in simple accommodations, but you must make reservations well in advance. Although the monastery can be reached from Silvermine Bay, it's best to go there via Peng Chau, a small community en route to Silvermine Bay (*see* below).

Visitors may also stay overnight at a tea plantation or at the Precious Lotus Monastery. The HKTA has an information sheet on these and other accommodations available on Lantau.

㉘ For a gentle two-hour trip into what rural China must have been like in past centuries wander across **Lamma Island,** which faces the fishing port of Aberdeen on Hong Kong Island's south side. Farmers, shielded from the sun by black-fringed straw hats, grow vegetables, while fishermen gather shellfish, much as their ancestors did before them. Ignore the power station and cement factory and seek out the small bays along narrow paths that offer changing views of the ocean and of Hong Kong Island.

㉙ ㉚ Allow time to stop for a meal at either of Lamma's two ferry villages: **Sok Kwu Wan** and **Yung Shue Wan.** In both villages, lines of friendly, open-air harborside restaurants, some with amazingly diverse wine lists, offer feasts of freshness that put many restaurants on Hong Kong Island to shame.

㉛ Dining out is a major joy on **Cheung Chau,** which lies south of Lantau. Almost every Western visitor's favorite Hong Kong island, it has dozens of good, open-air cafés on either side of its ㉜ crowded sand bar township—both on the **Praya Promenade** along the waterfront and overlooking the main public beach on ㉝ **Tung Wan.**

Cheung Chau is Hong Kong's most crowded outlying island, with 30,000 or more people, most of them living on the sand bar that connects the dumbbell-shaped island's two hilly tips. It has a Mediterranean flavor to it that has attracted artists and writers from around the world, some of whom have created an expatriate's artist's colony here. The entry into Cheung Chau's harbor, through lines of gaily bannered fishing boats, is an exhilarating experience. Also colorful is the island's annual springtime Bun Festival, one of Hong Kong's most popular community galas. There is also history on Cheung Chau—pirate caves, ancient rock carvings, and a 200-year-old temple built to protect the islanders from the twin dangers of plagues and pirates.

Throughout the year, small sampans provide ferry service from Hong Kong Island to beaches on Cheung Chau—beaches that are virtually deserted and have beautiful, clear water.

With the opening of the island's first hotel, **Cheung Chau Warwick Hotel** on Tung Wan Beach, it is now possible to stay on the island in reasonable comfort.

㉞ The tiniest of Hong Kong's four major islands, **Peng Chau** was once home for a few farmers, fishermen, and a fireworks factory. Although the factory is now closed and the villagers have built three-story weekend retreats for Hong Kong's city folks, the community feeling remains.

Stand on the Peng Chau ferry quay and watch the *kaido* (ferryboat) for Lantau's Trappist monastery sputter toward dark green hills. Choose your fresh shellfish from baskets held aloft by local fishermen bobbing in boats below the quay, and take it back to a café to be cooked. Then breathe in that stirring ambience of Hong Kong's islands—a mix of salt air, shrimp paste, and dried fish, combined with a strong dose of local pride and a sense of independence that has been lost or never found in urban Hong Kong.

Major Sights and Attractions

Museums, libraries, parks, and beaches are listed separately below.

Hong Kong Island

Central District   **Cat Street.** Once the center of Hong Kong's underworld, this is now one of the island's prime shopping areas.

Hollywood Road. Here, between Arbuthnot Road and its junction with Lyndhurst Terrace, is the most important street for antiques and flea-market merchandise. Each step of nearby **Ladder Street** is filled with hawkers.

Hongkong and Shanghai Banking Corporation Building. Hong Kong's largest bank has its headquarters in this glass-and-steel structure with towers and modular walls—an example of high-tech architecture at its best.

The Landmark (Pedder St. and Des Voeux Rd.). This is one of the territory's best shopping centers, home of some of the classiest boutiques in town. There is free entertainment daily.

Legislative Council Building (Chater and Jackson Rds.). This is one of the few historic buildings in Central that is still standing (though vibrations from the drills during construction of the MTR subway nearly caused it to collapse). It was built in 1910 and once housed the Supreme Court.

Mandarin Oriental Hotel. Located at the end of the Star Ferry pedestrian underpass, the hotel is frequently mentioned as one of the world's finest. It is a splendid place for people-watching, particularly in the **Captain's Bar,** where billion-dollar deals are negotiated over brandy.

Man Mo Temple (Hollywood Rd.). Hong Kong's oldest temple dates back to the 1840s.

Peak Tram Terminal (Garden Rd., behind the Hilton Hotel). Built in 1888, this is the starting point for trips up the funicular railway to the top of 1,805-foot Victoria Peak. From here you'll enjoy breathtaking views of Hong Kong Harbour, the outer islands, and sometimes even the Chinese border.

Poor Man's Nightclub. Located next to Macau Ferry Pier, this night market is open from about 6:30 PM to 1 AM.

Star Ferry Terminal. This is the starting point for one of the world's most famous harbor ferry rides. The journey takes only about 10 minutes, but is unforgettable.

St. John's Cathedral. The official Anglican church, completed in 1849, still shows off its early Victorian-Gothic elegance. Open daily 10–8. Sunday services are open to the public.

Wing On Street. This is the main street for cloth and clothing. Others are Li Yuen Street East and Li Yuen Street West, which run between Queen's Road Central and Des Voeux Road.

Wanchai/ Causeway Bay

Causeway Bay. This is a top shopping area with big Japanese and Chinese department stores, street hawkers, and lots of little shops. Prices are cheaper than in Central.

Food Street. This street in Causeway Bay boasts some three dozen restaurants serving everything from abalone to zabaglione.

Tai Wong Temple (Queen's Rd. East area). The temple is filled with mirrors left by people who have prayed for cures.

Noonday Gun. Tourists come here every day, next to the Excelsior Hotel, to hear the famous gun go off.

Victoria Park. This great park has been built entirely from land reclaimed from the sea. Open 14 hours a day, it is filled with people practicing t'ai chi at dawn, as well as joggers, tennis players, and strollers.

Wanchai Post Office (Queen's Rd. East area) is one of the few surviving and preserved historical buildings in Hong Kong.

Happy Valley

Happy Valley Race Course. This is one of two race tracks in Hong Kong. Though built in 1841, it is continually being modernized and includes a huge outdoor video screen for close-ups, slow motion, and instant replays.

Aw Boon Haw (Tiger Balm) Gardens. A veritable Disneyland of gardens and Chinese mythology spread over eight acres.

Mid-levels, Upper Western, Peak

Hong Kong Zoological and Botanical Gardens. Opened in 1871, the gardens have a superb aviary, a fair zoo, and, of course, fine plants and flowers. In the morning the 12.5-acre site is filled with people practicing t'ai chi.

Hong Kong University. You'll find good examples of Victorian-Colonial architecture here, and an excellent museum and library.

The Peak. Visitors enjoy a scenic tram ride from the Botanical Gardens to Victoria Peak.

South Side **Aberdeen.** This is one of the two oldest settlements on Hong Kong Island, and still a spectacular waterfront, with some 5,000 people living in sampans and fishing boats. Although Aberdeen is becoming more industrialized, it still presents a colorful sight. The famous floating restaurants are open until midnight, but they are not the best place to sample Cantonese food, nor are they known for their courtesy.

Ocean Park and Water World. This is one of the most popular family outing places in Hong Kong. The 170-acre park is divided into two sections linked by a cablecar. One section has parks and playgrounds; the other, the *Ocean Theatre*, with performing dolphins and a killer whale, a wave cove and an aquarium, plus an amusement park and a walk-through aviary. The adjacent 65-acre Water World is an aquatic fun park with slides, rapids, and pools. The new Middle Kingdom attraction takes the visitor through 3,000 years of Chinese history and culture. *Ocean Park and Middle Kingdom open year-round; Water World open May–October.*

Stanley. This was the largest town on the island in 1841, when the British arrived. Today it is a fairly posh seaside village. The **Tin Hau Temple** is venerable, for Hong Kong; the market has good bargains in rattan, clothing, porcelain, and bric-a-brac.

Kowloon

Tsimshatsui **Ocean Centre/Ocean Terminal/Harbour City.** Even in this city of shopping centers, the two "Oceans" and their "Harbour" are the biggest. You can buy everything from emerald-laden abacuses to gold-encrusted zircons through miles of air-conditioned comfort. A luxury liner may be parked right by the second floor of Ocean Terminal. Take a stroll along the veranda for some unparalleled views across the harbor.

Peninsula Hotel. Once rated by the *Wall Street Journal* as one of the "10 most exciting hotel lobbies in Asia," the huge colonnaded lobby still has charm, grandeur, celebrities (though with the opening of the Regent Hotel, no longer a monopoly on them), string quartets playing music, and a British "high tea." Rest your shopping feet in style.

Space Museum. Just opposite The Peninsula, the Space Museum has a fine planetarium, a hall of solar sciences, and good exhibitions.

New World Centre. Another huge shopping center, adjacent to New World and Regent hotels. Although it seems to be a baffling maze, you can find everything you want, from bookshops to a kosher delicatessen.

Tsimshatsui East. Ten years ago, Tsimshatsui East was just a few wharves, empty lots, even a quarry or two. Today, the area houses four first-class hotels, a dozen shopping centers, and restaurants. The latter run the gamut from pizzas to Peking duck.

Nathan Road. The so-called "Golden Mile," runs up through Kowloon to Boundary Street and New Territories. While the shopping is excellent on the main road, the best specialty shops are in the streets and alleys running at right angles to the main thoroughfare.

Yaumatei and Northern Kowloon

Bird Market, Hong Lok Street. Here are teahouses and shops filled with all kinds of birds, singing, playing on tables, even being taken for walks.

Kansu and Reclamation streets. Here's where you'll find the **Jade Market**—curbs and pavements virtually carpeted with jade bangles, pendants, and stones. Most of the jade is exceptionally inexpensive, but you must bargain hard and know what you're doing or you're liable to end up with fakes. The colors of the jade stones, in every shade of green imaginable, are magnificent. The market is open daily from 10 to 3:30. Arrive early for the best buys.

Lei Yue Mun. This old fishing village, once the haunt of pirates, sits at the eastern end of Kowloon. You choose your fare (live fish) from the markets and the restaurants cook it for a nominal price.

Shanghai Street. All the streets in this area are fascinating, day and night. During the daytime, search around Shanghai Street, Temple Street, and Public Square Street for old wine shops, market stalls, and street barbers. On Battery Street, you see nothing but shops selling goods made from paper. Public Square Street has little lanes filled with fortune tellers. The Tin Hau Temple is old and dazzling.

Sung Dynasty Village. This miniature village recreates life during the Sung Dynasty (AD 960 to 1279). It has interesting architecture, costumes (the people who work in the village dress in Sung fashions), restaurants, street performances, and a wax museum.

New Territories

Kam Tin Walled Villages. On the western side of New Territories are the villages of **Kat Hing Wai, Wing Lung Wai,** and **Shui Tau.** They are all some 500 years old and known collectively as the Kam Tin Walled Villages. All are interesting, though Kut Hing Wai is very tourist-oriented. **Hung Shing Temple** is in Shui Tau Village, a 30-minute walk from Kut Hing Wai Village.

Museums and Libraries

Museums

Most museums in Hong Kong specialize in the arts and crafts of China. A few collections, however, stress the colony's history and cultural traditions.

Hong Kong Island

Fung Ping Shan Museum. Run by the University of Hong Kong, the museum has the world's largest collection of Nestorian Crosses of the Yuan Dynasty (1279–1644). It also has superb pieces from pre-Christian periods: ritual vessels, decorative mirrors, and painted pottery. This museum is a bit out of the way, but a must for lovers of Chinese art. *University of Hong Kong, 94 Bonham Rd., Western District, tel. 859–2114. Admission free. Open Mon.–Sat. 9:30–6. Closed Sun. and major holidays.*

Hong Kong Museum of Art. An excellent collection of Chinese art and antiquities, including fine ceramics, quality paintings, drawings, and a pictorial record of Sino-British relations. Interesting temporary exhibitions usually change monthly. *City Hall, High Block, 10th–11th floors, Connaught Rd. Central, tel. 522–4127. Admission free. Open Mon.–Wed. and Fri.–Sat. 10–6; Sun. 1–6. Closed Thurs. and major holidays.*

Museum of Chinese Historical Relics. Ancient Chinese relics are on display. *Causeway Centre, 28 Harbour Rd., Wanchai, tel. 574–2692 or 831–8831. Admission free. Open weekdays 9:30–5, Sat. 9:30–1. Closed Jan. 1, Chinese New Year, Oct. 1 (Chinese National Day), and during the setting up of new exhibitions.*

Museum of Tea Ware. Built in 1845, this is the oldest Western-style building in Hong Kong. The museum opened in 1984 and has displays of tea ware, including Yi Xing tea ware, the most famous tea sets from Jiangsu Province, China. There are also slide shows and exhibitions on tea planting and harvesting. This is a branch of the Hong Kong Museum of Art, located in Flagstaff House. *Hong Kong Park, Cotton Tree Dr., Queensway, tel. 869–0690. Admission free. Open 10–5. Closed Wed.*

Kowloon **Hong Kong Museum of History.** This is the most comprehensive museum in the colony, with permanent and temporary displays on local history and traditions, archaeology, and arts and crafts. It also houses a photographic collection that traces Hong Kong's history. *Haiphong Rd., Kowloon Park, Tsimshatsui, tel. 367–1124. Admission free. Open Mon.–Thurs. and Sat. 10–6, Sun. 1–6. Closed Fri. and bank holidays.*

Hong Kong Space Museum. The main **Exhibition Hall** has several exhibits at one time, and the **Hall of Solar Sciences** has a solar telescope that permits visitors a close look at the sun. The museum also has a Space Theatre for Omnimax shows on space travel, sports, and natural wonders. *Salisbury Rd., Tsimshatsui, opposite Peninsula Hotel, tel. 721–2361. Space Theatre show: Admission: HK$20 adults, HK$13 students (children under 6 not admitted). Exhibition Hall: Admission free. Open Mon. and Wed.–Fri. 2–9:30, Sat. 1–9:30, Sun. 10:30–9:30. Closed Tues. For times of Space Theatre shows, tel. 721–2361.*

Lei Cheung Uk Museum. This is actually a burial vault from the late Han Dynasty (AD 25–220), discovered in 1955. The four barrel-vaulted brick chambers form a cross around a domed vault. The funerary objects are typical of the tombs of this era. *41 Tonkin St., Lei Cheng Uk Resettlement Estate, Shamshuipo, tel. 386–2863. Admission: HK10¢. Open Mon.–Sat. 10–1 and 2–6, Sun. 1–6.*

Science Museum. Opened in 1991, this is a high-tech, hands-on museum where you can play surgeon or car mechanic, or explore outer space. Exhibits include an energy machine, a miniature submarine, and the DC3 that launched Cathay Pacific airlines. The buildings look like giant Lego blocks. *Science Museum Rd., Tsimshatsui East, Kowloon, tel. 732–3232. Admission: HK$25 adults, HK$15 children and those over 60. Open Tues.–Sat. 1–9, Sun. 9–9. Closed Monday.*

Sung Dynasty Wax Museum. A visit here is included in the guided tour of the Sung Dynasty Village. The museum depicts life in the Sung Dynasty (960–1279), one of the great periods in Chinese history. *11 Kau Wa Keng, Laichikok, tel. 741–5111. Group tours daily, 10, 12:30, 3, and 5:30; individuals can tour* *weekends and public holidays 12:30–5. Admission: HK$75–HK$110 adults, HK$30–HK$60 children.*

New Territories **Chinese University.** The Arts Gallery of the Institute of Chinese Studies displays the work of Cantonese artists from the last 300 years along with bronze seals, pre-Christian stone rubbings, and jade flower carvings. *Shatin, tel. 695–2218. Admission free. Open Mon.–Sat. 10–4:30. Closed Sun. and major holidays and between exhibitions.*

Libraries

Hong Kong Island **City Hall Libraries** has three libraries of general interest: the fifth-floor **Reference Library,** which has over 400,000 volumes, half in English, half in Chinese, plus microfilm collections of rare books from the Peking National Library, and back-dated Hong Kong newspapers; the **Children's Library,** fourth floor; and the **General Reading Library,** third floor. Only residents are allowed to check out books. Take your passport; the museum is meticulous about checking identification. *City Hall High Block, near Star Ferry, Hong Kong Island, tel. 526–2747. Open Mon.–Thurs. 10–7, Friday 10–9, Sat. 10–5, and Sun. 10–1.*

American Library. This is the place to go for current and back issues of American magazines and books. Microfilm editions of *The New York Times* are also available. It takes one week to process your library card for checking out materials. *1st floor, United Centre, 95 Queensway Rd., Queensway, next to Admiralty Centre MTR Station, tel. 529–9661. Open weekdays 10–6.*

Parks

About 40% of Hong Kong's tiny land mass is given over to 21 country parks on Hong Kong Island, Lantau Island, and New Territories. These areas are very popular with Hong Kong residents, especially on weekends and holidays, so try to go on a weekday. Maps and publications on the flora and fauna of Hong Kong are available at the Government Publications Office in the General Post Office building (Connaught Pl., by the Star Ferry, on the Hong Kong Island side).

Hong Kong Island

Tai Tam Country Park spreads around the magnificent Tai Tam Reservoir, near Tai Tam Bay on the south side of the island. *Take bus no. 2 or no. 20 from Central, in front of Jardine House (Connaught Centre) or Star Ferry Pier, or outside City Hall; get off at Shaukiwan terminal, walk a short distance to the main road, and catch No. 14 bus to the reservoir. Alternate route: no. 6 or no. 260 bus from Central to Stanley; transfer to no. 14 to the reservoir.*

Hong Kong Park is a new 25-acre marvel in the heart of Central. In addition to Flagstaff House, it contains a walk-in rain-forest aviary of 500 birds, a greenhouse for 2,000 tropical and arid region plants, lakes, gardens, and sports areas. *Entrance on Cotton Tree Drive, behind the Bank of China. Admission free.*

If you want beautiful, manicured gardens instead of nature trails, head for the **Zoological and Botanical Gardens** in Central (across from Governor's Residence, Upper Albert and Garden roads). The gardens are small but beautifully laid out, and the zoo has a small but very fine collection of animals, including jaguars, and an aviary with cranes and flamingos.

Another beautiful city park is **Victoria Park** in Causeway Bay (Victoria Park Rd.), which holds fairs and other events throughout the year.

New Territories

The **MacLehose Trail,** named after a former governor, stretches 60 miles (100 km) and links eight of the area's most beautiful parks. The trail starts at **Pak Tam Chung** on the Saikung Peninsula and is split into 10 sections, ranging from three to nine miles (5–16 km), each graded according to difficulty. Most parts of the trail can easily be reached by public transportation. From **Pak Tam Chung to Long Ke** is a seven-mile (11-km) hike. At Long Ke you can either return on a circular route (about 11 mi or 18 km), or continue along the coast until you reach **Pak Tam Au**—15 miles (24 km) of hard walking. The scenery is magnificent, with dramatic coastline and sweeping landscapes, and views all the way to China. *No. 5 bus from Star Ferry to Choi Hung; change to No. 92, which takes you to Saikung; pick up no. 94 to Pak Tam Chung; take first section of the trail to Long Ke.*

You can also stay on the bus past Pak Tam Chung and start the trail at **Pak Tam Au.** The rough four-mile (6.5 km) walk to **Kei Ling Ha** offers breathtaking views of the entire Saikung Peninsula. The path takes you uphill, through a forest and past some beautiful tree nurseries, to an area with a stunning glimpse of the entire peninsula, as well as High Island, and Ma On Shan Mountain, 2,100 feet above sea level. The walk downhill will take you to Kei Ling Ha Road where you can catch a bus for Tsimshatsui, Kowloon. *No. 94 bus from Choi Hung to Pak Tam Au. Return trip: no. 99 bus from Kei Ling Ha Rd. to Tsimshatsui.*

The **Shing Mun Reservoir,** on the western side of New Territories, is also a popular walking and picnic spot. The trail around the reservoir is easy and pleasant, with many picnic areas along the way. *Mass Transit Railway (MTR) to Tsuen Wan; change to no. 32A bus and get off at Cheung Shan Housing Estate; trail crosses main road and leads to reservoir. Return trip: no. 32B bus from Cheung Shan Housing Estate to Tsuen Wan Ferry Pier; hoverferry back to Central, Hong Kong Island. Hoverferry fare: HK$6 (HK$5 off-peak hrs).*

Beaches

Few tourists think of Hong Kong as a place for swimming or sunbathing. Yet Hong Kong has hundreds of beaches, mostly unused, and most with clear water and clean sand. About 30 of them are "gazetted"—cleaned and maintained by the government, with services that include lifeguards, floats, and swimming-zone safety markers. Almost all the beaches can be reached by public transportation, but knowing which bus to catch and where to get off can be difficult. Most bus drivers have neither the time nor the ability to give instructions in English. If you want to try the double-decker buses, call the HKTA (tel. 801–7177) and ask for the bus route to a certain beach. Otherwise, use the MTR and then a taxi, or take a taxi all the way. Beaches on outlying islands are reached by HKF ferry from Central and are often a short walk from the pier.

Many beaches listed below were closed at press time because of severe pollution. Check with the HKTA before taking the plunge.

If the red flag is hoisted at a beach, stay out of the water; it indicates pollution or an approaching storm. The red flag is often flying at Big Wave Bay (on Hong Kong Island, south side) because of the rough surf. Check with the HKTA or listen to announcements on radio or TV before heading out there.

Hong Kong Island

Repulse Bay is Hong Kong's answer to Coney Island. It has changing rooms, showers, toilets, swimming rafts, swimming-safety zone markers, and playgrounds. There are also several Chinese restaurants, and kiosks serving light refreshments. The beach has an interesting building at one end resembling a Chinese temple, with large statues of Tin Hau, goddess of the sea, and Kwun Yum, goddess of mercy. Small rowboats are available for rent at the beach. *Take bus no. 6, 61, 260, or 262 from Central. All drivers on this route speak English and can tell you when to get off. Fare: HK$5 or less.*

At **Deep Water Bay** the action starts at dawn every morning, winter and summer, when members of the "Polar Bear Club" go for a dip. The beach is packed in summer, when there are lifeguards, swimming rafts, and safety-zone markers, plus a police reporting center. Barbecue pits, showers, and restrooms are open year-round. *20 min from Central by taxi or take no. 7 bus to Aberdeen and change for no. 73, which passes the beach en route to Stanley.*

Middle Bay is about a mile (1.6 km) from Repulse Bay. Because the beach has few public facilities, it is relatively quiet and rarely crowded, except on Sundays, when it is a haven for pleasure boats. *Take the bus from Central to Repulse Bay, exit one stop after Repulse Bay beach, and walk down South Bay Rd. for about 1 mi (1.6 km); or take a taxi from Central.*

South Bay is a bigger edition of Middle Bay. Far from the noise and traffic of the main beaches, it is quiet and rarely crowded, except on Sundays. There are kiosks with light refreshments, barbecue pits, swimming rafts, changing rooms, showers, and toilets. *Take a bus from Central to Repulse Bay, exit one stop past the beach, walk down South Bay Rd. past Middle Bay for 1.5 mi (2.4 km); or take a taxi from Central to Repulse Bay.*

Chung Hom Wan is a short but nice beach between towering cliffs; it has kiosks with light refreshments, barbecue pits, swimming rafts, changing rooms, showers, and toilets. *Take a taxi or bus no. 262 from Central.*

Stanley Main, a wide sweep of beach, is popular with the Hobie Cat crowd, and has a refreshment kiosk, swimming raft, changing rooms, showers, and toilets. *Take a taxi from Central, or bus no. 6 or 260.*

St. Stephen's, about one mile (1.6 km) from Stanley Village, has lifeguards, a refreshment kiosk, barbecue pits, swimming raft, changing rooms, showers, and toilets. *Take a taxi from Central* *via Stanley Village; or take a bus to Stanley Main Beach and then walk or take a taxi.*

Turtle Cove, isolated but picturesque, has lifeguards and rafts in summer, plus barbecue pits, a kiosk, changing rooms, showers, and toilets. *From Central take the MTR to Saiwanho and change to bus no. 14; get off on Tai Tam Rd. after passing the dam of Tai Tuk Reservoir.*

Shek O is almost Mediterranean in aspect. A fine, wide beach with nearby shops and restaurants, it has kiosks, barbecue pits, lifeguards, swimming rafts, playgrounds, changing rooms, showers, and toilets. This is one of the few beaches directly accessible by bus. *Take bus no. 2 from Central to the end of the line in Shaukiwan, then bus no. 9 to the end of the line.*

Big Wave Bay, Hong Kong's only surfing beach, often lives up to its name and is frequently closed for swimming because of high surf. When the red flag goes up, signaling dangerous waves, get out of the water. The beach has kiosks, barbecue pits, a playground, changing rooms, showers, and toilets. *Take no. 9 bus to Big Wave Bay Rd., then walk for about 20 min.*

Hoi Mei is a gem of a beach, with white sand and gently lapping waves, ideal for young children. It has shower and bathroom facilities, but no swimming rafts, playgrounds, or tents.

New Territories

New Cafeteria has no cafeteria, but it does have a decent beach, with a kiosk serving light refreshments, and with barbecue pits, changing rooms, showers, and toilets. *MTR to Tsuen Wan, then bus no. 52 or 53 from Tsuen Wan.*

Kadoorie is a tiny beach, but it has most of the standard amenities. The small sandy strip is guarded by ancient cannons. *MTR to Tsuen Wan, then bus no. 52.*

Lido is popular with schoolchild. .n on outings. It has rafts, tents for rent, barbecue pits, a kiosk, changing rooms, showers, and toilets. *MTR to Tsuen Wan, then bus no. 34B.*

Silverstrand is the most popular beach on Saikung Peninsula and is always crowded on summer weekends. Although a little rocky in spots, it has good, soft sand and all the facilities, including changing rooms, showers, and toilets. *MTR to Choi Hung, then bus no. 92 or taxi.*

Tai Au Mun, also on the Saikung Peninsula, has two beaches, both on the edge of Clearwater Bay and accessible by footpaths from Tai Au Mun Village. They have all the usual facilities. *MTR to Choi Hung, then bus no. 91 to the end of the line; or take a taxi.*

Camper's (or **Tai Po Tsai**), near the Saikung Peninsula, is a lovely beach, but can be reached only by sampan from Pak Sha Wan Village on Hiram's Highway. *Take MTR to Choi Hung, then bus no. 91 to Pak Sha Wan, then a sampan.*

Kiu Tsui and Hap Mun are on an island that can be reached only by small boat or sampan from Sai Kung Town. Both beaches have most of the amenities. *Take the MTR to Choi Hung, then bus no. 92 to Saikung, and walk to the waterfront to pick up a boat.*

Pak Sha Chau is a gem of a beach with brilliant golden sand located on a grassy island near Saikung Town. Amenities include barbecue pits and toilets. It can be reached only by sampan. *Take MTR to Choi Hung, then bus no. 92 to Saikung.*

At **Sha Ha** the water is sometimes dirty; but because it is rather shallow far out from shore, it's ideal for beginning windsurfers. You can take lessons or rent a board at the Kent Windsurfing Centre. Facilities include refreshment stands, a coffee shop, and a Chinese restaurant in the adjacent Surf Hotel. *Take MTR to Choi Hung, then bus no. 92 to the end of the line at Saikung, and walk or take a taxi for 1 mi (1.6 km).*

The Outer Islands

Hung Shing Yeh on Lamma Island is very popular with local young people. There are no swimming rafts, but there are tents to rent, and showers, toilets, changing rooms, barbecue pits, and a kiosk. *Take the ferry from Central to Yung Shue Wan and then walk over a low hill.*

Lo So Shing, also on Lamma Island, is a good beach, but to get there requires a rather strenuous hike over hills or along the rocky shore from Yung Shue Wan. Facilities include a kiosk, barbecue pits, swimming rafts, changing rooms, showers, and toilets. *Take a ferry from Central to Sok Wan and then walk for 20–30 min.*

Pui O, also on Lantau Island, is a tiny but popular beach around the headland from Silvermine Bay ferry pier. It has a kiosk, barbecue pits, changing rooms, showers, and toilets. *Take the ferry from Central to Silvermine Bay and walk.*

Cheung Sha is a very popular beach located only a short taxi or bus ride from Silvermine Bay ferry pier. It has a sandy beach one mile (1.6 km) long and is excellent for swimming. All the standard facilities are available. *Take the ferry from Central to Silvermine Bay. Buses meet the ferry every half-hour on weekdays; on Sun. and holidays buses leave when full.*

Tung Wan is the main beach on Lantau Island, and the wide sweep of golden sand is hardly visible on weekends because it's so crowded with sunbathers. At one end is the Warwick Hotel. There are plenty of restaurants along the beach for refreshments, seafood, and shade. The standard amenities are available. *Take the ferry from Central to Silvermine Bay ferry pier and walk 5 min through the village to the beach.*

Kwun Yum Wan is not far from Tung Wan and is a popular spot with young people on summer weekends. It has all the amenities including showers, changing rooms, and toilets. *Take the ferry from Central to Silvermine Bay ferry pier. It's about a 30-min walk along narrow footpaths and over hills.*

Hong Kong for Free

Considering what a materialistic and profit-conscious place Hong Kong is, it's surprising how many activities are free. Many museums, for example, do not charge admission. Among the most interesting of these are the **Hong Kong Museum of History,** the **Museum of Art,** and the **Tea Ware Museum** in historic Flagstaff House. Among the best free sightseeing experiences are the garishly elaborate **Aw Boon Haw Gardens,** also known as "Tiger Balm" gardens because they belong to two brothers who invented the popular balm. The **Hong Kong Zoological and Botanical Gardens** are also free and well worth a visit.

Free entertainment, including concerts, Chinese opera excerpts, film, traditional dancing, and acrobatics, is offered in shopping centers such as **Cityplaza, New World,** and **The Landmark.** These performances do not have regular schedules but are listed in the tourist newspapers given away at hotel front desks.

Perhaps the best free shows of all are the colorful **street markets,** where everything from vegetables to jade is sold. And in the midst of these you'll find Buddhist and Taoist **temples,** which do not charge admission.

What to See and Do with Children

Since most visitors seem intent on squeezing as much shopping or business as they can into a brief stay (the average visit is 3½ days), activities for children are usually ignored. Yet they needn't be.

For example, if you are going to shop in **Cityplaza** (Taikoo Shing, Hong Kong Island), you can time your trip to coincide with the free cultural shows performed there under the auspices of the Hong Kong Tourist Association (HKTA). In addition, the **Landmark** (Central, Hong Kong) has its own schedule of daily events. If you take your children with you to **Cityplaza** you will find roller-skating and ice-skating rinks, and the newly opened "World of Whimsy" with exciting rides and games.

The **Sung Dynasty Village,** with its acrobats and jugglers, is fun for kids (*see* Exploring Kowloon, above). Specific tour details are available at the HKTA. Next door is the **Laichikok Amusement Park.** It is not as fancy as the theme parks in the United States, but it can be a pleasant diversion. The park also has a small zoo—though there's an even better one at the **Botanical and Zoological Gardens,** Mid-Levels (Hong Kong Island).

Three all-weather options are the new **Science Museum, Hong Kong Park,** and the tried-and-true **Space Museum.**

Two of the best places to take children are the **Ocean Park** and **Water World** theme parks (south side of Hong Kong Island). The Headland section of **Ocean Park,** reached by an exciting cable-car ride, has the **Ocean Theatre,** with performing dolphins and a killer whale; a wave cove, where you can watch seals, sea lions, penguins, and other marine animals frolic; and Atoll Reef, a giant aquarium filled with hundreds of fish, including sharks. Also in the Headland is the "Dragon," one of the world's longest roller coaster rides. The bottom section of the park has a Golden Pagoda with a display of various kinds of goldfish, a large-screen theater, and trained bird and animal shows. There is also a huge, walk-through aviary. **Water World** (open May–October) is a water play park adjacent to Ocean Park with swimming pools and water slides. *Ocean Park: tel. 552–0293. Admission, including rides: HK$140 adults, HK$70* *children. Open 10–6 daily. Water World: tel. 555–6055. Admission: HK$60 adults, HK$40 children. Opening and closing times vary. Direct transport by Citybus from Admiralty MTR Station. Fare: HK$156 adults, HK$76 children, includes admission to Ocean Park.*

While you are on the south side of the island, you may want to visit the nearby beaches of **Deep Water Bay** or **Repulse Bay** (*see* Beaches, above) or the **Aberdeen Floating Restaurants**. If the kids are old enough, head for **Stanley Village,** where they can go windsurfing while you visit the village's famous market.

Tennis, golf, squash, scuba diving, boating, water skiing, and many other sports are available in Hong Kong. If you have the time and money, look into the **Sports and Recreation Tour** offered by the Clearwater Bay Golf and Country Club (*see* Chapter 5).

A few Borneo Mountain ponies and horses are available at the **Lantau Tea Gardens.** Since these animals are not for beginners, your children will have to prove their equestrian skills before they may ride. *Lantau Island, tel. 985–5161.*

Off the Beaten Track

A place worth a visit but not open to the public is the **Royal Hong Kong Yacht Club** in Causeway Bay (off Hung Hing Rd., tel. 832-5972). Try to find a local resident who is a member, or who knows one. If you belong to a yacht club at home, you may have reciprocal guest privileges. Once inside you are surrounded by glass-fronted cabinets containing silver prize trophies and a delightfully old-fashioned bar with magnificent views of the harbor. The menu in the members' restaurant is excellent. On weekends the place hums with activity, especially when there are races being held, a common event from the spring through the fall.

For the freshest seafood, cooked to order, visit **Lei Yue Mun,** a village in Kowloon situated where the harbor narrows, east of the airport. You can make your selection in the market from tanks filled with live fish and shellfish, and then take it to a restaurant for preparation to your specifications. *Take the North Point Ferry or a ferry from the public ferry pier in Central to Kwun Tong. From here, take a taxi or No. 14C bus along Yue Lei Mun Rd.*

Visit the 1,600-year-old **Han Dynasty burial vault** at Lei Cheng Uk, in Sham Shui Po, Kowloon. It was discovered in 1955, during excavations for a huge housing estate that now surrounds it. *41 Tonkin St., Lei Cheng Uk Resettlement Estate. Take No. 2 bus from Kowloon Star Ferry terminal to Tonkin St., or MTR to Cheung Sha Wan Station. Admission: HK10¢. Open Mon.–Wed. and Fri.–Sat. 10–1 and 2–6, Sun. 1–6. Closed Thurs.*

4 Shopping

Major Shopping Areas

Hong Kong Island From the edge of Central to Kennedy Town (Sheung Wan MTR
Western District or Western Market tram stop) is **Western District,** one of the
oldest and most typically Chinese areas of Hong Kong. Here
you can find craftsmen making mah-jongg tiles, opera costumes, fans, and *chops* (seals carved in stone with engraved initials); Chinese medicine shops selling ginseng, snake musk,
shark fins, and powdered lizards; rice shops and rattan furniture dealers; and cobblers, tinkers, and tailors. Here, too, you
will find alleyways filled with knickknacks and curios.

Also in Western, opposite Central Market, is the huge **Chinese
Merchandise Emporium** (92-104 Queen's Rd. Central) with a
vast display of goods made in China. Next to the Emporium, on
Pottinger Street, are stalls selling every kind of button, bow,
zipper, and sewing gadget. Cloth Alley, or Wing On Street, is
nearby and so is Wellington Street, where you'll find a variety
of picture framers, mah-jongg makers, and small boutiques.
Going west, don't miss Man Wa Lane, where you can buy your
personal Chinese chop. In this area you will also find Western's
two largest department stores: **Sincere** (173 Des Voeux Rd.
Central) and **Wing On** (211 Des Voeux Rd. Central).

The streets behind Western Market are where you will really
feel you're in a traditional Chinese world. Wing Lok Street and
Bonham Strand West are excellent browsing areas, with their
herbal shops and snake gall bladder wine shops (visit **She Wong
Yuen,** 89-93 Bonham Strand, for a taste), and shops selling rice,
tea, and Chinese medicines. Heading uphill, don't miss the
stalls selling bric-a-brac on **Ladder Street,** which angles from
Queen's Road in Central to Hollywood and Caine roads. For
genuine antiques, **Hollywood Road** is the place. If you are in
Western at night, try the **Night Market** by the Macau Ferry
Pier.

Central District The financial and business center of Hong Kong, **Central** offers
an extraordinary mixture of boutiques, department stores, ho-
tel shopping arcades, narrow lanes in which vendors sell copies
of designer goods, and alleys full of inexpensive clothing.

Lane Crawford (70 Queen's Rd. Central), east of the Chinese
Emporium, is Hong Kong's most luxurious department store.
Other exclusive shops can be found in Central's major business
and shopping complex, the **Landmark;** in the adjoining **Central
Building,** in nearby **Prince's Building,** in **Swire House,** and in
the mall of **Pacific Palace,** opposite Admiralty. The shopping
arcades of the **Mandarin, Hilton,** and **Furama Kempinski** hotels
also have luxury shops. A branch of **Chinese Arts & Crafts**
(Shell House, 28 Queen's Rd., with entrance on Wyndham St.)
is in this area. It has a small collection of upscale clothing,
linens, silks, jewelry, and art objects.

The two most interesting alleys in Central for clothing and accessories are **Li Yuen streets East and West** (between Queen's
Rd. and Des Voeux Rd.). **Wyndham** and **On Lan** streets have
several good embroidery and linen shops, and **D'Aguilar Street**
has interesting boutiques.

Wanchai District More famous for its "Suzie Wong" nighttime meanderings than
for daytime shopping, this district still has some interesting
spots for the curious or adventurous shopper. Tattoos, for instance, are available on **Lockhart Road,** and traditional Chi-

nese bamboo bird cages on **Johnston Road.** Wandering through the lanes between Johnston Road and Queen's Road East, with their vegetable and fruit markets, you can find dozens of stalls selling buttons and bows, and inexpensive clothes. In tiny **Spring Garden Lane,** you will also find several small factory outlets. **Queen's Road East** (near its junction with Queensway) is famous for shops that make blackwood and rosewood furniture and camphorwood chests. There are more furniture shops on **Wanchai Road,** off Queen's Road East.

Happy Valley This area is a good place to shop for shoes. Follow Wong Nai Chung Road around the eastern edge of the race course to Leighton Road. At the intersection of these two roads you will find several shops that make shoes, boots, and handbags to order, at reasonable prices. The nearby **Leighton Centre** (77 Leighton Rd., between Matheson St. and Percival St.) has several fashionable boutiques, toy shops, and accessory shops. But prices are higher here than they are in nearby Causeway Bay, Hong Kong Island's large shopping area.

Causeway Bay Four large Japanese department stores dominate Causeway Bay: **Mitsukoshi** (corner Hennessy and Lee Garden Rds.), **Sogo** (545-555 Hennessy Rd., East Point Centre), **Daimaru** (corner Great George and Paterson Sts.), and **Matsuzakaya** (2-20 Paterson St.). The main branch of the **China Products Company** chain (31 Yee Wo St., next to Victoria Park) is here, and a branch of **Lane Crawford** is in nearby Windsor House (311 Gloucester Rd.). **Hennessy Road** is filled with shops selling jewelry, watches, hi-fis, cameras, and electronic goods. Surrounding the nearby Lee Gardens Hotel are hundreds of small boutiques and tailors. **Lockhart Road,** parallel to Hennessy Road, has some good shoe shops; the nearby **Excelsior Hotel Shopping Centre** features a wide range of art, gift, and souvenir shops. Don't miss the street called **Jardine's Bazaar,** with its bustling stalls and shops filled with inexpensive clothing.

Eastern District This area, which includes North Point, Quarry Bay, and Shaukiwan, is more of a residential and restaurant area than an exciting shopping area. Although there are a few large department stores along King's Road, the best shopping is found farther east on King's Road in the huge shopping complexes of **Cityplaza I & II** (at Taikoo Shing MTR), which house Hong Kong's largest department store, **UNY.**

Stanley Village The best and most popular shopping area on the south side of the island is **Stanley Market,** a mecca for bargain hunters, particularly those looking for sportswear and casual clothing. It's also a good place to shop for handicrafts, gifts, curios, and linens. The area around Main Street has a trendy, artsy ambience. On the way to Stanley Market, stop at Repulse Bay, which has a shopping arcade filled with boutiques. Nearby, on Beach Road, is the **Lido Bazaar,** a series of stalls selling souvenirs, curios, jewelry, and clothing.

Kowloon Known for its "Golden Mile" of shopping along Nathan Road,
Tsimshatsui Tsimshatsui is justifiably popular with tourists because of its
District hundreds of hi-fi, camera, jewelry, cosmetic, fashion, and souvenir shops. Also investigate the streets east of Nathan Road, such as **Granville Road,** with its clothing factory outlets, and its embroidery and porcelain shops; and **Mody Road,** with its souvenir-shop alleys. In Tsimshatsui you'll also find three large and well-stocked branches of **Chinese Arts & Crafts,** the Japa-

Shopping

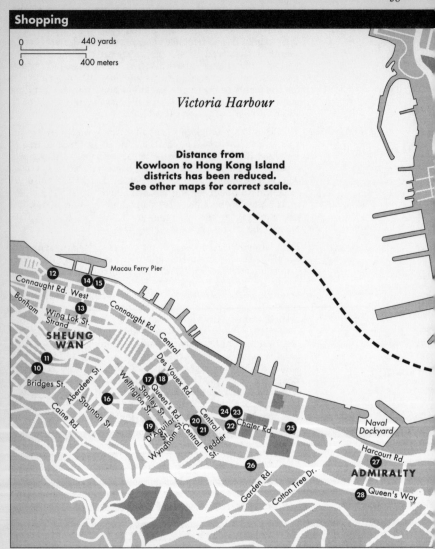

0 _____ 440 yards
0 _____ 400 meters

Victoria Harbour

**Distance from
Kowloon to Hong Kong Island
districts has been reduced.
See other maps for correct scale.**

Macau Ferry Pier

Connaught Rd. West

Bonham

Wing Lok St.
Strand

**SHEUNG
WAN**

Connaught Rd. Central

Des Voeux Rd.

Bridges St.

Aberdeen St.

Staunton St.

Caine Rd.

Wellington St.

Stanley St.

Queen's Rd.

D'Aguilar St.

Wyndham St.

Central

Central

Pedder St.

Chater Rd.

Garden Rd.

Cotton Tree Dr.

*Naval
Dockyard*

Harcourt Rd.

ADMIRALTY

Queen's Way

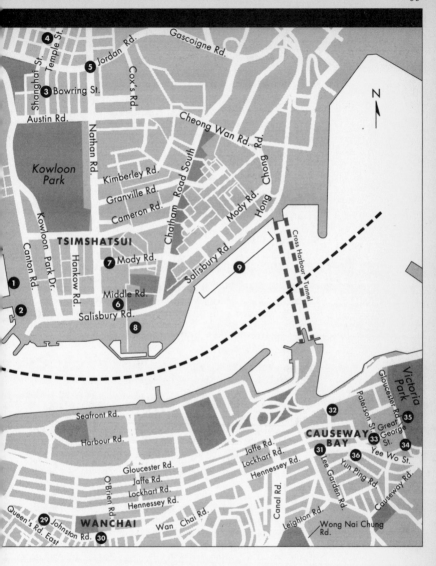

Gascoigne Rd.

4 Temple St.

Shanghai St.

5 Jordan Rd.

Cox's Rd.

3 Bowring St.

Austin Rd.

Nathan Rd.

Cheong Wan Rd.

Kowloon
Park

Chatham Road South

Hong Chong Rd.

Kimberley Rd.

Granville Rd.

Cameron Rd.

Mody Rd.

Kowloon Park Dr.

TSIMSHATSUI

Canton Rd.

Hankow Rd.

7 Mody Rd.

Salisbury Rd.

9

N

1

2

Middle Rd.

6

Salisbury Rd.

8

Cross Harbour Tunnel

Victoria
Park

Seafront Rd.

32

Gloucester Rd.

Paterson St.

Great George St.

35

Harbour Rd.

CAUSEWAY
BAY

33

34

Jaffe Rd.

Lockhart Rd.

Hennessy Rd.

31

Yee Wo St.

Gloucester Rd.

36

Yun Ping Rd.

O'Brien Rd.

Jaffe Rd.

Lockhart Rd.

Hennessey Rd.

Lee Garden Rd.

Canal Rd.

Causeway Rd.

Queen's Rd. East

29 Johnston Rd.

WANCHAI

Wan Chai Rd.

Leighton Rd.

Wong Nai Chung
Rd.

30

nese **Isetan** department store (in the shopping arcade of the Sheraton Hotel), the multistory maze of the **New World Shopping Centre**, and the vast, air-conditioned shopping complex of **Ocean Terminal-Ocean Centre-Harbour City-Hong Kong Hotel** (next to Star Ferry). The new **Tsimshatsui East** area provides a host of other air-conditioned shopping complexes.

There are two good Chinese stores near the Jordan MTR station (where Jordan and Nathan Rds. meet): **Chinese Arts & Crafts** and **Yue Hwa Chinese Products Emporium.** Nathan Road leads north to the Shamshuipo area. Here you'll find the **Golden Shopping Centre** (Fuk Wa St.), filled with Hong Kong-made computer goods.

Hunghom, the center of Hong Kong's jewelry and textile-manufacturing industries, offers a tremendous choice in designer and factory-outlet bargains. **Man Yue Street** (Kaiser Estate) is where many of the outlets are clustered.

Shopping Centers

Hong Kong Island **Admiralty.** This complex (MTR Admiralty Station) features a large selection of shops clustered in four shopping centers: **Queensway Plaza, United Centre, Pacific Place,** and **Admiralty Centre.** An open-air walkway connects them to the Hilton Hotel in Central. In Pacific Place the new multilevel **Seibu** department store includes upmarket products and a vast, varied food department. In the Admiralty Centre you will find optical shops and men's tailors.

Cityplaza I & II. This is one of Hong Kong's busiest shopping centers (above Taikoo Shing MTR Station), popular with families because of its ice- and roller-skating rinks, bowling alley, and weekly cultural shows. Many shops feature children's clothing, with labels such as Les Enfants, Crocodile, Peter Pan, and Crystal. With more than 400 shops, there are also plenty of toy shops and fashion shops for men and women.

The Landmark. One of Central's most prestigious shopping sites, The Landmark (Des Voeux Rd. and Pedder St., above Central MTR Station) is filled with boutiques and galleries. It's a multistory complex featuring names such as Celine, Loewe, D'Urban, Gucci, Joyce Boutique, and Hermès of Paris. There are also art galleries and fine jewelry shops. The information board on the mezzanine near the top of the escalators will help you find a specific boutique or gallery. A pedestrian bridge links The Landmark with shopping arcades at the **Swire House, Jardine House, Prince's Building,** and the **Mandarin Oriental Hotel.**

Shun Tak Centre. The MTR stops at Sheung Wan Station, where you'll find yourself at the Shun Tak Centre Shopping Arcade (at Macau Ferry Terminal). This also offers a good choice of boutiques featuring clothing, handbags, toys, and novelties.

Kowloon **New World Shopping Centre.** Another harborfront shopping center is the New World Shopping Centre (next to the New World Hotel). This boasts four floors of fashion and leather boutiques, jewelry shops, restaurants, optical shops, tailors, hi-fi stores, arts and crafts shops, and the Japanese **Tokyu Department Store.** The **Regent Hotel Shopping Arcade,** featuring mostly designer boutiques, can be reached through the center.

Ocean Terminal-Ocean Centre-Hong Kong Hotel-Harbour City. Located next to the Star Ferry Terminal, it is one of the largest shopping complexes in the world; if you can't find it here, it probably doesn't exist. Harbour City alone is Asia's largest shopping, office, and residential complex, with about 140 clothing shops, 36 shoe shops, 31 jewelry and watch stores, and 46 restaurants. It is connected by moving sidewalk to Ocean Terminal and Ocean Centre, which lead into the Hong Kong Hotel Shopping Arcade. The complex contains a vast **Toys R Us** and large branches of Britain's **Marks & Spencer's** and **Habitat.**

Tsimshatsui East. From the Kowloon Star Ferry you can take a mini-bus to Tsimshatsui East, an area of hotels, shops, and offices east of Chatham Road. There are 15 different shopping plazas clustered in this area, including *Wing On Plaza, Tsimshatsui Centre, Empire Centre, Houston Centre, South Seas Centre,* and *Energy Plaza.* Prices are reasonable and the atmosphere is lively.

Department Stores

Chinese The various Chinese-product stores give shoppers some of the most unusual and spectacular buys in Hong Kong—and often at better prices than in China. Whether you are looking for pearls, gold, jade, silk jackets, fur hats, Chinese stationery, or just a pair of chopsticks, you cannot go wrong with these stores. Most are open seven days a week but tend to be very crowded on Saturdays, Sunday sale days, and weekday lunchtimes. These shopkeepers are expert at packing, shipping, and mailing goods abroad, but are not so talented in the finer arts of pleasant service.

Chinese Arts & Crafts is a chain that's particularly good for silk-embroidered clothing, jewelry, carpets, and art objects, but prices may be a bit higher than at other stores. There are six branches. *Shell House in Central; New World Centre, Silvercord Bldg., and 233 Nathan Rd. in Tsimshatsui; 26 Harbour Rd. in Wanchai; and Whampoa Garden in Hunghom, Kowloon.*

China Products Company offers an excellent selection of goods, including household items. *19-31 Yee Wo St., next to Victoria Park, and 488 Hennessy Rd., both in Causeway Bay.*

Chinese Merchandise Emporium (92-104 Queen's Rd., Central) serves a bustling local clientele. The fabric, toy, and stationery departments are particularly good here. **Yue Hwa Chinese Products Emporium** (301-309 Nathan Rd., Yaumatei; 143–161 Nathan Rd.; and 54-64 Nathan Rd., Tsimshatsui) features a broad selection of Chinese goods and has a popular medicine counter. **Chung Kiu Chinese Products Emporium** (17 Hankow Rd. and 530 Nathan Rd., Kowloon) specializes in arts and crafts but also has a good selection of traditional Chinese clothing and fine silk lingerie. The **Taiwan Man Sang Product** stores (777 Nathan Rd., Kowloon) stock goods from Nationalist China.

Japanese Japanese department stores are very popular in Hong Kong. Several located in Causeway Bay include: **Daimaru** and **Matsuzakaya** (both on Paterson St.), **Mitsukoshi** and **Sogo** (both on Hennessy Rd.), and **UNY** (Cityplaza II, Taikoo Shing, Quarry Bay). Look for **Seibu** (tel. 868–0111) in Pacific Place. On the

Kowloon side, **Isetan** (Sheraton Hotel, 20 Nathan Rd.) is smaller but equally popular. Opposite, in the New World Centre, is **Tokyu Department Store.**

Western Of the department stores that stock large selections of Western goods at fixed prices, the oldest and largest chains are **Wing On** (9 branches), **Sincere** (173 Des Voeux Rd., Central and 83 Argyle St., Kowloon), and **Shui Hing** (23 Nathan Rd., Tsimshatsui). **Lane Crawford** is the most prestigious department store of all, with prices to match. Special sales here can be exhausting because everyone pushes and shoves to find bargains. The main store (70 Queen's Rd., Central) is the best. Branches are in Windsor House, Causeway Bay and Pacific Place, Central, on Hong Kong; and Manson House, 74 Nathan Rd., and Ocean Terminal in Kowloon.

The **Dragon Seed** chain has two department stores (39 Queen's Rd., Central; 2–6 Granville Rd., Tsimshatsui). The one in Central has a wide range of classic European clothing and shoes. The Kowloon store has clothes, furniture, and interior design products.

Some of these department stores hold Sunday sales, and all hold seasonal sales. But stay clear of these unless you have stamina.

Markets, Bazaars, and Alleys

These give you some of the best of Hong Kong shopping—good bargains, exciting atmosphere, and a fascinating setting. The once-famous Cat Street, the curio haunt in Upper Lascar Row, running behind the Central and Western districts, has fallen to office development. But there are still plenty of other alleys and streets filled with bazaars. Some of the best are listed here.

Cloth Alley (Wing On St., west of Central Market). This alley has fantastic bargains in all kinds of fabrics.

Jade Market (Kansu St., off Nathan Rd., Yaumatei). Jade in every form, color, shape, and size is on display in the Jade Market. This is *the* place for jade. The market is full of traders carrying out intriguing deals and keen-witted sellers trying to lure tourists. Some trinkets are reasonably priced, but unless you know a lot about jade, don't be tempted into buying expensive items.

Jardine's Bazaar. Located in Causeway Bay, this area merges a fruit and vegetable market with a tightly packed cluster of clothing stalls. The shops behind them sell attractively priced clothing and sportswear.

Kowloon City Market (No. 5 or 5C bus from Star Ferry in Kowloon, and get off opposite the airport). This market near the airport is a favorite with local bargain hunters because of its huge array of clothes, porcelain, household goods, and electrical gadgets.

Li Yuen Streets East and West (between Queen's and Des Voeux Central Rds.). This area offers some of the best bargains in fashions, with or without famous brand names. Many of the shops also feature trendy jewelry and accessories. You can also find traditional Chinese quilted jackets. Bags of every variety, many in designer styles, are particularly good buys here. Watch out for pickpockets in these crowded lanes.

Lido Bazaar (Beach Rd., Repulse Bay). This bazaar is a series of small stalls selling souvenirs, costume jewelry, bags, belts, and some clothing.

Poor Man's Nightclub (in front of the China Ferry Terminal and the Shun Tak Centre). This small market operates at night and is so called because of stalls of inexpensive food available here. Its popularity has diminished due to the many building sites nearby, but it is still worth a visit if you are after jeans, sequinned sweaters, "designer" watches, or beaded bags. It is a fun place, but avoid eating at the food stalls.

Stanley Village Market (take the no. 6 or 260 bus from Central). This is a popular haunt for Western residents and tourists looking for designer fashions, jeans, T-shirts, and sportswear, all at factory prices and in Western sizes. **Stanley's Selection** (11B New St.) usually has a good choice of sportswear, as does **Fashion Shop** (53 Stanley Style House), which is always piled high with jeans. Also interesting are the shops selling curios and household items from throughout Asia. **Manor House Collection** (17 Stanley Main St.) has a large choice of lacquerware, Korean chests, and Thai carvings. A variety of arts and crafts shops stock mostly Chinese products, such as rosewood boxes, porcelain dolls, and traditional tea baskets. **Oriental Corner** (125A Stanley Main St.) has Chinese wedding boxes and other carved items. Stanley Village Market is also a good place to buy linen. There are four linen shops here, and they are all worth exploring. The market is at its most enjoyable on weekdays when it's less crowded.

Temple Street. In Kowloon (near the Jordan MTR Station), this is another nighttime marketplace, filled with a colorful collection of clothes, handbags, electrical goods, gadgets, and all sorts of household items. By the light of lamps strung up between stalls, hawkers try to catch the eye of shoppers by flinging clothes up from their stalls; Cantonese opera competes with pop music, and there's a constant chatter of hawkers' cries and shoppers' bargaining. The market stretches for almost a mile (1.6 km) and is one of Hong Kong's liveliest nighttime shopping experiences.

Specialty Stores

Antiques Bargains and discoveries are much harder to find these days than they were a few years ago. If you want to be sure of your purchase, patronize shops such as **Charlotte Horstmann and Gerald Godfrey** (Ocean Terminal, Tsimshatsui, tel. 735–7167), **Eileen Kershaw** (Peninsula Hotel, Tsimshatsui, tel. 366–4083), **Zitan** (43-55 Wyndham St., Central, tel. 523–7584), **Gallery 69** (123 Edinburgh Tower, The Landmark, tel. 522–2456), or **Lane Crawford** (70 Queen's Rd., Central, tel. 526–6121).

For shoppers with more curiosity than cash, Hollywood Road is a fun place to visit. The street, running from Central to Western, is undeniably the best place for poking about in shops and stalls selling antiques from many Asian countries. Treasures are hidden away among a jumble of old family curio shops, sidewalk junk stalls, slick new display windows, and dilapidated warehouses.

Eastern Dreams (corner of Lyndhurst Terr. and Hollywood Rd., Central, tel. 524–4787 and 544–2804) has two floors of antique and reproduction furniture, screens, and curios. **Yue Po Chai Antique Co.** (132-136 Hollywood Rd., Central, tel. 540–4374) is one of Hollywood Road's oldest, and has a vast and varied stock. **Schoeni Fine Arts** (27 Hollywood Rd., Central, tel. 542–3143) sells Japanese, Chinese, and Thai antiques, Chinese silverware, such as opium boxes, and rare Chinese pottery.

In the Cat Street area, once famous for its thieves' market of secondhand stolen goods, there is now almost nothing of interest for antiques hunters. However, **Cat Street Galleries** (38 Lok Ku Rd., Sheung Wan, Western, tel. 541–8908) has a collection of dealers, all under one roof. You'll find them tucked away among the high-rise office buildings that are the result of the area's redevelopment.

In the unlikely event that you cannot find anything to interest you on Hollywood Road, there are several other fascinating but contemporary emporiums worth investigating. **Amazing Grace Elephant Co.** (New Town Plaza in Shatin; Tuen Mun Town Plaza in the New Territories; Ocean Centre in Tsimshatsui; Excelsior Hotel and Cityplaza on Hong Kong Island, tel. 567–3180) has a wide range of Asian antiques, curios, and gifts at reasonable prices. The **Banyan Tree** (Shop 214, Prince's Building, Central, tel. 523–5561; Ocean Galleries, Harbour City, Tsimshatsui, tel. 730–6631) also has a huge choice of things Asian, both old and new. **Treasures of China** (312 Ocean Terminal, Tsimshatsui, tel. 736–0089; 238, 304, and 322 and 331 Pacific Place, Hong Kong Island, tel. 845–3610) stocks art and antiques from most of the dynasties.

If you know what you are after, keep an eye out for auction announcements in the classified section of the *South China Morning Post*. **Lammert Brothers** (9th floor, Malahon Centre, 10–12 Stanley St., Central, tel. 522–3208) holds regular carpet and antiques sales. **Victoria Auctioneers** (Century Sq., D'Aguilar St., Central, tel. 524–7611) has sales of a more general nature.

For antique embroidered pieces, try **Teresa Coleman** (7th floor, Seabird House, 37 Wyndham St., Central, tel. 526–2450). For Japanese art, mostly prints and lithographs, look in **Koto Arts** (1/F, Arts Centre, 2 Harbour Rd., Wanchai, tel. 865–6029), which often has ceramics, fans, and other attractive items.

It may be worth having your artwork framed in Hong Kong, because prices are much lower than in Europe and the United States. Shops in Central that do excellent work include **Man Fong** (41 Wellington St., tel. 522–6923) and **Wah Cheong** (15 Hollywood Rd., tel. 523–1900).

If you are interested in seeing the latest developments in the East-meets-West art of local painters, visit **The Touchstone Gallery and Studio; The Arts Centre** (2 Harbour Rd., Wanchai, tel. 524–3078 and 823–0200), which often has exhibitions with works for sale; or the **Hong Kong Museum of Art** (City Hall High Block, Connaught Rd., Central, tel. 522–4127).

Cameras/Lenses/ Binoculars Many of Hong Kong's thousands of camera shops are clustered on the Lock Road/lower Nathan Road area of Tsimshatsui, in the back streets of Central, and Hennessy Road in Causeway Bay. Two well-known and knowledgeable dealers are **Williams Photo Supply** (Prince's Bldg. and Furama Kempinski Hotel, Central) and **Photo Scientific Appliances** (6 Stanley St., Central). If you are interested in buying a number of different items in the shop (most also stock binoculars, calculators, radios, and other electronic gadgets), you should be able to bargain for a good discount.

If in doubt about where to shop for such items, stick to the HKTA member shops. Pick up its *Official Guide to Shopping, Eating Out & Services* at any of its information centers and authorized dealers. All reputable dealers should give you a one-year, worldwide guarantee. Unauthorized dealers, who obtain their camera gear legally from sources other than the official agent, may not provide a proper guarantee—although you may pick up better bargains in these outlets.

Carpets and Rugs Regular imports from China, Iran, India, Pakistan, Afghanistan, and Kashmir make carpets and rugs a very good buy in Hong Kong. There are also plenty of carpets made locally. Though prices have increased in recent years, carpets are still cheaper in Hong Kong than they are in Europe and the United States. For Chinese carpets, branches of **China Products** and **Chinese Arts & Crafts** shops give the best selection and price range. For locally made carpets, **Tai Ping Carpets** (Shop 110, G/F, Hutchinson House, 10 Harcourt Rd., Central) is highly regarded, especially for custom-made rugs and wall-to-wall carpets. The store takes four to six weeks to make specially ordered carpets; customers can specify color, thickness, and even the direction of the weave. There is a showroom on the ground floor of Hutchinson House. Tai Ping's occasional sales are well worth attending. Check the classified section of the *South China Morning Post* for dates. **Peking Carpets** (402 Hennessy Rd., Wanchai) and **Carpet World** (Ocean Terminal, Tsimshatsui) both carry good selections.

In Upper Wyndham Street, Central, you will find several shops selling Persian, Turkish, Indian, Pakistani, Tibetan, and Afghan rugs—though don't expect miraculously low prices. **Oriental Carpet Trading** (31B Wyndham St.), **Mir Oriental Carpets** (71 Wyndham St.), **Tribal Arts & Crafts** (41 Wyndham St.), and **Tribal Rugs Ltd.** (Unit 66, 2/F at Admiralty Centre, Central) are all reputable dealers.

Ceramics Fine English porcelain dinner, tea, and coffee sets are popular buys in Hong Kong and are best found at **Craig's** (St. George's Bldg., 2 Ice House St., Central, tel. 522–8726; Shop 342 in Ocean Centre, Tsimshatsui, tel. 730–8930). Royal Worcester and Royal Crown Derby are among the fine china stocked at Craig's. **Hunter's** (Pacific Place Mall, in Admiralty, tel. 845–5422; Ocean Terminal, Kowloon, tel. 730–0155), **Wedgwood Shop** (Landmark, tel. 523–8337), and **Dragon Seed** (Ruttonjee Centre, Duddell St., Central, tel. 521–2233) are other shops selling top-quality porcelain.

For a full range of ceramic Chinese tableware, visit the various **China Products Company** stores. They also offer fantastic bargains and attractive designs on vases, bowls, and table lamps. Inexpensive buys can also be found in the shops along Queen's Road East in Wanchai, in the streets of Tsimshatsui, in the shopping centers of Tsimshatsui East and Ocean Terminal/Centre, and in such street markets as **Kowloon City Market.**

Factory outlets are also a good source. Two of the most popular, offering good bargains, are **Overjoy Porcelain** (1st floor, 10–18 Chun Pin St., Kwai Chung, New Territories, tel. 487–0615) and **Ah Chow Factory** (Block B, 7th floor, 1&2 Hong Kong Industrial Centre, Castle Peak Rd., Laichikok, tel. 745–0209). For Overjoy Porcelain, take MTR to Kwai Hing Station, then a taxi. For Ah Chow, take MTR to Laichikok Station and follow exit signs to Leighton Textile Building/Tung Chau West.

For antique ceramic items, visit **Yue Po Chai Antique Co.** (132– 136 Hollywood Rd., next to Man Mo Temple). For good repro- ductions, try **Sheung Yu Ceramic Arts** (Vita Tower, 29 Wong Chuk Hang Rd., Aberdeen, tel. 555–1881). For unusual and very beautiful reproductions of Chinese vases and bowls, try **Mei Ping** (Wilson House, 19–27 Wyndham St., Central, tel. 521–3566). Ceramic elephant stools from Vietnam make de- lightful table bases, stools, or decorative items, and can be found at **Amazing Grace Elephant Co.** (Excelsior Shopping Centre, Causeway Bay; Cityplaza, Quarry Bay; New Town Pla- za, Shatin; Tuen Mun Town Plaza, New Territories; Ocean Cen- tre, Tsimshatsui).

Children's Clothing There are plenty of stores in Hong Kong that sell Western- style, ready-to-wear children's clothing. Among the best are **G2000** (Queen's Rd., Central, and New World Centre, Tsimshatsui) and **Cacharel** (Landmark, Central and Ocean Centre and New World Centre, Tsimshatsui). For traditional English-style smocks and rompers, go to **Baba's** (Mainslit Bldg., 42 Stanley and Potter Sts.), or **Even Chance** (Far East- ern Exchange Bldg., Wyndham St., Central). Another good place for smocks and rompers is Britain's **Mothercare** (Windsor House, 311 Gloucester Rd., Causeway Bay; Ocean Terminal, Tsimshatsui). You can also find fabulous, traditional Chinese- style clothing for tots in two clothing alleys in Central—Li Yuen streets East and West. Branches of the **Welfare Handi- craft Shops** (Basement of Jardine House, Central; Salisbury Rd., Tsimshatsui) have interesting selections of Eastern and Western children's wear.

Chocolates **See's Candies,** flown fresh from California daily, are available in their outlets in Landmark (Central District), Ocean Terminal (Kowloon), and City-Plaza (Quarry Bay, Hong Kong Island) daily. **Peninsula Chocolates,** from the hotel of the same name, are also sold in the Lucullus outlets and have an excellent repu- tation.

Computers and All of the big names—Apple, Sinclair, Osbourne, IBM, BBC/
Peripheral Devices Acorn—sell in Hong Kong. If you are going to buy, make sure the machines will work on the voltage in your country—an IBM personal computer sold in Hong Kong will work on 220 volts, while the identical machine in the United States will work on 110 volts. Servicing is a major concern, too.

The real bargains in computers are the locally made versions of the most popular brands. But be forewarned: Even though the prices are lower than in Europe and the United States, you may have trouble getting your Hong Kong computer past customs on your return.

The Asia Computer Plaza (Silvercord, Canton Rd., Tsim- shatsui) has 40,000 square feet devoted to everything con- nected with computers. Most big names have outlets here. There are also three shopping centers into which are crammed dozens of small computer shops. On Hong Kong Island, the most accessible are the **Ocean Shopping Arcade** (128 Wanchai Rd.) and the **Hong Kong Computer Centre** (54 Lockhart Rd., Wanchai). The **Golden Shopping Centre** (Shamshuipo, Kowloon), is more difficult to reach. Take the MTR to Shamshuipo Station, and use the Fuk Wah Street exit. The shopping center is across the street. You will find countless stalls here selling everything related to computers.

Electronic Gimmicks and Gadgets For those electronic devices that shoppers love to take home, the **Special Interest Electronic Co.** (Hutchison House, 10 Harcourt Rd., Central) has hundreds of strange and not-so-strange items.

Factory Outlets For the best buys in designer clothes, visit some of the factory outlets and pick up high-fashion (almost indiscernibly damaged seconds or overruns) at a fraction of the normal price. One of the best areas for silks is Man Yue Street in Hunghom, Kowloon (take a taxi to Kaiser Estate, Phase I, II, and III). Here are factories such as **Camberley, Four Seasons, Vica Moda,** and **Bendini,** all of which produce for the fashion houses of Europe and the United States.

Furniture and Furnishings Home decor has boomed tremendously in Hong Kong in recent years, and manufacturers of furniture and home furnishings have been quick to expand their activities. **Design Selection** (39 Wyndham St., Central) has a good choice of Indian fabrics. **Interiors** (38 D'Aguilar St., Central) and **Furniture Boutique** (3 Tin Hau Temple Rd., Causeway Bay) stock imported and locally made goods. **The Banyan Tree** (Prince's Bldg., Central; and Harbour City, Tsimshatsui) sells ready-made or made-to-order rattan furniture and some antique Chinese, Korean, and Filipino pieces. Queen's Road East, in Wanchai, has several furniture shops specializing in rattan.

Rosewood furniture is a very popular buy in Hong Kong. Queen's Road East, in Wanchai, the great furniture retail and manufacturing area, offers everything from full rosewood dining sets in Ming style to furniture in French, English, or Chinese styles. Custom-made orders are accepted in most shops on this street. **Choy Lee Co. Ltd** (1 Queen's Rd. East) is the best known. Other rosewood furniture dealers, such as **Cathay Arts** (Shop 305 at Ocean Centre), can also be found in the Ocean Terminal complex at Tsimshatsui.

There are a number of old-style shops specializing in the rich-looking blackwood furniture (chairs, chests, and couches made in Southern China at the turn of the century). These are in the Western end of Hollywood Road, near Man Mo Temple. Queen's Road East and nearby Wanchai Road are also good sources for camphorwood chests, as is Canton Road in Kowloon.

Luk's Furniture (52–64 Aberdeen Main Rd., Aberdeen) is a bit off the beaten path, but offers a huge range of rosewood and lacquer furniture on three floors at warehouse prices. It also will make to order.

Reproductions are common, so "antique" furniture should be inspected carefully. Some points to look for include: a mature sheen on the wood, slight gaps at the joints that have resulted from natural drying, signs of former restorations, and signs of gradual wear, especially at leg bottoms.

Blackwood, like rosewood and teak, must be properly dried, seasoned, and aged to prevent future cracking in climates that are less humid than Hong Kong's.

Furs   It seems bizarre that Hong Kong, with its tropical climate, should host so many fur shops. But furs are a good buy here, with high-quality skins, meticulous tailoring, excellent hand-finishing, and competitive prices. Some of the largest and most popular shops are **Siberian Fur Store** (21 Chatham Rd., Tsimshatsui, and 29 Des Voeux Rd. Central); **Stylette Models** (L2–38B New World Centre, Tsimshatsui; the Excelsior Hotel at Causeway Bay), and **Jindo Fur Salon** (Harbour City, Tsimshatsui), which offers a wide range at factory prices.

Handicrafts and Curios   The traditional crafts of China include a fascinating range of items: lanterns, temple rubbings, screen paintings, paper cuttings, seal engravings, and wooden birds. The HKTA publishes a useful pamphlet, *Culture*, listing places where you can buy these specialty items; it is available at all HKTA information centers.

The Welfare Handicrafts Shop (Jardine House, Central) stocks a good collection of inexpensive Chinese handicrafts for both adults and children. All profits go to charity. For contemporary gifts, T-shirts, dolls, posters, and hats try **Startram (HK) Ltd.** (Star House, by Kowloon Star Ferry; Regal Meridien Hotel, Tsimshatsui; and Peak Tower, on the Hong Kong side). Small and inexpensive curios from other parts of Asia are on sale at **Amazing Grace Elephant Co.** (Ocean Centre, Tsimshatsui; Fleet House, Excelsior Hotel, Causeway Bay; and Cityplaza, Quarry Bay, Hong Kong).

Mountain Folkcraft (12 Wo On La., Central) offers a varied collection of fascinating curios. **The Forms Folkcrafts** (1/F, 37 Wyndham St., Central) is worth a visit if you like goods from China, Nepal, and Tibet. **Banyan Tree** (Harbour City, Tsimshatsui; and Prince's Bldg., Central) features a slightly more pricey but attractive selection of items from different Asian countries. More can be found in **Tribal Arts & Crafts** (41 Wyndham St., Central). For Filipino goods, visit **Collecciones** (61 Wyndham St., Central); for Indonesian goods, **Vincent Sum Designs Ltd.** (19 Lyndhurst Terr., Central); for Thai crafts, **Thai Shop** (Silvercord, Haiphong and Canton Rds., Tsimshatsui); and for New Zealand products, **Kiwi Shop** (166 Wanchai Rd., Hong Kong Island).

Stanley Market is also worth visiting for ethnic goods. Some of the more interesting shops there are **Manor House Collections** (17 Stanley Main St.) and **Oriental Corner** (125A Stanley Main St.).

Hi-fis, Stereos, Tape Recorders   Hennessy Road in Causeway Bay has long been the mecca for finding hi-fi gear, although many small shops in Central's Queen Victoria and Stanley streets and in Tsimshatsui's Nathan Road offer a similar variety of goods. Be sure to compare prices before buying, as they can vary widely. Also make sure that guarantees are worldwide and applicable in your home town or country. It helps to know exactly what you want, since most shopkeepers don't have the room or inclination to give you a chance to test and compare sound systems. However, some major manufacturers do have individual showrooms where you can test the equipment before buying. The shopkeeper will be able to direct you. Another tip: Though most of the export gear sold in Hong Kong has fuses or dual wiring that can be used in any country, it pays to double check.

Ivory   Although Hong Kong officially participates in the ban on trading ivory, there is still new and antique ivory for sale. It is subject to seizure at many foreign entry ports, however.

Jewelry   Jewelry is the most popular item among visitors to Hong Kong. It is not subject to any local tax or duty, so prices are normally much lower than they are in most other places of the world. Turnover is fast, competition fierce, and the selection fantastic. As one of the world's largest diamond-trading centers, Hong Kong offers these gems at prices that are at least 10% lower than world-market levels. Settings will also cost less here than in most Western capitals, but check your country's customs regulations, as some countries charge a great deal more for imported set jewelry than for unset gems.

If you are not a gemologist, shop only in reputable outlets—preferably one recommended by someone who lives in Hong Kong or listed in *The Official Guide to Shopping, Eating Out and Services in Hong Kong.* You might want to invest in a booklet, *Gems & Jewelry—in Hong Kong—A Buyer's Guide.* Hong Kong law requires all jewelers to indicate on every gold item displayed or offered for sale both the number of carats and the identity of the shop or manufacturer—make sure these marks are present. Also, check the current gold prices, which most stores will have displayed, against the price of the gold item that you are thinking of buying.

When buying diamonds, check the "Four C's": color, clarity, carat (size), and cut. For information or advice on diamonds, call the Diamond Importers Association, Hong Kong Island (tel. 523-5497).

Pearls, another good buy, should be checked for color against a white background. Colors vary from white, silvery white, light pink, darker pink, to cream. Cultured pearls usually have a perfect round shape, semi-baroque pearls have slight imperfections, and baroque pearls are distinctly misshapen. Also check for luster, which is never found in synthetics. Freshwater pearls from China, which look like rough grains of rice, are inexpensive and look lovely in several twisted strands. For jewelry appraisals, contact **S.P.H. De Silva** (Pacific Pl., Central, tel. 522-0639).

Jade is Hong Kong's most famous stone. But beware. Although you will see "jade" trinkets and figurines everywhere in Hong Kong, the good jade is rare and expensive. Its quality is determined by the degree of translucency and by the evenness of color and texture.

Jade is not only green; it comes in shades of purple, orange, yellow, brown, white, and violet. The most expensive color is a deep, translucent emerald green. Be careful not to pay jade prices for green stones sold as "jade" (such as aventurine, bowenite, soapstone, serpentine, and Australian jade). Inexperienced shoppers are well advised to buy only from reputable shops. However, a visit to the **Jade Market** (Kansu St., Kowloon) is a must. Walking among the many dealers you will get an excellent idea of the range of jade's many colors, shapes, and forms.

If you are wary of spending your money on Kansu Street, visit **Jade House** (Regent Hotel Shopping Arcade, tel. 721-6010) or **Jade Creations** (Lane Crawford House, Queen's Rd., Central, tel. 522–3519). The more opulent, big-name, and reputable jewelers include **Kevin Jewellery** (Hilton Hotel, tel. 523–3097); **Larry Jewelry** (Landmark, Central, tel. 521–1268; 33 Nathan Rd. and Ocean Terminal, Tsimshatsui, tel. 730–8081 and 721–8133); **Dickson Watch and Jewellery** (Peninsula and Holiday Inn Golden Mile hotels, Tsimshatsui), **S.P.H. De Silva** (Pacific Pl. Central, tel. 522–0639); **Manchu Gems** (Shop 120D in Ocean Terminal, tel. 730–3034); **Dabera** (Shop 2801 in Admiralty Centre, tel. 527–7722); **King Fook** (30 Des Voeux Rd., tel. 523–9424); and **House of Shen** (Peninsula Hotel, tel. 721–5483). **Chinese Arts & Crafts** (Star House, Kowloon, tel. 735–4061) has a wide collection of jade, pearls, and gold as well as porcelain, jewelry, and enamelware.

For pearls, try **The Pearl Gallery** (1/F New World Tower, Queen's Rd., Central, tel. 526–3599) or **Amerex** (702 Tak Shing House, 20 Des Voeux Rd., Central, tel. 523–9145). Famous international jewelers with shops in Hong Kong include **Van Cleef & Arpels** (Landmark, and Peninsula and Regent Hotels in Tsimshatsui, tel. 522–9677 and 367–5544), **Cartier** (Peninsula Hotel, tel. 368–8036; Prince's Bldg. in Central, tel. 522–2964), and **Ilias Lalaounis** (Regent Hotel lobby, in Tsimshatsui, and Landmark, tel. 721–2811). For modern jewelry with an Oriental influence, take a look at the fabulous designs by **Kai-Yin Lo** (Mandarin Oriental Hotel, Central, tel. 524–8238).

Kung-fu Supplies There are hundreds of kung-fu schools and supply shops in Hong Kong, especially in the areas of Mongkok, Yaumatei, and Wanchai, but often they are hidden away in back streets and up narrow stairways. The two most convenient places to buy your drum cymbal, leather boots, sword, whip, double dagger, studded wrist bracelet, Bruce Lee kempo gloves, and other kung-fu exotica are **Kung Fu Supplies Co.** (188 Johnston Rd., Wanchai) and **Shang Wu Kung Fu Appliance Centre** (366 Lockhart Rd., Wanchai).

Leather From belts to bags, luggage to briefcases, leather items are high on the list for the Hong Kong shopper. The best and most expensive leather goods come from Europe, but locally made leather bags in designer styles go for a song on Li Yuen streets East and West, in Central, and in other shopping lanes. The leather-garment industry is a growing one, and although most of the production is for export, some good buys can be found in the factory outlets in Hunghom, Kowloon.

For top-brand international products, visit department stores such as **Lane Crawford** (70 Queen's Rd., Central, is the best branch), **Wing On** (Des Voeux Rd., Central and in other locations, tel. 852–1888), and **Sincere** (Des Voeux Rd., Central, tel. 544–2688). Also visit the Japanese stores in Causeway Bay: **Daimaru** (tel. 576–7321), **Mitsukoshi** (tel. 576–5222), **Matsuzakaya** (tel. 529–5671), and **Sogo** (tel. 833–8338). All stock designer brands, such as Nina Ricci, Cartier, Lancel, II Bisonte, Comtesse, Guido Borelli, Caran d'Ache, Franco Pugi, and Christian Dior.

Linens, Silks, Embroideries Pure silk shantung, silk and gold brocade, silk velvet, silk damask, and printed, silk crepe de Chine are just some of the exquisite materials available in Hong Kong at reasonable prices. The best selections are in the **China Products Emporiums, Chinese Arts & Crafts,** and **Yue Hwa stores.** Ready-to-wear silk garments, from mandarin coats and cheongsams to negligees, dresses, blouses, and slacks are good buys at Chinese Arts & Crafts.

Irish linens, Swiss cotton, Thai silks, and Indian, Malay, and Indonesian fabrics are among the imported cloths available in Hong Kong. Many of them can be found on Wing On Lane in Central. **Vincent Sum Designs** (5A Lyndhurst Terr., Central) specializes in Indonesian batik. A small selection of Indonesian batik can also be found in **Mountain Folkcraft** (Ocean Terminal, Tsimshatsui; and 12 Wo On La., Central). Thai silks are about the same price in Hong Kong as they are in Bangkok. A large range of selections can be found in branches of **China Arts & Crafts** and in **V Thailand** (Sheraton Hotel Mall in Tsimshatsui). Attractive fabrics from India are available from **Design Selection** (39 Wyndham St., Central) and **The Thai Shop** (Silvercord, Canton Rd., Tsimshatsui).

The best buys from China are hand-embroidered and appliquéed linens and cottons. You can find a magnificent range of tablecloths, place mats, napkins, and handkerchiefs in the **China Products Company** and **Chinese Arts & Crafts** stores, and in linen shops in Stanley Market. Also, look in the various shops on Wyndham and On Lan streets in Central. The art of embroidery is said to have originated in Swatow, a port city in China's Kwangtung Province. A shop named after this city, **Swatow Drawn Work** (G2–3 Worldwide House, Central) sells some of the best examples of this delicate art form. When buying hand-embroidered items, be certain the edges are properly overcast and beware of machine-made versions being passed off as handmade.

Miscellaneous Chinese Gifts If you are really stuck for a gift idea, think Chinese. Some of the most unusual gifts are often the simplest. How about a pair of chopsticks, in black lacquer and finely painted? Or how about a Chinese chop, engraved with your friend's name in Chinese? These are available at shops throughout Hong Kong. For chop ideas, take a walk down **Man Wa Lane** in Central (opposite Wing On Dept. Store, 26 Des Voeux Rd.). For those who live in cold climates, wonderful *mien laps* (padded silk jackets) are sold in the alleys of Central or in the various shops featuring Chinese products. Another unusual item for rainy weather—or even as a decorative display—is a hand-painted Chinese umbrella, available very inexpensively at **Chinese Arts & Crafts** and **China Products Company** stores. Chinese tea, packed in colorful, traditional tins, can be picked up in the teahouses in Bonham Strand and Wing Lok Street in Western. A bit more expensive, but a novel idea, are the padded tea baskets with teapot and tea cups; or tiered bamboo food baskets, which make good sewing baskets. All can be found in China Product stores.

Optical Goods There are a vast number of optical shops in Hong Kong, and some surprising bargains, too. Soft contact lenses, hard lenses, and frames for glasses go for considerably less than in many other places. All the latest styles and best quality frames are available at leading optical shops at prices generally much lower than in Europe and the United States. **The Optical Shop** (branches throughout Hong Kong) is the fanciest and probably the most reliable store. An eye test using the latest equipment is provided free.

Perfume and Cosmetics Although aromatic ointments were believed to have been used by the Egyptians over 5,000 years ago, it was Asia that made the major contributions to the art of perfumery. Today, Chinese perfumes are hardly a match for Western fragrances. Scented sandalwood soap is the one exception (the "Maxam" label in China-product stores is prettily packaged). For Western perfumes, the best buys are in department stores such as **Wing On** and **Sincere**, drugstores such as **Manning's** and **Watson's**, and branches of **Fanda Perfume Co. Ltd** (21 Lock Rd., Kowloon; World Wide House, Pedder St., Central; and 71 Des Voeux Rd., Central).

Shoes The place to buy shoes in Hong Kong is on **Wongneichung Road**, in Happy Valley, next to the race course. Here you will find many shoe shops selling inexpensive, locally made shoes and Japanese-made shoes. Shoes from Europe are available occasionally, but most are brought in solely for the purpose of copying. If you have small feet, these shops can offer excellent buys. If you wear large sizes, you'll probably have trouble finding shoes that fit well.

Top-name Italian and other European shoes can be found in the department stores and shopping centers. But don't expect prices for designer shoes to be much less than they are back home.

Custom-made shoes for both men and women are readily and quickly available. Cobblers, even those with names such as **Lee Kee Boot & Shoe Makers** (65 Peking Rd., Tsimshatsui, tel. 367–4903), are renowned for their skill in copying specific styles at reasonable prices. **Mayer Shoes** (Mandarin Hotel, Central, tel. 524–3317) has an excellent range of styles and leathers. If you like cowboy boots in knee-high calfskin, try the **Kow Hoo Shoe Company** (Hilton Hotel, Central, tel. 523–0489). The shops in Happy Valley will also make shoes and boots to order, and are particularly good at making shoes and bags, covered with silk or satin, to match an outfit. If you leave your size chart, you can make future purchases through mail order.

Sporting Goods Hong Kong is an excellent place to buy sports gear, thanks to high volume and reasonable prices. Tennis players and golfers can find a good range of equipment and clothing in the many outlets of **Marathon Sports** (Cityplaza, Taikoo Shing; 1 D'Aguilar St., 29 Percival St., Queensway Plaza, Hong Kong Island; Ocean Terminal, Silvercord, Park Hotel, Kowloon). Watersports enthusiasts will find sailing, waterskiing, surfing, and snorkeling gear (including wet suits) at **Bunns Diving Equipment** (188 Wanchai Rd., Wanchai). Fishermen can get outfitted at **Po Kee Fishing Tackle Company** (Ocean Terminal, Tsimshatsui). For a comprehensive range covering a variety of sports, visit the **World Top Sports Goods Ltd.** (351–352 Ocean Centre, Harbour City; 49 Hankow Rd.; and 9 Carnarvon Rd., all in Tsimshatsui).

Tailor-made Clothing Despite the number of ready-to-wear clothing shops and off-the-peg fashion stores, you can still find Chinese tailors to make Western suits, dresses, and evening gowns. Here are some do's and don'ts.

For a suit, overcoat, or jacket, give the tailor plenty of time—at least three to five days, and allow for a minimum of two proper fittings plus a final one for finishing touches. Shirts *can* be done in a day, but again you will get better quality if you allow more time. Some shirtmakers like to give one fitting.

Choose a tailor whose shop is near your hotel, so you won't be too inconvenienced when you need to return for one or more fittings. Tailors located in hotels or other major shopping centers may be more expensive, but they will be more accustomed to Western styles and fittings.

Have a good idea of what you want before you go to the tailor. Often the best method is to take a suit you want copied. Go through the details carefully, and make sure they are listed on the order form, together with a swatch of the material ordered. When you pay a deposit (which should not be more than 50% of the final cost) make sure the receipt includes all relevant details: the date of delivery, the description of the material, and any special requirements. All tailors keep records of clients' measurements, so satisfied customers can make repeat orders by mail or telephone. Keep a copy of the original measurements in case you need to change them.

There are a number of reputable and long-established tailors in Hong Kong who provide for both men and women. **Sam's** (Burlington House, 94 Nathan Rd., Kowloon, tel. 367–9423) has been patronized by members of the British Forces since 1957; one of the company's regular customers is the Duke of Kent. Another tailor is **Cheng and Cheng** (Regal Meridien Hotel, 71 Mody Rd., Tsimshatsui, tel. 723–9151). **Ascot Chang** (Peninsula and Regent hotels, Kowloon; and Prince's Bldg., Central, tel. 523–3663) has specialized in shirtmaking since 1949. Clients have included George Bush and Andy Williams.

Tea If you want to buy a ton of tea, you can probably do so in Hong Kong's most famous tea area—Western district on Hong Kong Island. Walk down Queen's Road West and Des Voeux Road West and you will find dozens of tea merchants and dealers, such as **Cheng Leung Wing** (526 Queen's Rd. W). If you want to enjoy a cup of *cha* (tea) in traditional style, stroll along Stanley Street in Central, where Hong Kong's greatest selection of teas is served in traditional teahouses. The beautiful **Luk Yu Teahouse** (24 Stanley St.) is the oldest and best known. Also, try the **Wan Lai** (484 Shanghai St., Yaumatei, Kowloon) for the experience of having *yam cha* (tea with small snacks called *dim sum*). As you sip your tea, you'll be able to watch "bird walkers" who come here with their caged birds after taking them for a morning stroll.

You can buy packages or small tins of Chinese tea in the tea shops of the Western district or at the various **China Product** stores and leading supermarkets, such as **Park'n Shop.**

For more sophisticated tea shopping go to the **Fook Ming Tong Tea Shop** (211, Prince's Bldg., Central). There you can buy superb teas in beautifully designed tins, or invest in some antique clay teaware.

Teas fall into three types: green (unfermented), black (fermented), and oolong (semifermented). Various flavors include jasmine, chrysanthemum, rose, and narcissus. Loong Ching Green Tea and Jasmine Green Tea are among the most popular, often available in attractive tins. These make inexpensive but unusual gifts.

TVs and Video Recorders Color TV systems vary throughout the world, so it's important to be certain the TV set or video recorder you purchase in Hong Kong has a system compatible to the one in your country. Hong Kong, Australia, Great Britain, and most European countries use the *PAL* system. The United States uses the *NTSC* system, and France and Russia use the *Seacam* system. Before you buy, tell the shopkeeper where you will be using your TV or video recorder. In most cases you will be able to get the right model without any problems. The HKTA has a useful brochure called: *Shopping Guide to Video Equipment.*

Watches You will have no trouble finding watches in Hong Kong. Street stalls, department stores, and shops overflow with every variety, style, and brand name, many of them with irresistible gadgets. (But remember Hong Kong's remarkable talent for imitation. A super-bargain gold "Rolex" may have hidden flaws—cheap local or Russian mechanisms, for instance, or "gold" that rusts). Stick to officially appointed dealers carrying the manufacturers' signs if you want to be sure you are getting the real thing. When buying an expensive watch, check the serial number against the manufacturer's guarantee certificate and ask the salesman to open the case to check the movement serial number. If an expensive band is attached, find out whether it is from the original manufacturer or locally made, as this will dramatically affect the price (originals are much more expensive). You should obtain a detailed receipt, the manufacturer's guarantee, and a worldwide warranty for all items.

For top-of-the-market buys, try **Artland Watch Co. Ltd.** (corner of Ice House St. and Des Voeux Rd., Central; and 62A Nathan Rd., Tsimshatsui). For less expensive brands, visit any of the 11 branches of **City Chain** (127–131 Des Voeux Rd. and Queen's Rd., Central; 10 stores on Nathan Rd., in Kowloon).

Women's Clothing Hong Kong is more Western than many first-time visitors imagine. Nowhere is this more obvious than in fashions, especially in areas such as Central, where everyone wears Western-style clothing.

Some of the leading stores are **Green & Found** (Swire House, Landmark, and Peninsula Hotel), **Joyce Boutique** (Landmark and Peninsula Hotel), **Issey Miyake** (Swire House and Kowloon Hotel), **Boutique Bazaar** (Landmark and Peninsula hotels), **Celine Boutique** (Peninsula Hotel, Landmark, Repulse Bay Shopping Arcade), **Chanel Boutique** (Peninsula and Regent hotels and Prince's Bldg.), **D'Urban** (Landmark; Kowloon Hotel, Ocean Terminal, Isetan Department Store), **Giorgio Armani** (Mandarin Hotel and Landmark), **Christian Dior** (Landmark and Peninsula and Kowloon hotels), **Gucci** (Sogo, Peninsula Hotel, and Landmark), **Hermès of Paris** (Landmark and Peninsula Hotel), **Loewe** (Landmark), and **Nina Ricci** (Peninsula and Regent hotels).

For trendy or unusual fashions (though fairly expensive), **Jenny Lewis** (Shop 5, G/F Swire House) features exquisite, modern Asian-style fashions. Also try **Pavlova** (Shop 115, Swire House and Shop 20, G/F at Ocean Centre), **Diane Freis** (Shop 259D and 3258 at Ocean Terminal; UG 25 Prince's Bldg.; Shop 223 Pacific Place Mall; and Shop 56 and 216 at the Tsimshatsui Centre), and **Michel Rene** (Shop B11 at Landmark; Shop 5 at Prince's Bldg.; Shop 258 at Ocean Centre; Shop 2 at Paterson Plaza, Causeway Bay; and Shop 281 at Ocean Galleries, Harbour

City). **Kinsan Collections** (29 Wyndham St., Central) features the printed styles of Laura Ashley.

Medium-priced fashions in the latest styles for the young and young-at-heart can be found in such stores as **Toppy** (Shell House, 28 Queen's Rd., Central; Shop 64–66 at Landmark Shop G9 at New World Centre, Tsimshatsui; Shop 287 Ocean Terminal; and Shop 281 Ocean Galleries, Harbour City).

Other well-known designers located in Hong Kong include **Esprit** (88 Hing Fat St., at North Point; Park Lane Shopper's Blvd. and in Prince's Bldg., Central), **Benetton** (B24 The Landmark, Central; the Hong Kong Hotel, Tsimshatsui; and boutiques at Ocean Terminal), and **The Cotton Collection** (26 Wellington St., Central, and Cityplaza I, Taikoo Shing).

For uniquely designed T-shirts, sweat shirts, mohair sweaters, plus a host of designer goods, try the **Ben Sprout Shop** (inside Kowloon and Hong Kong terminals of Star Ferry). Dancers, exercisers, and those who like the latest in sexy bathing suits can browse through **La Plume** (Shop 128, Tsimshatsui Centre, Tsimshatsui, and Shop 226, Edinburgh Tower, Central). For frothy negligees, try **Caetla** (Bank of East Asia Bldg., 10 Des Voeux Rd., Central).

For fancy hats, try **Peggy Boyd** (9 On Lan St., Central) and **Panache** (Shop 256, Ocean Terminal, Harbour City, Kowloon).

5 Sports and Fitness

Participant Sports

Golf Three clubs welcome visitors, but only those with reciprocal rights from a club at home.

The **Royal Hong Kong Golf Club** allows visitors to play on its nine-hole course at Deep Water Bay, Hong Kong Island, or on its three 18-hole courses at Fanling, New Territories. *Fanling, tel. 670–1211 for bookings, 670–0647 for club rentals. Deep Water Bay, tel. 812–7070. Weekdays only.*

The **Clearwater Bay Golf and Country Club.** in New Territories has tennis, squash, badminton, table tennis, and a health spa, in addition to golf. The Hong Kong Tourist Association (HKTA) and this club run a Sports and Recreation Tour for visitors. *Clearwater Bay Rd., Saikung Peninsula, tel. 719–1595. HKTA tour, tel. 801–7177. Cost: HK$260 per person.*

The **Discovery Bay Golf Club** on Lantau Island is open to visitors on weekdays. *Tel. 987–7271. Take hoverferry from Blake Pier in Central.*

Jogging Visitors can join members of the **Hong Kong Running Clinic** (a Far East chapter of the Honolulu Marathon Clinic) every Sunday morning, and two evenings each week. Beginners are especially welcome and looked after. These runs are in the Hawaiian tradition of conversation-speed jogging—if you can't talk to your neighbor, you must be running too fast. There is also a "Ladies Walking Group" for visitors, going along Bowen Road. *Meet in front of Adventist Hospital, 40 Stubbs Rd., Hong Kong Island, tel. 574–6211, ext. 888 (ask for director of health). Sun. 7:30 AM; Tues. and Thurs. 6–6:30 PM; Ladies Walking Tues. 8:30–10 AM.*

Victoria Park at Causeway Bay has an official jogging track.

Roller Skating and Ice Skating There are two first-class roller-skating rinks, one at **Cityplaza I** on Hong Kong Island, the other at **Telford Gardens** in Kowloon. Cityplaza also has an ice-skating rink. *Taikooshing, Quarry Bay, tel. 567–0400; Telford Gardens Housing Estates, Kowloon Bay, tel. 757–2211.*

Social and Health Clubs The following clubs have reciprocal facilities. **Royal Hong Kong Jockey Club:** free entry to the members enclosure during racing season, no use of the recreational facilities. **Royal Hong Kong Golf Club:** free greens fees 14 times a year. Other clubs: **Royal Hong Kong Yacht Club, Hong Kong Cricket Club, Kowloon Cricket Club, Hong Kong Football Club, Hong Kong Country Club, Kowloon Club, Hong Kong Club, Ladies' Recreation Club.**

Health clubs are another matter. With the exception of the **Tom Turk Fitness Club** (Bond Centre, West Wing, 13th Fl., Queensway, Hong Kong Isl., tel. 521–4541; and Albion Plaza, 2 Granville Rd., Tsimshatsui, Kowloon, tel. 368–0022), you must be a member to use a club's facilities. Guests of the Excelsior can use the facilities of the **Spa at the Square** in 1 Exchange Square.

Squash **Squash** is very much a club activity in Hong Kong. However, there are public courts at the **Hong Kong Squash Centre,** where you'll need a passport to make a booking, and the **Harbour Road Indoor Games Hall,** both on Hong Kong Island; and at Laichikok Park, in Kowloon. *Hong Kong Squash Centre, tel.*

869–0611. Laichikok Park, tel. 745–2796. Harbour Rd. Indoor Games Hall, tel. 893–7684.

Tennis You will probably have to make arrangements with a private club if you want to play tennis. Although there are a limited number of public tennis courts, they are heavily booked in advance. To book a public tennis court you will need identification such as a passport. *Victoria Park, tel. 570–6186; Bowen Rd., tel. 528–2983; Wongneichong Gap, tel. 574–9122; and Kowloon Tsai Park, tel. 336–7878.*

Water Sports **Junking**—dining on the water aboard large *junks* (flat-bottom Chinese fishing boats) that have been converted to pleasure craft—is unique to Hong Kong. This type of leisure has become so entrenched in the colony that there is now a fairly large junk-building industry that produces highly varnished, upholstered, and air-conditioned junks up to 80 feet long.

These floating rumpus rooms serve a purpose, especially for citizens living on Hong Kong Island who suffer "rock fever" and need to escape by spending a day on the water. Because so much drinking takes place, the junks are also known as "gin-junks," commanded by "weekend admirals." They also serve as platforms for swimmers, waterskiers, and snorkelers. If anyone so much as breathes an invitation for junking, grab it. To rent a junk, call **Detours Ltd.** (tel. 311–6111) or **Simpson Marine Ltd.** (tel. 555–8377). The junks, with crew, can hold up to 45 people, and cost HK$2,500 per day or HK$150 per person for a 90-minute harbour tour.

To **waterski** you will need a speedboat and equipment. Contact the **Waterski Club** (tel. 812–0391) or ask your hotel front desk for names and numbers.

Windsurfing is certainly not unique to Hong Kong, but the territory has welcomed it with open sails. A company called Pro-Shop operates four **Windsurfing Centres** throughout the territory, offering lessons and board rentals. The cost for lessons is about HK$250 for four hours (spread over two days). Cost for a windsurfing board is around HK$50 per hour. The centers are at **Stanley Beach** (tel. 723–6816); **Tun Wan Beach** on Cheung Chau (tel. 981–8316 or 981–4872); **Tolo Harbour**, near Taipo in New Terrorities (tel. 658–2888); and **Sha Ha Beach**, in front of the Surf Hotel, Kowloon (tel. 792–5605).

Swimming is extremely popular with the locals, which means that most beaches are packed on summer weekends and public holidays. The more popular beaches, such as Repulse Bay, are busy day and night throughout the summer (*see* Beaches in Chapter 3). Shortly after the Mid-Autumn Festival in September, local people stop using the beaches. This is a good time for visitors to enjoy them, especially since the weather is warm year-round.

Public swimming pools are filled to capacity in summer and closed in winter. Most visitors use the pools in their hotels, although not all hotels have them.

To go **sailing** you must belong to a yacht club that has reciprocal rights with one in Hong Kong. Contact the Royal Hong Kong Yacht Club (tel. 832–2817) to make arrangements.

A number of clubs have **scuba diving** trips almost year-round, but it is usually difficult for visitors to join them unless introduced by a friend. However, **Bunn's Divers Institute** offers outings for qualified divers. *188 Wanchai Rd., Hong Kong Island, tel. 891-2113. Cost is HK$130-HK$160 per person. Tanks and weights are HK$55, regulators HK$75.*

Spectator Sports

Horse Racing and Gambling Horse racing is the nearest thing in Hong Kong to a national sport. It is a multi-million-dollar-a-year business, employing thousands of people and drawing crowds that are almost suicidal in their eagerness to rid themselves of their hard-earned money.

The Sport of Kings is run under a monopoly by the Royal Hong Kong Jockey Club, one of the most politically powerful entities in the territory. Profits go to charity and community organizations. The season runs from September or October through May. Some 65 races are held at two race courses—**Happy Valley** on Hong Kong Island and **Shatin** in New Territories. Shatin's race course is only a few years old and is one of the most modern in the world. Both courses have huge video screens at the finish line so that gamblers can see what is happening each foot of the way.

Races are run at one track on Wednesday nights, and at one or the other on either Saturday or Sunday. Even if you're not a gambler, it's worth going just to see the crowds.

Tourists can view races from the Members' Stand at both tracks by showing their passports and paying HK$50 for a badge.

In a place where gambling has developed into a mania, it may come as a surprise to learn that most forms of gambling are forbidden. Excluding the stock market, which is by far the territory's biggest single gambling event, the only legalized forms of gambling are horse racing and the lottery. Nearby Macau is another story—there you can get your fill of casino gambling (*see* Chapter 9).

The ancient Chinese sport of cricket fighting (that's cricket as in insect, not as in the sport) is hidden from visitors, so you'll have to ask to get directions from a local friend. If you see someone wandering in a market, carrying a washtub, and softly calling, "tau, chi choot," follow him.

6   Dining

Introduction

by Jack Moore

*Jack Moore is the
restaurant
columnist for the
South China
Morning Post's
weekly* T.V &
Entertainment
Times *magazine
and a regular
contributor to*
Epicure *magazine.*

Anywhere you go in Hong Kong, any direction you'd care to look, you're liable to see a restaurant sign. Establishments that sell prepared food are as old as Chinese culture itself, and the fact that most local people live in small apartments and have little space for home entertaining means that restaurants are usually the chosen venues for special occasions and family get-togethers.

Nowhere in the world is the cooking more varied than in this city, where Cantonese cuisine (long regarded by Chinese gourmets as the most intricate and sophisticated in Asia) is augmented by cookery from many other parts of China and virtually every other culinary region on earth.

French, German, Italian, Portuguese, Japanese, Korean, Indian, Thai, and even specialty American food is served up by literally thousands of restaurants. Others feature exotic fare from places like Burma, Mexico, Holland, the Caribbean, Switzerland, Sri Lanka, and the Philippines. In Hong Kong, the traditional deeply rooted Chinese love of good food flourishes in a cosmopolitan setting, and the city offers almost any gourmet cuisine you'd care to experience.

Be advised, however, that while Hong Kong contains some of Asia's best restaurants, it also contains some of the worst—so don't expect just any old neighborhood restaurant to turn out to be a gourmet's dream.

The words "Chinese cuisine" don't mean much more than "European cuisine." The largest country in the world has dozens of different styles, though only five are prominent in Hong Kong. These are as follows:

Cantonese. As 94% of the population comes from Guangdong (or Canton) Province, this is the most popular style by far. This is fortunate, because the semitropical province has the largest selection of fruits, vegetables, and meats. And speaking of *great* Chinese styles, Cantonese is the finest. The styles of cooking are simple: The wok is used to stir-fry, boil, or steam. When oil is poured into the bottom and heated up, the food can be dipped in quickly or left for just a few seconds. The result is a natural taste. Says international gourmet William Mark: "Only Cantonese chefs understand simplicity, purity, and variety." The menus are enormous.

Shanghai. Shanghai is a city of immigrants, not unlike New York, and its cosmopolitan population has several different styles of food. Lying at the confluence of several rivers on the South China Sea, it has especially good seafood. Shanghai crabs (actually from Suzhou) are winter favorites. Many dishes are fried in sesame or soy sauce. Some find the dishes a bit oily, but nobody can forget the famous beggar's chicken or squirrel fish, so-called because the sauce poured over the fish sizzles or "chatters" like a squirrel. Again, this dish originated in Suzhou, but Shanghai restaurants feature it.

Peking. Of course Peking duck is a favorite, and nowhere is it better than in Hong Kong. This was an Imperial Mongolian favorite, and its two (or three) courses are inevitably ordered. This is a northern "noodle" culture rather than a rice one. The

Peking noodles, along with Mongolian barbecue and onion cakes, are always ordered.

Szechuan. The spiciest Chinese food is now a favorite around the world. Rice, bamboo, wheat, river fish, shellfish, chicken, and pork dishes all have plenty of salt, anise, fennel seed, chili, and coriander. The ingredients are simmered, smoked, stirred, and steamed. Szechuan cuisine has integrated flavors—the opposite of Cantonese food, where each ingredient has its own taste.

Chiu Chow. Coming from near Canton, the Chiu Chow people have a gutsy, hearty cuisine, which has never caught on in the West. It begins with "Iron Buddha" tea, goes on to thick shark's-fin soup, soya goose, whelk, bird's nest, and the irresistible "chuenjew leaves" usually served with chicken.

A few more hints:

Dim-sum restaurants serve tasty Chinese hors d'oeuvres and must be tried at lunch (or a bit earlier, to avoid the crowds). The staff push trolleys around calling out the names of the dishes, and you point to what you want. Some dishes, such as congealed blood and giblets, are rather esoteric, but others, such as steamed pork buns or spring rolls, are readily acceptable to all.

Always check the prices of anything that says "market price." Anything from a typhoon to heavy traffic can determine the cost. Ask for the exact price for your party rather than a *catty* (Chinese weight system).

The most highly recommended restaurants in each price category are indicated by a star ★.

At press time there were 7.8 HK dollars to the U.S. dollar.

Category	Cost*
Very Expensive	over HK$500
Expensive	HK$300–HK$500
Moderate	HK$100–HK$300
Inexpensive	under HK$100

**per person plus 10% service charge*

In more traditional Chinese restaurants, tips are not expected. However, it is customary to leave small change.

Although major credit cards are widely accepted, many smaller establishments do not accept them. Ask before you sit down.

The following credit-card abbreviations are used: AE, American Express; DC, Diners Club; MC, MasterCard; V, Visa.

American

Moderate–Expensive **California.** A very upmarket and well-patronized establishment in trendy Lan Kwai Fung, this is as much a chic bar as a restaurant, and it stays open after midnight. Here a half dozen monitors constantly show old movies and music videos, and the place cultivates the general air of a surfer's hangout somewhere just south of Malibu. The food is good if not great, especially the fresh salads you make at the salad bar. Burgers are grossly overpriced by local standards but are delicious. The fettuccine with three cheeses is a true indulgence, and the Santa Fe steak comes with an interesting mild horseradish/mustard sauce. *Lan Kwai Fung, Central, Hong Kong Island, tel. 521–1345. Dress: anything you want, from jeans to black tie. AE, DC, MC, V.*

★ **San Francisco Steak House.** For more than 20 years, this mock Barbary Coast eatery has been pleasing both locals and traveling Americans with a combination of down-home atmosphere (if your home runs to dark paneled walls, red flock wallpaper, and replicas of Powell Street cable cars) and American fare. The clam chowder, for instance, is an original Boston recipe. Steaks are Angus beef and are treated with the respect good meat deserves. The California-style cioppino seafood stew comes straight from Fisherman's Wharf. Also excellent is the Canadian salmon, served as a whole baked baby coho. *101 Barnton Court, Harbour City, 9 Canton Rd., Tsimshatsui, Kowloon, tel. 735–7576. Reservations advised. Dress: informal. AE, DC, MC, V.*

Inexpensive– Moderate
Beverly Hills Deli. There are two locations (one on each side of the harbor), but the one in Central's Lan Kwai Fung restaurant district is marginally better. Neither is memorable for its ambience. Service is rushed at noon and not all that good at dinnertime either, but the food keeps people coming back. Here you'll find all the deli specials and a kosher menu with imported ingredients. The overstuffed sandwiches are *huge,* and the chiliburgers or the matzoh ball soup remind many patrons of the fare in the best New York delis. *2 Lan Kwai Fung, Central, Hong Kong Island, tel. 801–5123 or Level 2, 55 New World Centre, Tsimshatsui, Kowloon. tel. 369–8695. Reservations strongly advised. Dress: casual. AE, DC, MC, V.*

Austrian

Moderate– Expensive
Mozart Stub'n. To get to this local gourmet hideaway, you either get a taxi or you toil up a long hill on foot. But the clientele thinks the haul is worth it, and the place is very popular with locals. It's comfortably decorated as a farmhouse kitchen with wood panels and old prints. Much of the service is done by the affable owner, which adds a pleasant personal touch. After an appetizer of cold cuts (bacon, salami, and smoked meats, with a taste of schnapps,) you might try the lentil soup with chunks of bacon and sausage. The boiled beef comes in thick pink slices with creamed spinach and apple horseradish. And for dessert, the homemade Viennese apfelstrudel in flaky pastry is a must. *8 Glenealy (via Ice House St.) Central, Hong Kong Island, tel. 522–1763. Reservations strongly advised. Dress: casual. Closed Sun. MC, V.*

Caribbean

Inexpensive
★ **Harcourt Kitchen.** Just where you least expect to encounter it is a restaurant that specializes in the fare you'd find more easily around the Gulf of Mexico than on the coast of China. A pleasant but far from posh decor runs to bright tropical colors, lots of foliage, murals of beach scenes, and potted coconut palms bearing coconuts. The Haiti starfish aren't real starfish, but they are much like deep-fried wonton filled with minced shrimp and

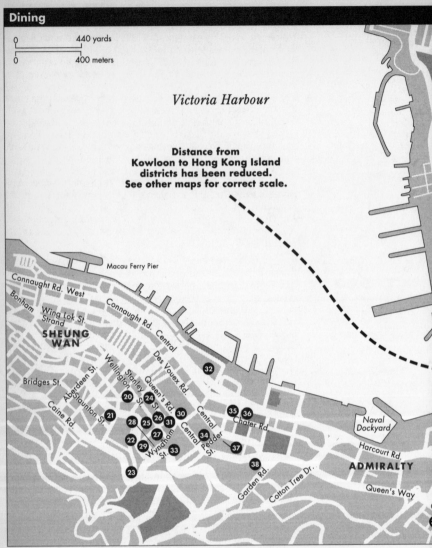

Dining

0 ——— 440 yards
0 ——— 400 meters

Victoria Harbour

Distance from Kowloon to Hong Kong Island districts has been reduced. See other maps for correct scale.

Macau Ferry Pier

Connaught Rd. West

Bonham

Wing Lok St.
Strand

SHEUNG WAN

Connaught Rd. Central

Bridges St.

Des Voeux Rd.

Aberdeen St.

Wellington St.

Stanley St.

Caine Rd.

Staunton St.

Queen's Rd.

Central

Central

Pedder St.

Chater Rd.

Wyndham St.

Garden Rd.

Cotton Tree Dr.

Naval Dockyard

Harcourt Rd.

ADMIRALTY

Queen's Way

American Restaurant, **40**

Ashoka, **29**

Au Trou Normand, **15**

The Baron's Table, **10**

Benkay Restaurant, **37**

Bentley's Seafood Restaurant and Oyster Bar, **35**

Beverly Hills Deli, **14, 31**

Bloom Restaurant, **34**

Bologna Ristorante Italiano, **52**

La Brasserie, **1**

Le Cafe de Paris, **27**

California, **30**

Casa Mexicana and Texas Rib House, **54**

Chesa, **3**

Chili Club, **42**

The Chinese Restaurant, **9**

Chiu Chow Garden, **51**

Eagle's Nest, **38**

Gaddi's, **4**

The Galley, **32**

Great Shanghai Restaurant, **18**

Harcourt Kitchen, **41**

Hugo's, **7**

Inagiku Restaurant, **2**

Jimmy's Kitchen, **5, 26**

Lai Ching Heen, **13**

Le Village, **12**

Luk Yu Tea House, **24**

Mabuhay Restaurant, **11**

Maxim's Palace, **53**

Il Mercato, **49**

Mozart Stub'n, **23**

Pep N' Chili, **47**

Pierrot, **36**

Rangoon Restaurant, **50**

Royal Thai Restaurant, **48**

Sagano Restaurant, **19**

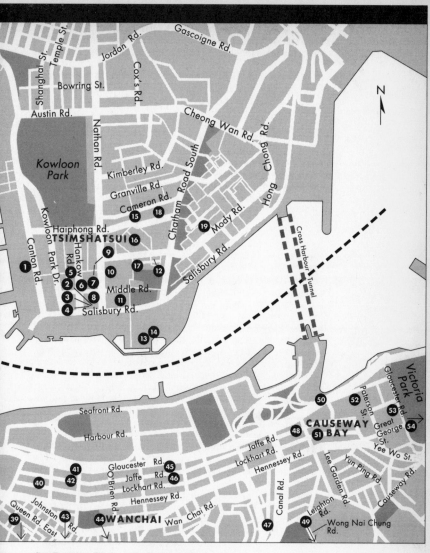

San Francisco Steak
House, **8**

Sawadee Thai
Restaurant, **17**

SMI Curry
Restaurant, **46**

Spice Island Gourmet
Club, **20**

Spices, **39**

Stanley's French
Restaurant, **44**

Supatra's Thai
Gourmet, **28**

Tandoor
Restaurant, **22**

La Taverna, **33**

Three-Five Korean
Restaurant, **6**

Le Tire Bouchon, **21**

La Toison d'Or, **45**

Valentino Ristorante
Italiano, **16**

The Verandah, **43**

Yung Kee, **25**

are delicious. Most unusual and flavorful is the Havana chicken, smoked over coffee beans; Brazilian beef sirloin in a sauce with lots of garlic and cilantro; and Jamaican pork stewed in rum, ginger, lime juice, and green peppercorns. *Harcourt House, Fenwick St. and Gloucester Rd., Wanchai, Hong Kong Island, tel. 865–0965. Reservations strongly recommended. Dress: casual. Closed Sun. AE, MC, V.*

Chinese

Very Expensive **The Chinese Restaurant.** It takes some nerve to call your establishment *the* Chinese restaurant in Hong Kong, but this one gets away with it. An art-nouveau design and a talented kitchen staff who explore new avenues in Cantonese cooking make the difference. The menu changes seasonally, though some much-ordered items (like the house papaya soup, crispy chicken skin, and stewed goose in brown ginger gravy) are always available and well worth tasting. *Hyatt Regency Hotel, 67 Nathan Rd., Tsimshatsui, Kowloon, tel. 311–1234. Reservations recommended. Jacket and tie advised. AE, DC, MC, V.*

★ **Eagle's Nest.** Atop the Hilton Hotel in Central district, this tourist-oriented eatery offers a spectacular view of Hong Kong harbor and also serves a fine selection of Cantonese and other Chinese regional dishes. With splendid premises in the best American hotel style, the Eagle's Nest offers first-rate service. Those who reserve find matchbooks printed with their names at the table, and a full-sized band provides dinner and dancing music. The menu features mostly well-known specialties—Peking duck, beggar's chicken, barbecued pork with plum sauce. Bird's Nest, shark's fin and abalone soup are available but costly. Fresh seasonal seafood dishes are always a specialty, along with an excellent Lotus Vegetable Platter. *Hongkong Hilton, 2 Queen's Rd., Central, Hong Kong Island, tel. 523–3111. Reservations recommended. Jacket and tie suggested but not mandatory. AE, DC, MC, V.*

★ **Lai Ching Heen.** This is a truly luxurious Cantonese restaurant (and one of the most highly regarded by Hong Kong's culinary critics) tucked away in the basement of the Regent Hotel. The subtly decorated dining room features a stunning view of the harbor near sea level, and opulent table settings include ivory chopsticks and jade spoons. There are special menus for each month of the Chinese lunar calendar, always featuring fresh steamed seafood dishes and seasonal Chinese fruits and vegetables. *The Regent Hotel, Salisbury Rd., Tsimshatsui, Kowloon, tel. 721–1211. Reservations necessary. Jacket and tie recommended. AE, DC, MC, V.*

Moderate– **Szechuan Lau.** A comfortable, cheerful restaurant popular for
Expensive many years among lovers of spicy, garlicky Szechuan food. Popular dishes include hot garlic eggplant, smoked duck, and prawns in hot peppers on a sizzling platter. Small helpings are available. Staff are accustomed to western guests. *466 Lockhart Rd., Causeway Bay, Hong Kong Island, tel. 891–9027. Reservations recommended. Dress: casual. AE, MC, V.*

Moderate **Chiu Chow Garden.** Chiu Chow cuisine, which emphasizes seafood, comes from the area around Swatow and Fukien on the China coast and is popular among Chinese gourmets, though not well known outside East Asia. In this big, spacious and well-lit restaurant service tends to be slow, and getting a waiter who speaks English is not always easy. Worthy of mention are the Iron Buddha tea (served in thimble-size cups and packed with caffeine), the cold roast goose on a bed of fried blood (better than it sounds), the Fukien abalone in a light ginger sauce, and the exquisite sautéed shrimp and crabmeat balls served over crispy prawn crackers. *Hennessy Centre, 500 Hennessy Rd., Causeway Bay, Hong Kong Island, tel. 577–3391. (Also branches in Jardine House and Vicwood Plaza, Hong Kong Island). Reservations recommended. Dress: casual. AE, DC, MC, V.*

Pep N'Chili. Let the name serve as a warning: This is the place for the peppery fare of Szechuan. This small and comfortable place has an upstairs and a downstairs dining room, and both feature smart European-style decor, though the food is Chinese. Don't miss the hot-and-sour seafood soup, presented in an earthenware jar, and the wonderfully creamy eggplant and garlic, spiked (as many Szechuan dishes are) with violent red chilis. Also recommended is the duck, smoked over camphor and tea leaves—sometimes a trifle dry, but always an unexpected and delightful taste. *Blue Pool Rd., Happy Valley, Hong Kong Island, tel. 573–8251. Reservations necessary. Dress: smart casual. AE, DC, MC, V.*

★ **Yung Kee.** Once rated by *Fortune* Magazine as one of the world's 15 best restaurants, this multistory eatery offers very good Cantonese food amid riotous Chinese decor featuring writhing golden dragons. Handy to hotels and the Central business district, the restaurant attracts clientele from office workers to visiting celebrities, and all receive the same cheerful high-energy service. Roast goose is the specialty, with the skin just beautifully crisp. Seafood fanciers should try the sautéed fillet of pomfret with chili and black bean sauce. *Wellington St., Central, Hong Kong Island, tel. 522–1624. Reservations advised. Dress: casual. AE, DC, MC, V.*

Inexpensive– Moderate
Great Shanghai Restaurant. Do not come for the decor unless you're really fond of dingy old restaurants. This is, however, an excellent spot both for culinary adventurers and for those who are already serious about Shanghai food, which tends to feature more blatant flavors than the delicate local Cantonese fare. You may not quite be ready for the sea blubber or braised turtle with sugar candy, but do try one of the boneless eel dishes, Shanghai-style yellowfish soup, beggar's chicken, and the excellent spiced and soyed duck. *26 Prat Ave., Tsimshatsui, Kowloon, tel. 366–8158 or 366–2683. Reservations strongly recommended. Dress: casual. AE, DC, MC, V.*

★ **Maxim's Palace.** A typical Hong Kong banquet hall—capacious, high-ceilinged, and full of moveable partitions that can segment the room into an amazing number of individual dinner parties. It's also generally full of people, doing everything from grabbing a quick lunch to holding huge wedding parties that include good-luck lion dances. The cuisine is mostly basic Cantonese fare, but with adequate notice, they'll prepare an Emperor's Feast that includes bear paw, camel hump, elephant trunk, and essence of tiger. Maxim's is a good place to enjoy daily dim sum and to try shark's fin at moderate prices. *World Trade Centre, Causeway Bay, Hong Kong Island, tel. 576–0288. Reservations strongly advised. Dress: casual. AE, DC, MC, V.*

Inexpensive
★ **American Restaurant.** Despite the name, the cuisine here is from Peking, which means hearty, stick-to-the-ribs fare suitable for the chilly climate of northern China. A typically over-

decorated Chinese restaurant full of red and gold fixtures and a gastronomic amenity in Hong Kong for 40 years, the American is noted for its hot-and-sour soup, fried and steamed dumplings, and noodle dishes. Every meal starts with complimentary peanuts and sliced cucumber in vinegar. It has delicious hot pots in winter and excellent beggar's chicken, cooked in clay and lotus leaves. Don't confuse this place with The American Cafe, which has branches all over town and is merely a fast-food chain. *20 Lockhart Rd., Wanchai, Hong Kong Island, tel. 527–7277 or 527–7770. Reservations recommended any time and essential on weekends. Dress: informal. No credit cards.*

Luk Yu Tea House. You don't go here for the food as much as the atmosphere. This place—where you can catch a rare glimpse of old colonial Hong Kong—has been in business for 60 years, and looks it. The decor—including handsome carved wood doors, hardwood paneling, marble facings, and, unfortunately, spittoons, which are noisily used by the clientele—is definitely worth seeing. One member of the staff speaks rudimentary English. The morning dim sum is popular with Chinese businessmen, though the fare is no more than standard Cantonese. *24–26 Stanley St., Central, Hong Kong Island, tel. 523–5464. Reservations impossible unless you speak Cantonese. Dress: casual or business. No credit cards.*

Continental

Very Expensive **Hugo's.** The Hyatt Hotel's showpiece restaurant since it
★ opened in 1969, Hugo's is a big space that still manages to make diners feel cozy. Done in warm colors and filled with lots of activity (including wandering Filipino minstrels), this is a place locals favor for celebratory dinners after a successful day at the racetrack and/or stock market. The food is renowned, for very good reasons. The lobster bisque and U.S. prime rib are exceptional. More distinctive, however, is the baked rack of lamb in an onion/potato crust with juniper-berry cream, and the salmon and scallops baked in flaky pastry with mango and spinach. *Hyatt Regency Hong Kong, 67 Nathan Rd., Tsimshatsui, Kowloon, tel. 311–1234. Lunch reservations advised. Jacket and tie required. AE, DC, MC, V.*

Moderate **Jimmy's Kitchen.** Probably the most famous (and still one of the
★ best) of the territory's restaurants, this China Coast institution first opened for business in 1928. It has been catering to a deeply devoted Hong Kong clientele in one location or another (currently there are two) ever since. Well but not spectacularly decorated, it looks like just what it is—a well-kept and comfortable old restaurant with booths, dark woodwork, lattice partitions and brasswork on the walls. Some of the dishes are as charmingly old-fashioned as the place itself (who else serves corned beef and cabbage?). Other specialties include borscht, stroganoff, and goulash, and the complimentary pickled onions are an international gourmet byword. The Kowloon branch, on Ashley Road, does not meet the same high standards. *South China Bldg., 1 Wyndham St., Central, Hong Kong Island, tel. 526–5293. Lunch reservations required. Dress: jacket and tie or smart casual. AE, DC, MC, V.*

English

Expensive **Bentley's Seafood Restaurant and Oyster Bar.** Here, in the
★ basement of an office building, you'll find an exact copy of a
well-known swank London restaurant, with cream-colored
walls, floral carpet, Dickensian prints, and the overall feeling
of an exclusive English club. There are even English oysters
from Colchester in season, and oysters from many other places
in the world as well. They are served up raw or cooked as oysters Kilpatrick with tomato, chili, and bacon; oysters Imperial
with champagne sauce; or oysters Bentley with tomato and
curry sauces. The Dover sole is the best in town, grilled simply
with lemon and butter, and the house fish pie is classic English
cooking at its rare best. *Prince's Bldg. (enter off Statue
Square), Central, Hong Kong Island, tel. 868–0881. Lunch
reservations required. Jacket and tie recommended. AE, DC,
MC. Closed Sun.*

Moderate **The Galley and Pier One.** Conveniently located in the basement
of Jardine House, this shipshape restaurant (with nautical decor that includes a moving horizon) is very popular at lunchtime. It serves the best fish and chips in Asia, plus great
swordfish steaks, fried squid, oxtail, and chili con carne. The
wine list is excellent, and the service is friendly and efficient.
*Basement, Jardine House, Central, Hong Kong, tel. 526–3061.
Reservations required for lunch, accepted for dinner. Dress:
casual. AE, DC, V. Closed Sun.*

Filipino

Inexpensive **Mabuhay Restaurant.** Filipino cuisine, a largely ignored yet
★ very exciting Asian cuisine, is served here mostly to Hong
Kong's large Filipino community, though there's a growing following among local gourmets as well. Small, clean, and well-
managed, the Mabuhay features quick, cheerful service in a
Spartan setting where the most obvious design features are
art-deco travel posters and a signed photo of Philippines President Corazon Aquino. If you're new to this fare, try standards
like the vinegar-based pork, chicken adobong stews, or the
beef steak cooked in onions and soy sauce. If you're already a
devotee, don't miss the dinuguan—a stew of pork entrails,
blood, chili, and vinegar. *11 Minden Ave., Tsimshatsui, Kowloon, tel. 367–3762. Reservations advised on weekends. Dress:
casual. MC, DC, V.*

French

Very Expensive **Gaddi's.** The classiest lunch or dinner venue in Hong Kong for
★ the last 40 years; a Rolls Royce among restaurants. The decor
includes huge chandeliers made in Paris and salvaged from
wartime Shanghai, ankle-deep Tai Ping carpets that exactly
match the napery, and a priceless Chinese coromandel screen,
made in 1670 for the Emperor's Summer Palace in Beijing and
on semipermanent loan from one of the hotel's owners, Lord
Kadoorie. The service is superlative, and the menu changes
frequently. Soufflés are always featured and are exquisite, a
favorite is orange-flavored and liberally laced with Grand
Marnier. *The Peninsula Hotel, Salisbury Rd., Tsimshatsui,
Kowloon, tel. 366–6251, ext. 3989. Reservations essential.
Dress: the best you have, black tie if possible. AE, DC, MC, V.*

Pierrot. A specially commissioned ceramic clown welcomes you to this restaurant, with windows overlooking the quintessential Hong Kong harbor panorama. The service is among the best in the world. The management often hosts visiting French chefs to prepare their specialties as part of food promotions. The regular menus change seasonally. Both lunch and dinner menus are small but exquisitely wrought, and the restaurant features one of the biggest and best-chosen wine lists in this part of the world. *Mandarin Oriental Hotel, Connaught Rd., Central, Hong Kong Island, tel. 522–0111, ext. 4028. Reservations a must. Jacket and tie mandatory. AE, DC, MC, V. Closed for lunch weekends.*

The Verandah. It's not quite the same as the lost and lamented veranda of the Repulse Bay Hotel, though it contains a number of that vanished hostelry's fixtures, such as the heavy cap wood doors and stained glass. This restaurant caters unabashedly to those seeking colonial nostalgia, paying less attention to service and prices. Featured dishes include bourguignonne snails in hazelnut and herb butter, grilled tuna steak on vegetables, and pigeon with creamed asparagus. It's worth finding somebody of similar tastes to share the two-person roast Angus beef tenderloin with creamy goose-liver filling and truffle sauce. *109 Repulse Bay Rd., Hong Kong Island, tel. 812–2722. Reservations strongly suggested. Dress: smart casual or business. AE, DC, MC, V.*

Expensive **Au Trou Normand.** For a quarter of a century this place has offered diners a chance to hide away in a typical French farmhouse–not an easy thing to arrange in the middle of bustling Tsimshatsui. Red checked tablecloths, a dark wood mantlepiece, and candlelight on shiny copper utensils create the atmosphere. You can be certain you're getting a series of authentic Gallic tastes. The tournedos Rossini is topped with Strasbourg pâté, the rack of lamb comes in a tangy and memorable Dijon mustard sauce, and there's an excellent chicken in Madeira sauce. *6 Carnarvon Rd., Tsimshatsui, Kowloon, tel. 366–8754. Reservations advised. Jacket and tie recommended. AE, DC, MC, V.*

La Toison d'Or. This eatery, which is very close to the HK Convention and Exhibition Centre and its two hotels, has a steady international clientele. It's decorated with pastel shades (pink and grey predominate), mirrored columns, and view windows (though the view is nothing special). The food, however, is remarkable. The goose-liver terrine is made on the premises and is superb, as is the escargot stew in a cream sauce. The lobster ragout with a rich herbal sauce is a much-ordered entrée, as is the perfectly medium-rare roast lamb. *147–149 Gloucester Rd., Wanchai, Hong Kong Island, tel. 838–3962. Reservations advised, especially for lunch. Dress: smart casual. AE, DC, MC, V. Closed Sun. for lunch.*

Moderate–Expensive **La Brasserie.** What might have been a boring basement coffee
★ shop has here been cleverly changed into a charming French restaurant, with lots of plants, etched glass, and framed prints of cartoon chefs engaged in various antics. Live music is supplied by an accordionist, and the chef's daily selection list is wheeled to your table on a huge mirror. French provincial cooking is the draw here, and a good place to start would be with the fresh crabmeat ravioli or salmon marinated in lime and olive oil. The bouillabaisse features local seafood and is outstanding. Strangely enough, this is one of the better places in town to find

California wine. *Omni Marco Polo Hotel, Harbour City, Canton Rd., Tsimshatsui, Kowloon, tel. 736–0888, ext. 113. Reservations recommended. Dress: casual. AE, DC, MC, V.*

★ **Le Cafe de Paris.** Le Cafe is a really excellent and affordable French restaurant that's also a stage for its flamboyant owner, former French movie star Maurice Gardett. Located in the trendy Lan Kwai Fung district, it has murals of Paris on the walls (painted by the owner) and windows overlooking the bustle of the streets outside. Not everything on the menu is always available (Maurice is also the chef, and a temperamental one) but whatever there is will be classic French cooking. Try the crusted veal and ham pâté, the rich Barbarie duck breast with wild mushrooms in a heavy, unforgettable sauce, or the quail garnished with raisins. *30-32 D'Aguilar St., Central, Hong Kong Island, tel. 524–7521. Reservations strongly advised. Dress: business or smart casual. AE, DC, MC, V. Closed Sun.*

Stanley's French Restaurant. This romantic spot is a converted seafront home with lots of hidden tables for intimate tête-à-tête dinners and verandas overlooking the bay. The Caesar salad is well-regarded and rightly so, as is the roast rock Cornish game hen, crisp-skinned and redolent with Continental spices. The grilled or poached Macau sole is a wonderful local seafood treat, and on Fridays and Saturdays only, there's fresh lobster from Boston, cooked with Parisian flair. *86-88 Stanley Main St., Stanley Village, Hong Kong Island, tel. 813–8873 or 813–9721. Reservations absolutely necessary. Dress: casual. AE, DC, MC, V.*

Moderate   **Le Tire Bouchon.** Something of a Hong Kong secret, this bistro is hidden on a steep hill on Old Bailey Street and is probably the nearest thing in the territory to a real Parisian neighborhood bistro. Decor is French without being overbearing, and the menu, while small, contains treasures like sautéed chicken livers, with raspberry vinegar and walnuts, and homemade goose-liver pâté with Armagnac. Consider also the chicken in cranberry sauce, calf's liver in red wine sauce, and beef tenderloin with pears and Saigon cinnamon. *9 Old Bailey St., Central. Hong Kong Island, tel. 523–5459. Reservations advised, but not always necessary. Dress: casual. MC, V. Closed Sun.*

German

Expensive   **The Baron's Table.** It's a good idea to be hungry when you head for this restaurant, because hearty Bavarian fare is headlined at this classy hotel dining room, which is decorated with lots of heraldic trappings in a bright mock-Middle-Ages style. Service is exceptional even for this part of the world. Cold smoked Balik salmon or pickled herring with apple, onion, and pickle slices make excellent starters. Game dishes are superb, especially the tournedos of venison with a haunting cranberry/cognac sauce, served with freshly made spaetzle dumplings and red cabbage. The cinnamon parfait is a memorable dessert. *Holiday Inn Golden Mile, 50 Nathan Rd., Tsimshatsui, Kowloon, tel. 369–3111. Reservations strongly recommended. Dress: dressy. AE, DC, MC, V.*

Indian

Moderate–Expensive ★ **Tandoor Restaurant.** This upstairs eatery, one of the classiest venues in town for Indian food, is exotically decorated with mirrors, Indian paintings, colorful cloth hangings, and musical instruments. A glass-fronted kitchen allows you to watch the chef at work. There's a rose for every lady and a cheroot for every gentleman after dinner. Dinner is likely to be superb. There are almost 100 dishes to choose from, but don't miss the tandoor (clay oven) specialties, the roast lamb sagwalla (covered with tasty spinach), and the lamb rogan josh, swimming in Kashmiri spices. Also featured are no fewer than 14 kinds of Indian bread, all worth tasting. *Carfield Commercial Bldg., 75–77 Wyndham St., Central, Hong Kong Island, tel. 521–8363. Reservations essential. Dress: smart casual. AE, DC, V.*

Inexpensive–Moderate **Ashoka.** A cramped but popular upstairs/downstairs premises just above the Central business district, this restaurant is a favorite of the local Indian community, which says a good deal about the authenticity of the food. Decorated tastefully with Indian art and mirrors to give the much-needed illusion of space, the restaurant offers a large menu. A local favorite is the chicken tikka (soaked in a spicy marinade and barbecued in a clay oven), and you shouldn't miss the stuffed tomato (not on the menu but available by request) filled with a complex mixture of raisins, rice, and lamb in a mild but fascinating sauce. *57–59 Wyndham St., Central, Hong Kong Island, tel. 524–9623 or 525–5719. Reservations strongly advised. Dress: casual. AE, DC, V. Closed Sun. for lunch.*

Inexpensive **SMI Curry Restaurant.** The initials in this restaurant's name are reputed to stand for Singapore, Malaysia, and India, but it's the Indian taste that predominates. The SMI is old, well-worn, and cozy, with comfortable rattan furniture and attentive service. Chicken curries here are famous, especially the mild mint curry and the chicken in black-pepper curry. Try the prawn curry with coconut and cucumber, and if you can order a day in advance, the dry masala crab curry with taste-shocking south Indian spices is a must. *81–85 Lockhart Rd., Wanchai, Hong Kong Island, tel. 529–9111 or 527–3107. Reservations advised. Dress: casual. DC, V.*

★ **Spice Island Gourmet Club.** This is a "club"—because the place has no back door and thus was unable to qualify for a restaurant licence. This means you have to join up (it's free); you get a membership card and then you're properly qualified to tuck into one of the best Indian buffets in the city. The place is small but there's elbow room, and the decor is basic but features some interesting old Victorian lithographs. There's a different buffet at lunch and dinner, where Indian chicken, lamb, and seafood dishes are always on offer. The club is located in the old district, just west of the business core. *63 Wellington St., Central, Hong Kong Island, tel. 522–8706. Reservations recommended. Dress: casual. MC, V. Closed Sun.*

Italian

Moderate–Expensive ★ **Valentino Ristorante Italiano.** This hideaway right in the middle of the otherwise-bustling Tsimshatsui district is one of the most romantic places in Hong Kong. Here behind a marble facade and a doorway flanked by potted cedar trees is a cozy place that could be an intimate Italian eatery in any city in the world. The decor runs to pinks and pastels, framed posters of Valentino, and lots of elbowroom between tables—a rare commodity in Hong Kong. Pastas feature *tagliatelle alla puttanesca* (said to have been invented by the streetwalkers of Naples) with anchovies, garlic, olives, red pepper, and tomato. The entrée list offers Macau sole grilled in lemon butter and Italian herbs as well as several veal dishes worth exploring. Daily specials are always good and worthy of attention. *16 Hanoi Rd., Tsimshatsui, Kowloon, tel. 721–6449. Reservations strongly advised. Dress: informal, smart casual. AE, DC, MC, V.*

Moderate **Bologna Ristorante Italiano.** This spacious restaurant is done in red, green, and white to match the Italian flag, and the decor features lots of plants, Roman pillars, a print of the Mona Lisa, and the almost-compulsory collection of emptied Chianti bottles. It's a trifle hokey but eminently comfortable and friendly. The fare is traditional Italian, with lots of pasta dishes and generous helpings of everything. Well worth exploring is the fish soup "Vaticana," full of prawns, clams, and Mediterranean spices; the veal scallopine with asparagus; and the braised veal knuckle with rice. A good Italian wine list (rare in these parts) is also offered. *Elizabeth House, 250 Gloucester Rd., Causeway Bay, Hong Kong Island, tel. 574–7282 or 574–6808. Reservations not always necessary. Dress: casual. AE, DC, MC, V.*

La Taverna. A long-established Hong Kong restaurant in a new location, this much-loved local establishment has a fiercely loyal clientele. The food is less than totally authentic Italian, though, being light on the cheese to please Chinese tastes. The decor runs to checked tablecloths and empty Chianti bottles— about what you'd expect from such a place anywhere in the world. Pastas are very good, especially the ravioli alla Bresciana, served in a savory cream sauce. Perennial favorites are the tagliata beef, seasoned with rosemary, and the hearty seafood soup with a shot of Pernod. *Shun Ho Tower, 24-50 Ice House St., Central, Hong Kong Island, tel. 523–8624. Reservations suggested. Dress: casual. AE, DC, MC, V.*

Inexpensive **Il Mercato.** The best place in town for American-style pizza,
★ this tiny 24-seat place (with room for a few more on an outdoor patio) is hidden away in bustling Stanley Market. It's often found by accident by delighted visitors who simply weren't expecting an Italian eatery (let alone a good one) in that location. The food is very good, though the menu is unpredictable, changing every three days. Usually there's excellent tagliatelle alla Bolognese with ground beef and fresh tomato, and wonderful roast chicken flavored with rosemary. Get there early if you want to sample the New York–style cheesecake. *Stanley Main St., Stanley Village, Hong Kong Island, tel. 813–9090. Reservations essential. Dress: extremely casual. AE, MC, V.*

Japanese

Very Expensive **Inagiku Restaurant.** Truly grandiose by Hong Kong standards, this elegant two-floor restaurant offers that rarest of local commodities—space—an indoor miniature rock garden, sweeping staircase, and eye-catching Oriental art-nouveau decor with lots of light. Inagiku is noted for its wide selection of sushi and sashimi and for its richly marbled Kobe beef, which is served either thinly sliced with a broth as the traditional shabu-shabu or simply charcoal grilled. This place also features seasonal menus that always offer fresh delights. *Peninsula Hotel, Salisbury Rd., Tsimshatsui, Kowloon, tel. 366-6251. Reservations strongly advised. Dress: casual. AE, DC, MC, V.*

★ **Sagano Restaurant.** Probably the most popular Japanese restaurant in Hong Kong, the Sagano features remarkable food, impeccable service, and as a bonus, a thoroughly engaging panoramic view of the constant activity in Hong Kong harbor. Seafood for sushi and sashimi are imported exclusively from Japan. The main offering of the house is Kansai cuisine from the region around Kyoto, which features light sauces and absolute freshness. Seasonal dishes should always be considered. Save some room for the special house dessert, plum sherbet. *Hotel Nikko Hong Kong, 72 Mody Rd., Tsimshatsui, Kowloon, tel. 739-1111. Reservations absolutely necessary. Dress: smart casual. AE, DC, MC, V.*

Expensive **Benkay Restaurant.** The elegant Japanese-style decor in this Central venue features light-toned wood and many panels and decorative screens. Those who aren't already familiar with Japanese food may require a little expert help from the staff to decipher the menu. For a delightful overview of this cuisine, try one of the set Kaiseki meals, in which 10 or more tiny portions of fried, steamed, or raw delicacies are served. For sheer entertainment, order a Teppanyaki meal, prepared before your eyes on a hot griddle. *The Landmark, Central, Hong Kong Island, tel. 521-3344. Reservations recommended. Dress: smart casual or business. AE, DC, MC, V.*

Korean

Inexpensive **Three-Five Korean Restaurant.** A genuine treasure, this tiny
★ but impressive eatery is tucked away on a minor Tsimshatsui street. The name of the restaurant is printed on the establishment's sign in Korean and Chinese. Inside it's sparsely decorated, spotlessly clean, and a trifle cramped; but the food makes up for any of the place's other shortcomings. The best dish is a Korean barbecue (which you cook yourself at the table) of beef, ribs, chicken, or fish. This is accompanied by many small dishes of Korean specialties like bean curd, marinated vegetables, dried anchovies, bean sprouts, and the traditional kimchi (cabbage preserved in brine, with black beans, red peppers, and more than enough garlic to make it a good idea for everybody in the party to sample some). *6 Ashley Rd., Tsimshatsui, Kowloon, tel. 721-0993. Reservations difficult to make (they don't always have somebody who speaks English) but advised anyway. Dress: extremely casual. No credit cards.*

Mexican

Inexpensive– **Casa Mexicana and Texas Rib House.** Yes, there *is* Mexican food
Moderate to be had in Hong Kong, and strangely enough a very good
★ Mexican restaurant in which to enjoy it. Half of this place is an American steak house with Alamo ambience. The rest is a good copy of a southwestern rancho interior where talented mariachis (from the Philippines, but who cares?) wear serapes, play guitars, and warble traditional south-of-the-border serenades. All the standard Mexican fare is available, from tacos and tamales to enchiladas and guacamole-laden nachos. The menu also features some true gourmet treats, such as a Mexican version of beggars' chicken, cooked in lotus leaves. *Victoria*

Centre, Watson's Estate, Causeway Bay, Hong Kong Island, tel. 566–5560. Reservations advised on weekends. Dress: casual. AE, DC, MC, V.

Pan-Asian

Moderate–Expensive **Spices.** The famed Repulse Bay Hotel is gone, but the classic colonial facade and this chic-but-affordable place remain. High ceilings, hardwood floors, and louvered windows give Spices' dining room an old-time East-of-Suez elegance. Just as interesting as the ambience is the food, which incorporates a number of Asian tastes ranging from spiced Arabic chickpea pâté to earthy Korean kimchi (fermented vegetables with lots of red pepper and garlic). Notable on the menu are stir-fried Filipino prawns with onions and garlic, Indian-style tandoori mixed grill, and Japanese steak or salmon teriyaki. The branch in Pacific Place is equally good. *109 Repulse Bay Rd., Hong Kong Island, tel. 812–2711; 1 Pacific Pl., Hong Kong, tel. 845–4798. Reservations strongly advised. Dress: casual. AE, DC, MC, V.*

Southeast Asian

Moderate **Rangoon Restaurant.** Interesting Burmese food is served here in a tidy atmosphere that features artifacts on the walls and Burmese pop music on the sound system. Primary spices and flavorings include tamarind, banana bark, dried shrimp, and coconut. Recommended are the king prawns in garlic sauce, a wide selection of Buddhist vegetarian dishes, and any of the spicy noodle dishes. *265 Gloucester Rd., Causeway Bay, Hong Kong Island, tel. 892–1182. Reservations recommended, especially on weekends. Dress: casual. AE, MC, V.*

Swiss

Expensive ★ **Chesa.** Lovingly fostered by a succession of Swiss hotel managers over 25 years, this is a perfect reproduction of an Alpine country tavern, with wood beams, tiny windows, hand-painted butter moulds, and real Swiss linen on the tables. The service is entirely up to Peninsula Hotel standards, which are very high indeed. You should sample the tassette Suisse, an aromatic beef broth with bone marrow, morels, and fresh herbs under a light pastry crust. Also worth mentioning is the pan-fried fillet of lake trout with roast almonds and the deep, rich oxtail stew with red wine. Fondues for two and a good selection of esoteric and excellent Swiss wines are also on offer. *The Peninsula Hotel, Salisbury Rd., Tsimshatsui, Kowloon, tel. 366–6251. Reservations strongly advised. Dress: smart casual/business suit. AE, DC, MC, V.*

Thai

Moderate–Expensive **Royal Thai Restaurant.** The decor here is upmarket Asian, restrained opulence in muted blues and whites, giving a contrasting cool feeling to balance the spicy food. Although the recipes are less authentic than at other Thai restaurants, the service is friendlier, which attracts a steady clientele of local European and Chinese customers. The chefs here are from Bangkok's famed Bussarakan Restaurant, and they prepare some dishes originally created for the Thai Royal Family (hence the place's name). Sample the charcoal-grilled chicken with Thai herbs, and the crab with extra-lively chili sauce or with rice noodles and black pepper. *Elizabeth House, 250 Gloucester Rd., Causeway Bay. Hong Kong Island, tel. 832–2111. Reservations recommended. Dress: smart casual. AE, DC, MC, V.*

Supatra's Thai Gourmet. This very trendy establishment is still new, but it has already collected a devoted clientele. Located in Central's fashionable Lan Kwai Fung restaurant district, it features a chic bar downstairs (where you can get ice-cold Singha beer from Bangkok), and an upstairs dining room with windows showing the passing parade—rare in local restaurants. The menu is small but strictly authentic, and there are seven (!) Thai chefs in the kitchen at dinnertime. Try the light but spicy seafood salad, the rich and creamy curries and the Thai-style, deep-fried fish cakes (the best and least rubbery in Hong Kong). *46 D'Aguilar St., Central, Hong Kong Island, tel. 522–5073. Reservations strongly advised. Dress: smart casual. AE, MC, V.*

Moderate **Chili Club.** This place is arguably the most popular Thai restaurant in a city where this cuisine is very popular indeed. It's above one of Wanchai's main thoroughfares, although there are no windows that show you the neighborhood. The dining room is Spartan, clean, and cramped. *Excellent* Thai food is served here. A must-try is the shrimp spicy/sour yom tum soup with the overriding taste of lemon grass. Don't miss the squid salad, filled with explosive tiny bits of chili pepper. If you like tastes that linger, try the durian-flavored ice cream for dessert. *68 Lockhart Rd., Wanchai, Hong Kong Island, tel. 527–2872. Reservations essential and not always possible. Dress: casual. MC, V.*

Sawadee Thai Restaurant. This is one of the few Thai restaurants in Hong Kong (or anywhere outside Thailand) that makes no concession to the fact that this cuisine is just too spicy for some people. Here they pride themselves on fresh and genuine foodstuffs from Thailand, and this has won a large and loyal following of purists. The restaurant's clean and modestly sized premises are decorated in royal blue, with Buddha figurines, and orchids on the tables. As an appetizer, you might fancy the pieces of marinated chicken wrapped in fragrant pandamus leaves and grilled, or maybe the shredded papaya salad. The chicken in green curry is a Hong Kong culinary standard as a main course. *1 Hillwood Rd., Tsimshatsui, Kowloon, tel. 722–5577. Reservations advised. Dress: casual. AE, V.*

Vietnamese

Inexpensive **Le Village.** This was the first Vietnamese restaurant in Hong Kong (it opened in the early '60s) and it is still considered the best. The room is small, the decor simple, and the menu great. Try the crab marinated in beer, sour fish and tomato soup, garlic pork, or *cha gio* spring rolls. *19 Hillwood Rd., Kowloon, tel. 721–2006. Reservations advised. Dress: casual. No credit cards.*

7   Lodging

Introduction

Until the early 1960s, Hong Kong didn't have a single international hotel. Today there are more than 75 hotels and some 33,000 hotel rooms in a city that welcomes almost 6 million visitors annually. These figures only include hotels and lodging facilities that belong to the Hong Kong Tourist Association (HKTA). With the exceptions of the two monasteries and the Silvermine Beach Hotel on Lantau Island, the hotels, guest houses, and hostels listed below belong to the HKTA.

As price ranges indicate, Hong Kong is hardly a budget traveler's paradise. Most of the hotels provide deluxe or firstclass accommodation and facilities, so it is not surprising that so many rooms are in the *Very Expensive* or *Expensive* categories. Visitors not on group tours should expect to pay at least HK$650 for a hotel room of normal international standards. For that price, visitors probably won't get harbor views, but they will get reliable facilities—bathrooms with hot and cold running water, color TV, radio, telephone, same-day valet laundry service, room service, secretarial service, safe deposit box, refrigerator and minibar, and air-conditioning. Most hotels also have at least one restaurant and bar, a travel and tour-booking desk, and limousine or car rental.

As one might expect in one of the world's most important financial centers, Hong Kong is a business executive's paradise. Most of the major hotels have business centers, which provide secretarial, translation, courier, telex, fax, and printing services—even word processors. Charges vary from hotel to hotel, but secretaries run HK$150–HK$200 per hour, typing HK$30–HK$45 per page, and word processing about HK$140 per hour. Each hotel prints a business-center tariff, so check before you act. Many hotels have ballrooms and most have smaller function meeting rooms. For an overview of Hong Kong meeting, convention, and incentive facilities, contact the **Convention and Incentive Department** (Hong Kong Tourist Association, 35th fl., Jardine House, Central, Hong Kong Island, tel. 801–7177).

Most hotels also have some sort of "guest recognition program." The Hyatt-Regency, for example, has its Regency Club floors while the Hilton has special Executive Floors. Recognition at the Sheraton is through its Sheraton Club International, at the Furama Kempinski through its Six Continents Club, and at the Holiday Inns through their Insider Club. Some hotels, like the Kowloon Ramada Renaissance Hotels, even have word processing facilities in the room. Have your travel agent or company make it known in advance that you are a business person; in Hong Kong, which thrives on commerce, that makes you a VIP.

In the busy period—spring and fall—advance bookings are strongly recommended. Even with the rash of new hotels, rooms can prove scarce during the high season of September through early December. Where available, we have provided toll-free (800) numbers for making reservations from the United States.

The HKTA publishes *Hotel Guide*, a listing of their hotel members and daily rates, services, and facilities. The brochure is published twice a year, so it is usually one price hike behind the current situation. The HKTA does not arrange hotel reservations. The Hong Kong Hotel Association (HKHA) does, and at no extra charge, but only through its reservations office at Kai Tak International Airport, which is immediately beyond the Customs area.

Choosing where to stay in Hong Kong depends on the purpose of your visit. Thanks to the harbor tunnel and the Mass Transit Railway (MTR) subway, it no longer matters whether you stay "Hong Kong-side" or "Kowloon-side." Either side of the harbor is only minutes away by MTR.

For those who want to escape the main tourist accommodation areas, there are a few places in the New Territories and outlying islands that provide alternatives, which are also generally less expensive than lodgings on Hong Kong Island or in Kowloon.

Our categories for hotel rates are based on the average price at press time for a double room for two people. All rates are subject to a 10% service charge and a 5% government tax, which is used to fund the activities of the HKTA. Lodgings are listed by three geographical areas (Hong Kong Island, Kowloon, and New Territories and Outlying Islands). Listings for each area are alphabetical within each price category.

The most highly recommended properties in each price category are indicated by a star ★.

At press time there were HK$7.8 to the U.S. dollar.

Category	Cost*
Very Expensive	over HK$1500
Expensive	HK$1000–$1500
Moderate	HK$700–$1000
Inexpensive	under HK$700

double room; add 15% for service charge and tax

The following credit card abbreviations are used: AE, American Express; DC, Diners Club; MC, MasterCard; V, Visa.

Our ratings are flexible and subject to change. Listings for hotels under renovation are soon outdated. But one thing that is not likely to change is the high standard of service. The city's top hotels provide the best all-around hotel services of any city in the world. The fact that they also contain some of Asia's finest restaurants is another major plus.

Hong Kong Island

People who need to be near the city's financial hub prefer the Central district on Hong Kong Island. Central is as busy as New York's Manhattan Island on weekdays, but it is quiet at night and on weekends. Wanchai, east of Central, was once a sailor's dream of "Suzie Wongs" and booze. Although it is still one of the city's more entertaining nightlife areas, land reclamation has given it an array of new harbor-fronting skyscrapers. Causeway Bay, farther east, is ideal for those who like to try lots of different restaurants or are on shopping trips; Happy Valley is near the racetrack.

Lodging

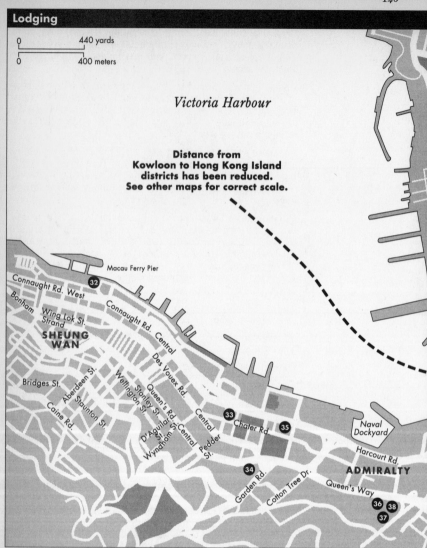

0 ___ 440 yards
0 ___ 400 meters

Victoria Harbour

**Distance from
Kowloon to Hong Kong Island
districts has been reduced.
See other maps for correct scale.**

Macau Ferry Pier

Connaught Rd. West 32

Bonham Strand · Wing Lok St.

Connaught Rd. Central

SHEUNG WAN

Des Voeux Rd.

Bridges St. · Aberdeen St. · Wellington St. · Stanley St. · Queen's Rd. Central

Caine Rd. · Staunton St. · D'Aguilar St. · Wyndham St. · Central · Pedder St.

33 · Chater Rd. · 35

Naval Dockyard

34 · Garden Rd. · Cotton Tree Dr. · Harcourt Rd.

ADMIRALTY

Queen's Way

36 · 38
37

Ambassador, **8**
Bangkok Royal, **13**
Caravelle, **45**
Chungking, **9**
Conrad, **37**
The Empress, **22**
The Excelsior, **46**
Furama Kempinski, **35**
Grand Hyatt, **43**
Guangdong, **23**
Harbour, **42**
Harbour View
International
House, **40**
Hilton, **34**

Holiday Inn Golden
Mile, **11**
Holiday Inn Harbour
View, **29**
Hyatt Regency, **7**
Imperial, **10**
International, **24**
Island Shangri-La, **36**
Kowloon, **6**
Lee Gardens, **47**
Luk Kwok, **41**
Mandarin Oriental, **33**
Marriott, **38**
Miramar, **12**

New Astor, **17**
New World, **20**
New World Harbour
View, **44**
Hotel Nikko, **30**
Omni The Hongkong, **4**
Omni Marco Polo, **1**
Omni Prince, **2**
Park Lane
Radisson, **48**
Peninsula, **18**
Ramada Inn Hong
Kong, **39**
Ramada Inn
Kowloon, **25**

Ramada
Rennaissance, **3**
Regal Airport, **31**
Regal Meridien, **28**
The Regent, **19**
Ritz, **15**
Royal Garden, **27**
Shamrock, **14**
Shangri-La, **26**
Sheraton Hong Kong
Hotel and Towers, **21**
Victoria, **32**
Windsor, **16**
Y.M.C.A., **5**

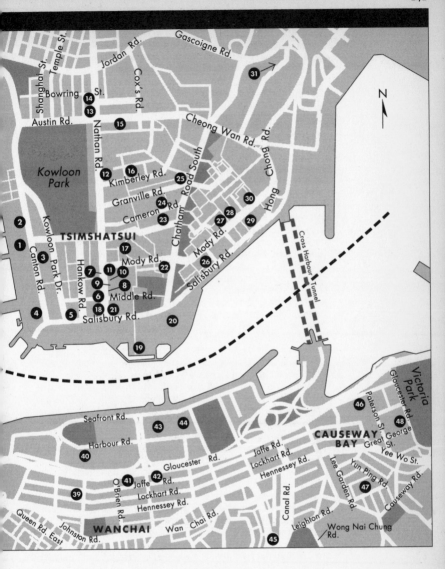

N

Gascoigne Rd.

Jordan Rd.

Temple St.

Shanghai St.

Bowring St.

Cox's Rd.

Austin Rd.

Cheong Wan Rd.

Nathan Rd.

Kowloon
Park

Kimberley Rd.

Granville Rd.

Chatham Road South

Hong Chong Rd.

Cameron Rd.

Kowloon Park Dr.

TSIMSHATSUI

Canton Rd.

Hankow Rd.

Mody Rd.

Mody Rd.

Middle Rd.

Salisbury Rd.

Salisbury Rd.

Cross Harbour Tunnel

Victoria
Park

Gloucester Rd.

Seafront Rd.

Paterson St.

**CAUSEWAY
BAY**

Great George St.

Yee Wo St.

Harbour Rd.

Jaffe Rd.

Lockhart Rd.

Hennessey Rd.

Yun Ping Rd.

Lee Garden Rd.

Causeway Rd.

Gloucester   Rd.

Jaffe   Rd.

O'Brien Rd.

Lockhart Rd.

Hennessey Rd.

Canal Rd.

Queen Rd. East

Johnston Rd.

WANCHAI

Wan Chai Rd.

Leighton Rd.

Wong Nai Chung
Rd.

Very Expensive **Conrad.** The first Conrad in Asia, this hotel opened in 1990 in a tower of the Pacific Place, on the edge of Central District. The rooms, located in the top 21 floors of the 61-story building, have dramatic views of the harbor and city. Business visitors will appreciate the four floors of executive rooms and the extensive business center. *Pacific Pl., 88 Queensway, Hong Kong, tel. 521–3838, fax 521–3888. 513 rooms. Facilities: business center, 4 restaurants, 3 bars, outdoor pool, health club, ballroom. AE, DC, MC, V.*

Grand Hyatt. No expense was spared in building this opulent hotel, which adjoins the Hong Kong Convention Centre. Located on the Wanchai waterfront, the facility has fabulous views that function as backdrops for various restaurants. Art deco touches give panache to the marble-clad, greenery-filled lobby, and the ballroom which is reminiscent of Old World Europe. The restaurants are very popular with locals, who will also stand in line to get into JJ's, the entertainment center. The hotel and the New World Harbour View share a vast recreation deck on the 11th floor with pools, gardens, golf driving, tennis courts, and health club facilities. *1 Harbour Rd., Wanchai, Hong Kong, tel. 861–1234, fax 861–1677. 575 rooms. Facilities: Chinese and Continental restaurants, lounges, disco/nightclub, ballroom, health club, pool, golf driving, tennis, beauty parlor, clinic, florist. AE, DC, MC, V.*

★ **Hilton.** The well-equipped business facilities, six executive floors, and Central district location make this elegant hotel an attractive choice for business travelers. The hotel also boasts tennis courts, a swimming pool, and its own 110-foot brigantine which makes regular lunch, cocktail, and dinner cruises and is available for weekend island picnics or private hire. Rooms are decorated in pastels and are modern and well-appointed. *2 Queen's Rd., Central, tel. 523–3111, fax 845–2590. 668 rooms; 83 suites. Facilities: health club with heated outdoor pool, business center, 9 restaurants, 2 nonsmoking floors, beauty salon, barbershop, gift shop, shopping arcade, florist. AE, DC, MC, V.*

Island Shangri-La. Part of the dramatic new Pacific Place complex of shops, offices, hotels, restaurants, and cinemas, this hotel (opened in 1990) has guest rooms between the 39th and 56th floors of a tower. Built by Shangri-La International (owners of the Shangri-La in Kowloon), the hotel has the highest standards of furnishings, decor, and service. Its spacious lobby and lounge face a 25-foot picture window, and the atrium in the upper floors features a 14-story mural. A music room and restaurant occupy the top floor. The pool and health club on the eighth floor overlook Hong Kong Park. *Pacific Pl. 2, 88 Queensway, Hong Kong, tel. 877–3838, fax 521–8742. 566 rooms. Facilities: Chinese, Japanese, and Western restaurants; music room; lounges; health club; pool; business center; conference rooms. AE, DC, MC, V.*

★ **Mandarin Oriental.** Much touted by travel writers as "one of the world's great hotels," the Mandarin Oriental represents the high end of hotel accommodation in Hong Kong. The vast lobby, decorated with antique gilded Chinese wall sculpture, and featuring a live band during afternoons and evenings, and the guest rooms, where the walls are decorated with antique maps and prints and there's always a plate of fresh fruit on hand, are all designed with the guest's comfort in mind. Centrally located next to the Star Ferry concourse on Hong Kong

Island, the hotel is definitely a place to spot visiting celebrities and VIPs. For more than 25 years, it has catered to the well-to-do and business travelers with hefty expense accounts. *5 Connaught Rd., Central, tel. 522–0111 or 800/526–6566, fax 529–7978. 489 rooms; 58 suites. Facilities: health club with heated indoor pool, business center, 4 restaurants, beauty salon, barbershop, gift shop, shopping arcade, florist. AE, DC, MC, V.*

★ **Marriott.** A cascading waterfall and glass walls make the garden lobby bright and impressive. With all the amenities and then some, this new (1989) luxury American-style hotel between Central and Wanchai districts is fast becoming a favorite of business travelers. *Pacific Place, 88 Queensway, Central, tel. 810–8366 or 800/228–9290, fax 845–0737. 564 rooms; 41 suites. Facilities: health club with heated outdoor pool, business center, 3 restaurants, beauty salon, barbershop, gift shop, shopping arcade, florist. AE, DC, MC, V.*

Ritz-Carlton. Opened in 1991 as a super deluxe Asian flagship of the American chain, the hotel is an art deco town house on the harbor front. Large rooms have marble bathrooms and honor bars. An outdoor pool affords harbor views. *Connaught Rd., Central, Hong Kong Island, tel. 877–6666. 187 rooms, 29 suites. Facilities: pool, fitness center, four restaurants, bar, ballroom. AE, DC, MC, V.*

Expensive **The Excelsior.** Located in Causeway Bay and overlooking the
★ Royal HK Yacht Club marina, the Excelsior offers a good selection of restaurants and entertainment. Jazz evenings in the basement bar and rooftop disco add to the hotel's appeal. Eighty percent of the 930 rooms have harbor views. Sports-minded guests can use the hotel tennis courts and the jogging track in the adjacent park. Business travelers are provided with many service amenities, and the World Trade Centre is only a short walk away through an air-conditioned walkway. *281 Gloucester Rd., Causeway Bay, tel. 894–8888, fax 895–6459. 903 rooms; 22 suites. Facilities: business center, 4 restaurants, nonsmoking areas, beauty salon, barbershop, gift shop, shopping arcade, florist. AE, DC, MC, V.*

Furama Kempinski. A contemporary, elegant, and full-facility hotel in the heart of the financial Central district, the Furama was managed by InterContinental Hotels until 1989 when it became the Asian flagship for Germany's Kempinski. Guests have their choice of two good views: Chater Garden and the Peak or City Hall and Victoria Harbour. The 18th to 28th floors offer the best vantage points, and diners get a 360° view in the revolving rooftop restaurant and bar on the 30th floor. *1 Connaught Rd., Central, tel. 525–5111, fax 845–9339. 522 rooms; 55 suites. Facilities: health club, business center, 5 restaurants, 2 nonsmoking floors, beauty salon, barbershop, gift shop, shopping arcade, florist. AE, DC, MC, V.*

Grand Plaza. An out-of-the-way location provides some advantages for guests here, not the least of which are the in-house recreational facilities: a 9-hole putting green, jogging track, billiard room, squash courts, aerobic dance room, and music/video/reading room. The hotel, built above the Taikoo Shing MTR in 1988, is connected to the massive Kornhill Plaza shopping mall. Evening barbecues are served in the garden terrace. *2 Kornhill Rd., Quarry Bay, tel. 886–0011, fax 886–1738. 306 rooms; 42 suites. Facilities: health club with heated indoor pool, business center, 2 restaurants. AE, DC, MC, V.*

Lee Gardens. This older hotel with Oriental-style rooms and Western amenities is popular with European and Australian travelers. The lobby has several small meeting areas furnished with Chinese straight-backed carved wood chairs and small tables. A short walk will bring you to the Causeway Bay MTR, shopping, and markets. *Hysan Ave., Causeway Bay, tel. 895–3311 or 800/223–9868, fax 576–9775. 800 rooms; 54 suites. Facilities: business center, 4 restaurants, beauty salon, gift shop, florist. AE, DC, MC, V.*

Luk Kwok. This new hotel/office tower has replaced the Wanchai landmark featured in the book *The World of Suzie Wong*. This new place garners appeal from its proximity to the Convention Centre, the Academy for Performing Arts, and the Arts Centre. *72 Gloucester Rd., Wanchai, Hong Kong, tel. 866– 2166, fax 866–2622. 198 rooms. Facilities: Western and Chinese restaurants, business center. AE, DC, MC, V.*

New World Harbour View. Sharing the Convention Centre complex with the Grand Hyatt, this hotel is more modest but just as attractive. It has excellent Chinese and Western restaurants, a cozy bar, and all the amenities of the recreation deck it shares with the Grand Hyatt. *1 Harbour Rd., Wanchai, Hong Kong, tel. 866–2288, fax 866–3388. 864 rooms. Facilities: 3 restaurants, 2 bars, pool, recreation center. AE, DC, MC, V.*

Park Lane Radisson. This elegant hotel, opposite Victoria Park and in the midst of the small shops and department stores of Causeway Bay, is in the center of Hong Kong Island's busiest shopping, entertainment, and business areas. *320 Gloucester Rd., Causeway Bay, tel. 890–3355 or 800/333–3333, fax 576–7853. 850 rooms; 25 suites. Facilities: health club, business center, 3 restaurants, beauty salon, shopping arcade, florist. AE, DC, MC, V.*

Victoria. This hotel is located near the Sheung Wan MTR, west of the island's financial and shopping area. It is also connected to Central district by a long overhead walkway. Most of the spacious rooms of this 40-story hotel have an unobstructed harbor view because guest rooms are located on the top 15 floors of the building. Guests have access to two floodlit tennis courts, as well as the outdoor pool. *Shun Tak Center, Connaught Rd., Central, tel. 540–7228 or 800/227–5663, fax 858–3398. 540 rooms; 55 suites. Facilities: fitness center with outdoor pool, business center, 5 restaurants, gift shop, shopping arcade, florist. AE, DC, MC, V.*

Moderate **Eastin Valley** (formerly **Asia**). Located near the Happy Valley racetrack, this modern hotel is convenient for horse-racing fans, but it is at least 5 to 10 minutes by taxi from the shopping area of Causeway Bay. *1A Wang Tak St., Happy Valley, tel. 574–9922, fax 838–1622. 108 rooms; 3 suites. Facilities: outdoor pool, fitness center, business center, 2 restaurants. AE, DC, MC, V.*

Harbour. This newly renovated hotel is bright and modern, but it lacks the extras such as in-house bars, live entertainment, and business and recreational facilities. It is popular with tour groups from the mainland and other Asian countries. *116–122 Gloucester Rd., Wanchai, tel. 574–8211, fax 572–2185. 188 rooms; 12 suites. Facilities: 2 restaurants. AE, DC, MC, V.*

Ramada Inn Hong Kong. Within walking distance of the new Convention and Exhibition Centre, this hotel is designed to appeal to the budget-conscious business traveler. The lobby is bright and modern, with adjoining bar and café. *61–73*

Lockhart Rd., Wanchai, tel. 861–1000 or 800/272–6232, fax 865–6023. 284 rooms; 2 suites. Facilities: indoor heated pool, Gymtonic health club, business center, restaurant. AE, DC, MC, V.

Inexpensive

★ **China Merchants.** Located in the island's waterfront district, 1½ miles west of the Central business core, this trim three-year-old medium-size hotel is part of a chain that also includes 10 properties in the People's Republic of China. It is owned by a Chinese company—which allows for easy arrangements for trips to China. As the name indicates, the hotel was built to cater to visiting business people, and the rooms are small, clean, comfortable, and entirely functional. Features include bidets in the bathrooms, a location handy to the China and Macau ferry piers, and views of Victoria Harbour or The Peak (depending on which side your room is on). *160–161 Connaught Rd., Central/Western, tel. 559–6888, fax 559–0038. 285 rooms; 3 suites. Facilities: health club, business center, 3 restaurants, nonsmoking areas, limited shopping arcade. AE, DC, MC, V.*

Emerald. A little far to the west of Central but a very good value with clean, comfortable rooms and fine harbor views. *152 Connaught Rd., West, Hong Kong Island, tel. 546–8111, fax 559–0255. 318 rooms. Facilities: two restaurants. AE, DC, MC, V.*

Harbour View International House. Located on the Wanchai waterfront, this YMCA property provides clean accommodation for economy-minded travelers. The best rooms face the harbor. The hotel provides free shuttle service to Causeway Bay and the Star Ferry. *4 Harbour Rd., Wanchai, tel. 520–1111, fax 865–6063. Facilities: restaurant. AE, DC, MC, V.*

Kowloon

Most of the hotels in Hong Kong are situated on the Kowloon peninsula, which includes "Old" Tsimshatsui, Tsimshatsui East, Harbour City, and the districts north of Tsimshatsui to the border of the New Territories. The fabled shopping "Golden Mile" of Nathan Road runs through Old Tsimshatsui. Back streets are filled with restaurants, stores, and hotels.

Tsimshatsui East is a grid of modern office blocks (many with restaurants or nightclubs) and luxury hotels. This area has been created on land reclaimed from the harbor in the last decade, so none of these hotels is very old.

There are three luxury hotels (all members of the Omni hotel chain) in Harbour City, on the western side of the Tsimshatsui promontory. This newly developed area is Asia's largest air-conditioned shopping and commercial complex.

Northern Kowloon contains more of the moderate, smaller, older hotels. Most are on or very near to Nathan Road and are probably the best bets for economy-minded visitors. Excellent bus service and the MTR make it possible to reach the center of old Tsimshatsui quickly.

Very Expensive **Holiday Inn Harbour View.** At the eastern end of Tsimshatsui East, this luxury hotel has an unobstructed harbor view from more than half its rooms. Taxis or limousines provide more convenient transportation than the MTR or Star Ferry, which are on the other side of the peninsula. *70 Mody Rd., Tsimshatsui East, tel. 721–5161 or 800/HOLIDAY, fax 369–5672. 588* *rooms; 9 suites. Facilities: health club with heated outdoor rooftop pool, business center, 3 restaurants, nonsmoking areas, beauty salon, shopping arcade, florist. AE, DC, MC, V.*

Hotel Nikko. Part of the Japanese Nikko chain, this luxury harborfront hotel is at the far end of Tsimshatsui East. The Sagano, the hotel's Japanese restaurant, is reputed to be the most popular of its kind in Hong Kong. *72 Mody Rd., Tsimshatsui East, tel. 739–1111 or 800/645–5687, fax 311–3122. 442 rooms; 19 suites. Facilities: health club with heated outdoor pool, business center, 4 restaurants, beauty salon, barbershop, gift shop, shopping arcade, florist. AE, DC, MC, V.*

★ **Kowloon Shangri-La.** Billed as one of the top 10 hotels in the world, this full-facility waterfront hotel, now managed by Shangri-La International, caters to the international business traveler. Twenty-one stories above the lobby is the executive floor with 24-hour services, personalized stationery, and complimentary breakfast and cocktails. The modern, pastel rooms are large by Hong Kong standards, and a variety of in-house restaurants, lounges, a bar, and a nightclub offer a range of live entertainment including string quartets and harp and piano music. Views are of Victoria harbor or the city. *64 Mody Rd., Tsimshatsui East, tel. 721–2111 or 800/228–3000, fax 723–8686. 689 rooms; 30 suites. Facilities: health club with indoor pool, business center, 5 restaurants, nonsmoking floor, barbershop, gift shop. AE, DC, MC, V.*

★ **Peninsula.** "The Pen", the grand old lady of Hong Kong hotels, was built in 1928, when travelers took many weeks (and trunks) to reach Hong Kong by boat and then by train from London. Almost a British colonial institution, with a lobby reminiscent of Europe's great railway lounges, this is the ultimate in colonial class. The Pen's glory as a monument to good taste and Old World style is in evidence everywhere: the columned and gilt-corniced lobby; the fleet of Rolls-Royces; the large, high-ceilinged bedrooms; attentive room valets; the French soaps and daily newspapers. Gaddi's, the hotel's French restaurant, is perhaps Hong Kong's most distinguished gourmet restaurant. *Salisbury Rd., Tsimshatsui, tel. 366–6251, fax 722–4170. 190 rooms; 20 suites. Facilities: business services, 6 restaurants, beauty salon, barbershop, gift shop, shopping arcade, florist. AE, DC, MC, V.*

Ramada Renaissance. The luxurious lobby features Louis XVI–style leather furniture, thick area rugs, and a barrel-vaulted ceiling. Guest rooms are decorated in salmon and peach or lavender and grey with mahogany trim. The best (and more expensive) rooms have a harbor view. *8 Peking Rd., Tsimshatsui, tel. 311–3311 or 800/272–6232, fax 311–6611. 474 rooms; 27 suites. Facilities: health club with outdoor heated pool, business center, 5 restaurants, nonsmoking floor, beauty salon, barbershop, gift shop, shopping arcade, florist. AE, DC, MC, V.*

★ **The Regent.** Built in 1980, this elegantly modern hotel on the most southern tip of Tsimshatsui offers luxurious guest rooms and spectacular ocean harbor views. The view can also be enjoyed from the restaurants or the cocktail lounge where windows rise 40 feet above the polished granite floor. A wide range of features, such as health spa with masseur, fine Oriental art displays, an oversize outdoor pool, and computerized guest histories to store information about guests' preferences, will appeal to those who want the best and are prepared to pay for it. *Salisbury Rd., Tsimshatsui, tel. 721–1211 or 800/545–4000,* *fax 739–4546. 530 rooms; 70 suites. Facilities: health club with heated outdoor pool, business center, 4 restaurants, beauty salon, barbershop, shopping arcade, florist. AE, DC, MC, V.*

Sheraton Hong Kong Hotel and Towers. Across the street from the Space Museum, at the southern tip of the fabled Golden Mile, is the newly renovated Sheraton. Make sure you visit the rooftop restaurant or lounge (accessible by various elevators, but use the exterior glass lift). *20 Nathan Rd., Tsimshatsui, tel. 369–1111 or 800/325–3535, fax 739–8707. 834 rooms; 26 suites. Facilities: health club with outdoor pool, business center, 9 restaurants, nonsmoking floor, beauty salon, barbershop, gift shop, shopping arcade, florist. AE, DC, MC, V.*

Expensive **Ambassador.** Recent renovations have given the Ambassador a modern look. The polished granite-and-marble lobby is new. Rooms are spacious by Hong Kong standards. Located in the heart of the Tsimshatsui shopping and business district, the hotel is 20 minutes from Kai Tak Airport and accessible from Central by Star Ferry or MTR. *26 Nathan Rd., Tsimshatsui, tel. 366–6321 or 800/227–5663, fax 369–0663. 313 rooms. Facilities: business center, 3 restaurants, shopping arcade, florist. AE, DC, MC, V.*

Holiday Inn Golden Mile. Located on the Golden Mile of Nathan Road, the hub of Kowloon's business and shopping area, this Western-style hotel has been popular with business and leisure travelers alike since it opened in 1975. *50 Nathan Rd., Tsimshatsui, tel. 369–3111 or 800/HOLIDAY, fax 369–8016. 591 rooms; 9 suites. Facilities: health spa with outdoor rooftop pool, business center, 5 restaurants, nonsmoking areas, beauty salon, barbershop, gift shop, shopping arcade, florist. AE, DC, MC, V.*

★ **Hyatt Regency.** Major renovations in 1987 have given the Hyatt a dramatic marble and teak lobby and plush, earth-toned guest rooms. The hotel boasts a gallery of Oriental antiques and an award-winning Chinese restaurant, but gourmets will also want to sample the classic Continental fare at Hugo's. The hotel is 5 minutes away from the Star Ferry, beside an MTR station. *67 Nathan Rd., Tsimshatsui, tel. 311–1234 or 800/228–9000, fax 739–8701. 706 rooms; 17 suites. Facilities: business center, 4 restaurants, nonsmoking rooms, beauty salon, barbershop, gift shop, shopping arcade, florist. AE, DC, MC, V.*

Miramar. Located in the middle of the Golden Mile, and across the street from Kowloon Park, the Miramar recently was remodeled. The lobby is still among the largest in the territory. *130 Nathan Rd., Tsimshatsui, tel. 368–1111, fax 369–1788. 542 rooms; 3 suites. Facilities: health club with heated indoor pool, business center, 4 restaurants, beauty salon, barbershop, gift shop, shopping arcade, florist. AE, DC, MC, V.*

New World. This hotel, with beautifully landscaped gardens and terraces, is part of a huge shopping complex on the southeast tip of Tsimshatsui. *22 Salisbury Rd., Tsimshatsui, tel. 369–4111 or 800/227–5663, fax 369–9387. 679 rooms; 41 suites. Facilities: health club with outdoor pool, business center, 6 restaurants, beauty salon, barbershop, gift shop, shopping arcade, florist. AE, DC, MC, V.*

★ **Omni The Hongkong.** Like the two other Omni hotels on the western side of Tsimshatsui (Omni Marco Polo and Omni Prince), this is part of the enormous Harbour City hotel, entertainment, and shopping complex. The Hongkong's Taipan Grill and new Gripps bar are very popular. The Star Ferry and bus terminals are next door, and old Tsimshatsui is just a short walk away. *Harbour City, Tsimshatsui, tel. 736–0088 or 800/ THE OMNI, fax 736–0011. 670 rooms; 84 suites. Facilities: heated outdoor pool, business center, 7 restaurants, nonsmoking floor, beauty salon, barbershop, shopping arcade, florist. AE, DC, MC, V.*

Omni Marco Polo. See Omni listing above. *Harbour City, Tsimshatsui, tel. 736–0888 or 800/THE OMNI, fax 736–0022. 384 rooms; 55 suites. Facilities: use of heated outdoor pool at Omni The Hongkong, business center, 3 restaurants, nonsmoking floor, barbershop, shopping arcade. AE, DC, MC, V.*

Omni Prince. See Omni listings above. *Harbour City, Tsimshatsui, tel. 736–1888 or 800/THE OMNI, fax 736–0066. 349 rooms; 50 suites. Facilities: use of heated outdoor pool at Omni The Hongkong, business center, 4 restaurants, nonsmoking floor, shopping arcade. AE, DC, MC, V.*

Regal Airport. This hotel, which is connected to the airport terminal by an air-conditioned walkway and is just three minutes away from the Customs area, has the greatest appeal for business travelers who are in transit or have airport-related business. The best rooms face the airport, as does the romantic top-floor restaurant. All rooms are fully soundproofed. There is a half-price day-use discount for transit passengers. *30 Sa Po Rd., tel. 718–0333 or 800/543–4300, fax 718–4111. 389 rooms; 11 suites. Facilities: business center, 3 restaurants, nonsmoking floors, beauty salon, barbershop, shopping arcade. AE, DC, MC, V.*

Regal Meridien. This was the first French-style hotel in Hong Kong. The lobby has an impressive tapestry and Louis XVI–style furniture graces one of the lounges and the guest rooms. Rooms are decorated in peach and green with chintz bedspreads and curtains. *71 Mody Rd., Tsimshatsui East, tel. 722–1818 or 800/543–4300, fax 723–6413. 600 rooms; 33 suites. Facilities: health spa, business center, 5 restaurants, nonsmoking rooms, beauty salon, barbershop, gift shop, shopping arcade. AE, DC, MC, V.*

★ **Royal Garden.** Named for the elegant garden atrium, this hotel's courtyard is the focus of the luxury balconied rooms which overlook it. Doors are soundproofed, and rooms are Oriental in style. Glass elevators, trailing greenery, live classical music, and trickling pools give the Royal Garden a serene atmosphere. For a contrast, head to the basement disco, which is a Victorian-style pub until 9 PM. *Tsimshatsui East, tel. 721–5215, fax 369–9976. 399 rooms; 34 suites. Facilities: business center, 6 restaurants, beauty salon, barbershop, gift shop, shopping arcade, florist. AE, DC, MC, V.*

Moderate
★ **The Empress.** This small hotel features private balconies, some of which overlook the harbor. Rooms are not luxurious, but they are contemporary, clean, and functional. Located in the heart of Tsimshatsui, the Empress is near numerous bars, nightclubs, and live entertainment but does not offer these features in-house. *17 Chatham Rd., Tsimshatsui, tel. 366–0211 or 800/223–9868, fax 721–8168. 186 rooms; 3 suites. Facilities: some business services, restaurant, gift shop. AE, DC, MC, V.*

Grand Tower. This new hotel (built in 1987) gives tourists a sense of the real Hong Kong. Bird Street (where many Chinese walk and talk together with their caged birds) and Lady's Market are a short walk away, as is the Mongkok MTR. Rooms are clean and functional. *627–641 Nathan Rd., Mongkok, tel. 789–*

0011, fax 789–0945. 536 rooms; 13 suites. Facilities: business center, 4 restaurants, beauty salon, barbershop, gift shop, shopping arcade, florist. AE, DC, MC, V.

Guangdong. This China Travel Service–managed hotel is popular among Southeast Asian and Chinese visitors. There are no bars or live entertainment in-house, but guests will not have to travel far to find evening activities. The best views are on or above the 9th floor. *18 Prat Ave., Tsimshatsui, tel. 739–3311, fax 721–1137. 234 rooms; 11 suites. Facilities: business center, 2 restaurants, gift shop. AE, DC, MC, V.*

Imperial. This relatively small but comfortable hotel lacks the bars, lounges, restaurants, and live entertainment common to most hotels in the territory. However, its location on the Golden Mile of Nathan Road means guests don't have to walk far for any product or service. The hotel is a minute from the MTR and a short walk from the Star Ferry. *30 Nathan Rd., Tsimshatsui, tel. 366–2201, fax 311–2360. 216 rooms; 7 suites. Facilities: limited business services, restaurant. AE, DC, MC, V.*

★ **Kowloon.** A shimmering mirrored exterior and a chrome, glass, and marble lobby reflect the Kowloon's aims for high efficiency and hi-tech amenities. Room TVs offer information on shopping, events, flights, and the guest's bill. It is on the southern tip of Nathan Road's Golden Mile, just minutes away from the Star Ferry and even closer to the MTR. Hotel guests have direct access to the facilities of the Peninsula across the street. *19 Nathan Rd., Tsimshatsui, tel. 369–8698, fax 369–8698. 704 rooms; 34 suites. Facilities: business center, 2 restaurants, nonsmoking rooms, beauty salon, barbershop, gift shop, shopping arcade, florist. AE, DC, MC, V.*

New Astor. A small, inviting, triangle-shape hotel on a busy corner of old Tsimshatsui. *11 Carnarvon Rd., Tsimshatsui, tel. 366–7261, fax 722–7122. 151 rooms; 2 suites. Facilities: 1 restaurant, gift shop kiosk. AE, DC, MC, V.*

Ramada Inn Kowloon. This modern hotel is relatively small and tries to appeal to business travelers with a home-away-from-home ambience. A fireplace in the lobby and comfortably furnished rooms with natural woods throughout add to the cozy atmosphere. *73-75 Chatham Rd., South Tsimshatsui, tel. 311–1100 or 800/272–6232, fax 311–6000. 205 rooms; 1 suite. Facilities: business center, 2 restaurants, gift shop, florist. AE, DC, MC, V.*

Windsor. This modern hotel offers clean, functional accommodation just east of the Nathan Road Golden Mile of shopping and entertainment. *39-43A Kimberley Rd., Tsimshatsui, tel. 739–5665, fax 311–5101. 167 rooms. Facilities: business center, 2 restaurants. AE, DC, MC, V.*

Inexpensive **Bangkok Royal.** Just off Nathan Road and steps away from the Jordan MTR, this hotel will appeal to the economy-minded tourist. Rooms are sparse and somewhat scruffy, but there is a good Thai restaurant off the lobby. Also lacking are in-house bars, lounges, and live entertainment—but all are within walking distance down Nathan Road. *2 Pilkem St., Yaumatei, tel. 735–9181, fax 730–2209. 70 rooms. Facilities: 2 restaurants. AE, DC, MC, V.*

Booth Lodge. This pleasant guest house, built in 1985, near the Jade market is operated by the Salvation Army. *11 Wing Sing La., Yaumatei, tel. 771–9266. 33 rooms. Facilities: restaurant.*

Caritas Bianchi Lodge. Just over 10 years old, this clean and friendly lodge is close to the Jade Market and the nightly Temple Street Market. *4 Cliff Rd., Yaumatei, tel. 388–1111, fax 770–6669. 90 rooms; 2 suites. Facilities: restaurant. AE, DC, MC, V.*

Chungking. Located between the Sheraton and Holiday Inn Golden Mile hotels, these are among the least expensive rooms in Hong Kong. If the noise and the spicy aromas from the building's Indo-Pakistani cafés don't deter you, you'll find the price and the central location a bargain. *40 Nathan Rd., Tsimshatsui, tel. 366–5362. 82 rooms. Facilities: restaurant. No credit cards.*

Concourse. One of the new series of budget hotels, the Concourse was opened in 1991 by the China Travel Service in Mongkok, reasonably close to public transport and active nightlife. *20 Lai Chi Kok Rd., Kowloon, tel. 397–6683, fax 381–3768. 402 rooms. Facilities: three restaurants, karaoke lounge. AE, DC, MC, V.*

Holy Carpenter Church Hostel. Situated in the center of the discount shopping and industrial district of Hunghom, this small, 15-year-old hostel is close to the airport and train station. The hostel will be most attractive to budget travelers who can book far enough in advance, just want a place to sleep, and don't mind the lack of in-house entertainment, restaurants, bars, and tour-booking facilities. *1 Dyer Ave., Hunghom, tel. 362–0301, fax 362–2193. 14 rooms. MC, V.*

International. This hotel provides the basics. The bright orange lobby helps prepare guests for the pink and orange color scheme of their rooms. The best rooms face Cameron Road and have balconies to view the bright lights, sounds, and nightlife of Tsimshatsui. *33 Cameron Rd., tel. 366–3381, fax 369–5381. 91 rooms; 2 suites. Facilities: restaurant. MC, V.*

Shamrock. With rooms that are more spacious than elegant and an atmosphere best described as pre-renovation rustic, this hotel is still a good choice for budget travelers. It is just north of Kowloon Park and steps away from the Jordan MTR. *233 Nathan Rd., Yaumatei, tel. 735–2271, fax 736–7354. 150 rooms. Facilities: restaurant. AE, DC, MC, V.*

Y.M.C.A. This is the most popular of the Ys, no doubt because of its excellent location (across the street from the legendary Peninsula Hotel and near the Star Ferry terminal). Recent changes have eliminated the swimming pool. The staff speaks English. *Salisbury Rd., Tsimshatsui, tel. 369–2211. 196 rooms; 17 suites. Facilities: restaurant, barbershop. AE, DC, MC, V.*

New Territories, The Outer Islands

Tsuen Wan's 950-room Kowloon Panda, which opened at the end of 1991, has helped alleviate the shortage of first-class accommodations in the fast-developing New Territories and has been welcomed by visitors involved in manufacturing here. Accommodations are still limited on the outlying islands, although some of them (such as Cheung Chau), have a booming business in rooms to rent, with agents displaying photographs of available rentals on placards that line the waterfront opposite the ferry pier.

Moderate **Kowloon Panda.** This massive new hotel is the first in the western New Territories. Located close to the subway, in bustling Tsuen Wan, it offers a variety of restaurants, pool, health club, and business and meeting facilities. The layout and decor are described as Ginza-style, with lots of glitter, open-plan lounges, and interconnected facilities. *Tsuen Wah St., Tsuen Wan, tel. 409–1111, fax 409–1818. 1026 rooms. Facilities: four restaurants, three lounges, pool, health club, business center, airport transfers. AE, DC, MC, V.*

★ **Regal Riverside.** Located in one of the territory's new towns, this large, modern hotel overlooks the Shing Mun River in the foothills of Shatin. Be prepared to spend at least 20 minutes getting to the Kowloon shopping district. The city-resort atmosphere comes not only from its location but also from such features as Hong Kong's largest hotel disco and the health club, which has Hong Kong's only float capsule, purported to soothe away the day's pressures. *Tai Chung Kiu Rd., Shatin, tel. 649–7878 or 800/543–4300, fax 649–7791. 389 rooms; 11 suites. Facilities: business center, 3 restaurants, nonsmoking floors, beauty salon, barbershop, shopping arcade. AE, DC, MC, V.*

Royal Park. Designed for those with business in Shatin, this new hotel adjoins Shatin's Town Plaza, which contains shops, restaurants, cinemas, and the train station. *8–18 Pak Hok Ying St., Shatin, tel. 601–2111, fax 601–3666. 442 rooms. Facilities: Chinese, Japanese, and Western restaurants, pool, health center, business center. AE, DC, MC, V.*

Inexpensive **Cheung Chau Warwick.** The eight-story hotel overlooks Tung
★ Wan Beach. The tennis court and swimming pool, and the fact that there are no cars on this island, which is only an hour away by ferry from Hong Kong Island, has made this hotel popular with local families. *East Bay, Cheng Chau, tel. 981–0081, fax 981–9174. 133 rooms; 17 suites. Facilities: swimming pool, 2 restaurants. AE, DC, MC, V.*

8 The Arts and Nightlife

The Arts

The best daily calendar of cultural events is the *South China Morning Post* newspaper, which has a daily arts and culture page. You can read previews in the *Sunday Post*. The *Hong Kong Standard* also lists events. Weekly listings are in the *TV and Entertainment Times*, which comes out on Thursdays. The government radio station, RTHK 3 (567AM), announces events during the 7 AM–10 AM "Hong Kong Today" program.

City Hall (by Star Ferry, Hong Kong Island) has posters and huge bulletin boards listing events and ticket availability, and booths where tickets can be purchased, although finding the right booth can be a bit confusing. The monthly *City News* newspaper, which also lists events, is free and available at City Hall. The following is a list of locales that present events and display posters of Hong Kong cultural events.

Performance Halls

Hong Kong Island **City Hall** (Edinburgh Pl., by Star Ferry, Central, tel. 522–9928). This complex has a large auditorium, a recital hall, and a theater. Classical music, legitimate theater, and films are presented here.

Hong Kong Arts Centre (2 Harbour Rd., Wanchai, tel. 823–0200). Here you will find 15 floors of auditoriums, rehearsal halls, and recital rooms. Local as well as visiting groups of entertainers perform here.

Hong Kong Fringe Club (2 Lower Albert Rd., Central, tel. 521–7251). Locally run, this has some of Hong Kong's most interesting visiting and local entertainment and art exhibitions. Shows and exhibits range from the blatantly amateur to the magically professional. It also has good jazz, avant-garde drama, and events for and by both young and old.

Queen Elizabeth Stadium (18 Oi Kwan Rd., Wanchai, tel. 891–1727). Although this is basically a sports stadium with a seating capacity of 3,500, it frequently presents ballet, orchestra concerts, and even disco.

Hong Kong Academy for Performing Arts. (1 Gloucester Rd., Wanchai, tel. 823–1500). This arts school has two major theaters seating 1,600 people, plus a 200-seat studio theater and outdoor theater.

Kowloon **Hong Kong Coliseum.** (Hunghom Railway Station, Hunghom, tel. 765–9211). This stadium has seating capacity for more than 12,000 and presents everything from basketball to ballet, from skating polar bears to international pop stars.

Hong Kong Cultural Centre (Salisbury Rd., tel. 734–2831). This newest venue for shows and conferences contains the Grand Theatre which seats 1,750, and a concert hall that accommodates 2,100. The center is used by visiting and local artists.

Academic Community Hall (224 Waterloo Rd., Kowloon Tong, tel. 338–6121. Take the MTR to Kowloon Tong Station, then a taxi). This is a very modern auditorium belonging to Baptist College. Mainly it has pop groups, but it offers dance and symphony concerts, too.

New Territories   **Tsuen Wan Town Hall** (tel. 414–0144. Take the MTR to Tsuen Wan Station). Although off the beaten track, this auditorium has a constant stream of performers. Groups include everything from the Warsaw Philharmonic to troupes of Chinese acrobats. It has seating capacity for 1,424 and probably the best acoustics in the colony.

  Shatin Town Hall (tel. 694–2536. It's a 5-min walk from the MTR at Shatin.). This is an impressive building attached to an enormous shopping arcade. It usually shares cultural events with Tsuen Wan through the Regional Council.

Festivals and Special Events

No other Asian territory has as many festivals as Hong Kong. Many festivals are ad hoc—somebody comes up with the idea for a Chinese dance festival or an Asian acrobatic festival, and suddenly it's there, taking even the residents by surprise. Following are the regular cultural festivals—but don't be surprised if a festival turns up that's not on the list.

Hong Kong Arts Festival (Jan.–Feb.). This includes four weeks of music and drama from around the world. Information abroad can be obtained through Cathay Pacific Airways offices. In Hong Kong, City Hall has all the schedules.

Hong Kong Fringe Festival (Jan.–Feb.). Running simultaneously with the Arts Festival, it starts off with Sunday street theater in Central. There are shows at the Fringe Club, near Star Ferry pier, and just about anywhere.

Hong Kong International Film Festival (Apr.). This includes two weeks of films from virtually every country in the world. Quality varies, but since this festival is neither for selling films nor for competition, the spectrum is far wider than anywhere else. It's difficult to get tickets for evening performances, but daily shows, beginning at 10:30 AM, are available (tel. 573–9595 for information). Brochures are available at City Hall.

Free Chinese Cultural Shows sponsored by the Hong Kong Tourist Association (HKTA) are performed in *Cityplaza* on Hong Kong Island. A monthly schedule and program is published by the HKTA.

Chinese Opera Fortnight (Sept.). This is two weeks of Cantonese, Peking, Soochow, Chekiang, and Chiu Chow opera presented in City Hall Theatre, Concert Hall, and Ko Shan Theatre.

Festival of Asian Arts (Oct.–Nov.). Perhaps Asia's major cultural festival, this draws over 150 artistic events from as far afield as Hawaii, Bhutan, and Australia. It is staged not only in concert halls but also at playgrounds throughout the territory. It occurs biennially in even-numbered years.

Performing Arts Ensembles

Several permanent arts ensembles are indigenous to Hong Kong, some with government support, some subsidized by private organizations. The following are the major groups:

Hong Kong Philharmonic Orchestra. More than 100 artists from Hong Kong, the United States, and Europe perform everything from classical to avant-garde to contemporary music by Chinese composers. Soloists have included Ashkenazy, Firkusny, and Maureen Forrester. Performances are mostly on Friday and Saturday at 8 PM in City Hall or recital halls in New Territories (tel. 721–2030 for ticket information).

Hong Kong Chinese Orchestra. Created in 1977 by the Urban Council, this group performs only Chinese works. The orchestra is divided into strings, plucked instruments, wind, and percussion. Each work is arranged and orchestrated especially for the occasion. Weekly concerts are given throughout Hong Kong.

Chinese Opera

Cantonese Opera. There are 10 Cantonese opera troupes in Hong Kong, as well as many amateur singing groups. Many perform "street opera," as in the Shanghai Street Night Market on Sundays, while others perform at temple fairs, in City Hall, or in playgrounds under the auspices of the Urban Council. Visitors unfamiliar with the form are sometimes alienated by the strange sounds of this highly complex and extremely sophisticated art form. Every gesture has its own meaning; in fact, there are 50 different gestures for the hand alone. Props attached to the costumes are similarly intricate and are used in exceptional ways. For example, the principal female will often wear five-foot-long pheasant tails attached to the headdress. Anger is shown by dropping the head and shaking it in a circular fashion so the feathers move in a perfect circle. Surprise is shown by "nodding the feathers." One can also "dance with the feathers" to show a mixture of anger and determination. The orchestral instruments punctuate the singing. It is best to have a friend translate the gestures, since the stories are so complex that they make Wagner or Verdi librettos seem almost simplistic.

Peking Opera. Some people like this less than Cantonese opera, because the voices are higher-pitched. This is an older opera form and more respected for its classical traditions. Several troupes visit Hong Kong from the People's Republic of China each year, and their meticulous training is of a high degree. They perform in City Hall or at special temple ceremonies.

Dance

Hong Kong Dance Company. The Urban Council created the Hong Kong Dance Company in 1981 to promote the art of Chinese dance and to present newly choreographed work on Chinese historical themes. They give about three performances a month throughout the territory and have appeared at the Commonwealth Arts Festival in Australia. The 30-odd members are expert in folk and classical dance.

Hong Kong Ballet (tel. 573–7398). This is Hong Kong's first professional ballet company and vocational ballet school. It is Western-oriented, both classical and contemporary, with the dancers performing at schools, auditoriums, and various festivals.

City Contemporary Dance Company (tel. 326–8597). This group is dedicated to contemporary dance inspired by Hong Kong and has very innovative programs.

Drama

The Fringe Club (tel. 521–7251). An enormous amount of drama, ranging from one-man shows to full dramatic performances, is presented by this club. Regular groups include Chung Ying Theatre Company, a professional company of Chinese actors performing plays in English and Cantonese, in regular public performances, as well as in most major festivals, schools, and churches.

Zuni Icosahedron (tel. 893–8419). The most important avant-garde group puts on new drama and dance in Cantonese and English at various locations.

Nightlife

Hong Kong's nightlife offers something for everybody. For some, a night out means a visit to a street market, a long dinner at a harborside restaurant, or a bout of window-shopping. For others, it means elegant piano bars and rollicking British pubs, funky jazz dens, high-tech, super-strobed discos, topless bars, and hostess clubs. For still others, it includes marble massage parlors, American-style bar-lounges, old-fashioned ballrooms, sing-along cafes, *karaoke* (sing-a-song) bars for amateur crooners, and cabaret restaurants.

All premises licensed to serve alcohol are subject to stringent fire, safety, and sanitary controls by police and local authorities. True clubs, as distinct from public premises, are less strictly controlled, and wise visitors should think twice before succumbing to the city's raunchier club hideaways. If you stumble into one, check out cover and hostess charges *before* you get too comfortable, pay for each round of drinks as it's served (by cash rather than credit card), and never sign any blank checks. As in every tourist destination, the rip-off is a well-practiced art. To be safest, visit spots that are sign-carrying members of the Hong Kong Tourist Association (HKTA). You can pick up its free membership listing (including approved restaurants and night spots) at any HKTA Information Office.

Take note, too, of Hong Kong's laws. You need to be over 18 to be served alcohol. Drugs, obscene publications, homosexual acts, and unlicensed gambling are ostensibly illegal. There is some consumer protection, but the generally helpful police, now mostly English-speaking, expect every visitor to know the meaning of "caveat emptor" (buyer beware!).

Following is a checklist of some suggested drinking and dancing spots (with telephone numbers where reservations are possible or wise). Many of Hong Kong's smarter night spots are located in hotels (*see* Chapter 7 for addresses and telephone numbers).

Fast-paced, competitive Hong Kong is a world of change where buildings seem to vanish overnight and new fads emerge weekly. Don't be surprised if our listing includes some spots that have changed their decor or name, or have closed down since these words were written.

Cabaret and Nightclubs

Some hotels have dinner shows on a now-and-then basis. The **Hilton** is the major dinner-theater destination, often featuring short seasons of British theater companies staging three-act comedies for nostalgic British expatriates.

Stand-up comedians, usually British, also visit Hong Kong, appearing at the **Sheraton, Holiday Inn Harbour View,** or **China Fleet Club** (6 Arsenal St., Wanchai, tel. 529–6001). Check newspaper listings or the weekly *TV & Entertainment Times* for details.

The biggest and best old-fashion nightclub-restaurants are Chinese. The cuisine is Cantonese, and so are most of the singers. Big-name local balladeers and "Cantopop" stars make guest appearances. Though modest by Las Vegas standards, the shows can be entertaining, as at the massive **Ocean City Restaurant & Night Club** in Peninsula Centre (Tsimshatsui East, tel. 723–3278).

Ocean Centre's **Ocean Palace Restaurant & Night Club** (tel. 730–7111) is another favorite for Hong Kong family and wedding parties.

On Nathan Rd., at 36 and 94, check out the **Capital** (tel. 368–0366) and **Golden Crown** (tel. 366–6291) nightclub-restaurants. Here you will see Hongkongers dining and dancing the night away.

One of the few hotel restaurants to feature a band and singers is the Hilton's **Eagle's Nest** Chinese restaurant (tel. 523–3111).

In Causeway Bay, the Lee Gardens Hotel's **Pavilion** (tel. 895–3311) is a less expensive dinner-dance Western-style restaurant, much favored by Australian and British tourists.

Nation 97 (tel. 810–9333) is a small, smoky, usually crowded nightclub in Lan Kwai Fong. It is open from 11 PM to 4 AM or later, as long as there are customers. The club charges HK$50 admission on Friday and Saturday.

Cocktail and Piano Bars

Every luxury hotel has at least one piano bar. Some serve food, and many have live music (usually jolly Filipino trios with a female singer) and a handkerchief-size dance floor. Hong Kong's Happy Hours usually run from late afternoon to early evening, with drinks at half price.

Harbor-gazing is the main attraction at the Shangri-La's **Tiara Lounge,** Sheraton's **Sky Lounge** (go up in the bubble lift), and Excelsior's **Talk of the Town.** Marvelous harbor views are also part of the appeal of **Gripps** (tel. 736–0088), the new night spot in the Omni Hong Kong and reminiscent of the bar cafés of the 1930s. There's piano music at night.

Feeling pampered is the pleasure at the Peninsula's clublike **Verandah** or the Mandarin Oriental's mezzanine **Clipper Lounge.** The socially aware go to the Peninsula's **Lobby** or Regent's two lobby lounges to see and be seen. Sit on the right of the Peninsula's entrance to be where the cream of society traditionally lounges; be ready to chat about the fashion industry if you sit in the Regent's lobby.

Pubs

Pubs have become popular with young beer-loving Hong Kongers as well as British residents and troops. Drinks are cheaper than in bars, pub "snacks" are filling fare, and there is usually a game of darts or chess, and some free musical entertainment.

Off-duty Central business folks flock to the pirate-galleon **Galley** at Jardine House (tel. 526–3061).

Central's oak-beamed, British-managed **Bull & Bear** is in Hutchison House, on Lambeth Walk (tel. 525–7436).

Another popular spot is **The Jockey Pub,** tucked away in Swire House (2nd-floor shopping arcade Chater Rd., tel. 526–1478).

In Wanchai, pub-hopping is practiced by the fit and less fastidious. **The Horse & Groom** (126 Lockhart Rd., tel. 527–2083) and its neighboring **Old China Hand Tavern** (104 Lockhart Rd., tel. 527–9174) are reliable starting points. End up at the Excelsior Hotel's **Dickens Bar** (go there first on a Sunday afternoon for its jazz sessions).

Cool off at an outdoor table at Causeway Bay's **King's Arms,** on Sunning Plaza (tel. 895–6557), one of Hong Kong's few city-center "beer gardens."

Over in Tsimshatsui, a mixed, happy crowd can be found in the window-fronted **Kangaroo Pub** (15 Chatham Rd., tel. 723–9439). The set-up includes the **Windjammer Restaurant.**

The **Blacksmith's Arms** (16 Minden Ave., tel. 369–6696) is a cozier gathering place. Go to 4 Hart Avenue to taste the atmosphere at **Rick's Cafe** (tel. 367–2939).

Neighboring **Grammy's Lounge** (2A Hart Ave., tel. 368–3823) features Filipino-led sing-alongs. **Ned Kelly's Last Stand** (11A Ashley Rd., tel. 366–0562) is Aussie-style, with beer and filling grub. One of Hong Kong's best drinking scenes for non-Asian visitors is in Central, in the Lan Kwai Fong area (*see* For Singles, below).

Wine Bars

Western stockbrokers and financial types unwind in Central's **Brown's Wine Bar** (Tower 2, Exchange Sq., tel. 523–7003). It has good food and a splendid bar. Accents tend to be British.

At **La Rose Noire** (8 Wo On, Central, tel. 526–5965), a chic little bistro, the owners are a formidable piano-singing team.

Even more intimate is **Le Tire Bouchon** (9 Old Bailey St., tel. 523–5459), whose owner dispenses tasty bistro meals and fine wines by the glass.

Jazz/Folk Clubs

Since 1989, jazz lovers have been enjoying great performances at the **Jazz Club** (34 D'Aguilar St., Central, tel. 845–8477). The house band gives professional backing to such luminaries as Nat Adderley, George Melly, and Dolly Baker.

Ned Kelly's Last Stand (11A Ashley Rd., Tsimshatsui, tel. 366–0562) is an Aussie-managed home for pub grub and Dixieland. Get there early, before 10 PM, to get a comfortable seat.

Sunday afternoon sessions at the Excelsior Hotel's **Dickens Bar** are always worth checking out. So are the Wednesday-night gigs at the **Godown** bar-restaurant, at the Admiralty Centre, Tower 2, street level (tel. 522–1608).

Wanchai's unpretentious alternative to the topless bar scene is **The Wanch** (54 Jaffe Rd., tel. 861–1621), known for its live local folk and rock performances.

There's a rousing Filipino version of Country Western music most evenings in **Bar City** in New World Centre, in Tsimshatsui (tel. 369–8571), which is popular with young Hong Kongers.

Hardy's Folk Club (35 D'Aguilar St., Central, tel. 522–4448) is another Hong Kong rarity—the singers tend to be selfconscious Western transients singing for their supper in a pub setting. Folk fans will enjoy **Someplace Else** in the Sheraton.

Discos

Hong Kong young people fill the discos, a major outlet for letting off steam. Entry prices are high by American standards, and you'll see thousands of fashionably dressed fun-seekers if you do a grand disco tour. Entrance to the smarter spots, around HK$100 or more (much more on major public holiday eves), usually entitles you to two drinks. The latest "in" night spot is **JJs** (Grand Hyatt, 1 Harbour Rd., Hong Kong, tel. 861–1234), the Grand Hyatt's entertainment center. It contains a disco, a nightclub with floor shows, and a pizza lounge with a pool table and a dart board. Still holding its own is **Canton** (World Finance Centre, Harbour City, Canton Rd., Tsimshatsui, tel. 735–0209), a two-story high-energy maze of gangways, video monitors, and gathering areas packed with a young crowd. Its members-only room is a live music lounge.

The new **Catwalk** in the New World Hotel (tel. 369–4111) attracts the night crowd with a disco, live band, and karaoke lounges.

Slightly older nightlifers frequent the adjacent **Hot Gossip** (tel. 730–6884), which has a separate café-style cocktail lounge.

Other discos on this side of Tsimshatsui, such as **Apollo 18** (Silvercord, Canton Rd., tel. 722–6188), attract milling crowds of local youngsters. There is a more cosmopolitan scene at **Hollywood East,** in the basement of Tsimshatsui East's Regal Meridien Hotel (tel. 311–9789). Smallish, it boasts everchanging light effects.

Its reliable neighbor is the Royal Garden Hotel's **Royal Falcon.** The daytime pub operation goes disco at night.

Japanese tourists gravitate to the Park Lane Radisson Hotel's **Starlight** disco, also in Causeway Bay. Some check out the self-styled Japanese high-tech **Zodiac** disco in the New World Centre's **Bar City** drinking complex (tel. 369–8571). One ticket admits you to the City's three operations. It's another place for Chinese youngsters enjoying a night out on the town.

Chuppies (Chinese yuppies) and conversationalists head upstairs, to the New World Hotel's **Faces,** which has quiet corners. Similar types, many of the boat-owning class, take a taxi or chauffeur out to **R.J.Casa Supper Club** for dancing to a live band in Aberdeen's Marina Club (tel. 554–0044) on the south side of Hong Kong Island.

The **Godown** disco bar-restaurant, in Tower 2 of Admiralty Centre (tel. 522–1608), is another popular night spot. **Joe Bananas** (23 Luard Rd., Wanchai, tel. 529–1811) is a high-ceiling, American-style disco café, busiest when the fleet's in town. The original trendsetter, and Hong Kong's first really mixed disco in which all classes and races mingled, is **Disco Disco** (40 D'Aguilar St., Central, tel. 523–5863). It is still popular with singles and, like almost all discos, has mid-week ladies' nights.

Topless Bars

With a few notable exceptions, most topless bars are scruffy dives. A beer may seem reasonably priced, at around HK$25, but the "champagne" the women drink is not. Charges for conversational companionship can also be unexpected extras.

Bottoms Up (14 Hankow Rd., Tsimshatsui, tel. 721–4509) was immortalized by its use in a James Bond film. Cozy circular bar counters are tended by topless women. This place is so respectable that visiting couples are welcomed.

Over in Wanchai, once known as "The World of Suzie Wong," the friendliest faces are those of off-duty Filipina *amahs* (household servants), either working or lounging on the dance floors of spots like the **San Francisco Bar** (129 Lockhart Rd., tel. 527–0468) and the **Club Mermaid** (96 Lockhart Rd., tel. 529–2113).

Other bars, with or without door touts, in Wanchai or old Tsimshatsui (on the side roads off Nathan Road), warrant sober assessment by potential visitors. Avoid the so-called "fishball stalls" farther out, in Kowloon, unless you are a Cantonese-speaking anthropologist who likes working in the dark. Ditto for massage parlors.

A popular cluster of Wanchai haunts are to be found on and off Wanchai's Fenwick Street—stick your nose in **An-An, Crossroads, Club Mikado, Club Pussycat**, and, of course, the **Suzie Wong Club**.

Hostess Clubs

These are clubs in name only. Hong Kong's better ones are multimillion-dollar operations, with hundreds of presentable hostess-companions of many races. Computerized time clocks on each table tabulate companionship charges in timed units—the costs are clearly detailed on table cards, as are standard drink tabs. The clubs' dance floors are often larger than a disco's, and they have one or more live bands and a scheduled line-up of singers. They also have dozens of fancily furnished private rooms with sofas or partitioned drinking lounges, often palatially comfortable. Local and visiting businessmen adore them—and the numbered, multilingual hostesses. Business is so good that the clubs are willing to allow visitors *not* to ask for companionship. The better clubs are on a par with deluxe hotels' music lounges, and they cost little more. Their Happy Hours start in the afternoon, when many have a sort of tea-dance ambience, and continue through to mid-evening. Peak hours are 10 PM–4 AM.

Club BBoss (formerly Club Volvo) is the grandest, in Tsimshatsui East's Mandarin Plaza (tel. 369–2883). Executives, mostly Hong Kongers, entertain here, tended by a staff of over 1,000. If one's VIP room is too far from the entrance, one can hire an electrified vintage Rolls and purr around an indoor roadway. Close by is another drinkers' dreamland, **China City Night Club,** in Peninsula Centre (tel. 723–3278). Along the harbor, in New World Centre, are **Club Cabaret** (tel. 369–8431) and **Club Deluxe** (tel. 721–0277), both luxurious dance lounges.

As its name implies, **Club Kokusai** (81 Nathan Rd., Tsimshatsui, tel. 367–6969) appeals to visitors from the land of the risen Yen.

Two comfortably grand Wanchai nightclubs are the **Mandarin Palace** (24 Marsh Rd., tel. 575–6551) and the **New Tonnochy** (1 Tonnochy Rd., tel. 575–4376).

For Singles

Many Westerners and Chuppies choose to meet in crowded comfort in the Lan Kwai Fong area, a hillside section around Central's D'Aguilar Street. It contains many appetizing bistros, wine bars, and ethnic cafés.

Singles mix happily at **Disco Disco** (*see* Discos, above) and around the bar of **California** (tel. 521–1345) a laid-back American-style restaurant for all ages. It has a late-night disco most nights.

The bar area of the cosy **Nineteen '97** restaurant (tel. 810–9333) is also favored by conversationalists, though they tend to arrive, and stay, in cliques. So does most of the cheery Western crowd in a Scottish-Victorian pub farther up the hill: **Mad Dogs** (33 Wyndham St., tel. 525–2383).

Schnurrbart (Winner Bldg., D'Aguilar St., tel. 523–4700) is a friendly German pub. Next door is **Hardy's Folk Bar.** One place nearby where the arts-minded can mingle is the **Fringe Club** (2 Lower Albert Rd., tel. 521–7251), in the historic red-brick building that also houses the Foreign Correspondents Club. The Club is Hong Kong's "alternative" arts scene.

Lonely businessmen can be talked to at hotel bars. The Hilton's **Dragon Boat,** Hyatt's **Chin Chin** or **Nathan's,** and Sheraton's **Someplace Else** have their fans.

Owing to the supposedly reserved natures of both the British and the Chinese, Hong Kong is one of the more difficult places for striking up conversations with strangers. Most Hong Kong singles go hunting in discos or pubs with same-sex friends, or wander in groups through the shopping complexes. Central's **Landmark,** on Des Voeux Road, is a favored place for "eye-talking," up to 6 PM. As in most destinations, singles usually meet during the day (on coach tours or on business assignments).

9 Macau

Introduction

*A British freelance
writer, Shann
Davies has lived
and traveled in
many countries,
but she always
comes back to
Macau, which she
first visited in
1962. She is the
author of* Viva
Macau!, Chronicles
in Stone, *and*
Macau *(Times
Edition).*

If history balanced its books, no one would today be skimming
over the 40-mile (64-km) waterway from Hong Kong to Macau.
After all, the Portuguese-administered enclave of six square
miles (15.6 sq km) tucked into China's back pocket ceased to
have any commercial or political significance a century and a
half ago.

How and why has it survived? One clue can be found on the vessel en route to Macau. Most of the passengers will be Hong
Kong Chinese heading for the casinos, which have provided the
territory with much of its revenue since legal gambling was introduced in the 1840s as an attempt to compensate for the loss
of entrepôt trade to newly founded Hong Kong.

Also on board might be Jesuit priests and Roman Catholic
nuns, both Chinese and European, who run vital, centuries-old
charities and tend to one of Asia's oldest and most devout
Christian communities. Just as likely, there are Buddhist
priests, who help maintain Macau's firm faith in its Chinese
traditions. Then there are the tourists—more than a million a
year—textile and toy buyers, British engineers, Swiss chefs,
French showgirls and bar hostesses from Southeast Asia. In
their different ways they all prove that there's plenty of life left
in the grande dame of the China Coast.

The voyage is a pleasant progress between hilly green islands,
some belonging to Hong Kong, some Chinese, and most uninhabited. As it appears on the skyline, Macau jolts the imagination. Hills crowned with a lighthouse and church spire, a blur of
pastel buildings, and tree-lined avenues all confirm that this is
a bit of transplanted Iberia, settled in 1557 by the Portuguese
as Europe's first outpost in China.

Macau is 90 miles (144 km) south of Canton, the traditional port
for China's trade with foreign "barbarians." In the 16th century, however, her traders were forbidden by the emperor to deal
with Japan, whose Shogun had imposed a ban on China trade.
The Portuguese saw their chance and soon were making fabulous fortunes from their command of trade between the two
Asian countries and Europe. Among the cargoes that passed
through Macau were silk, tea, and porcelain from China, silver
and lacquerware from Japan, spices and sandalwood from the
East Indies, muslin from India, gems from Persia, wild animals
and ivory from Africa, foodstuffs from Brazil, and European
clocks, telescopes, and cannons.

Macau's golden age came to an abrupt end with the closure of
Japan and the loss of Portugal's mercantile power to the Dutch
and English. The northern Europeans and the Americans sent
their India-men and clipper ships to Macau to barter ginseng,
furs, woolens, and opium for tea and silk. Their merchants
treated the city as their own but, with their rents and customs
duties, helped Macau survive. Then, in the mid-19th century,
Hong Kong was founded and the merchants moved out, leaving
Macau a backwater.

In the early part of this century, Macau was cast by movie producers and novelists as a den of sin, sex, and spies. True, it had
casinos, brothels, opium divans, and secret agents; but, in fact,
it was a small, pale shadow of Shanghai or even Hong Kong. To-

day, any traveler in search of wild and wicked Macau will be disappointed, and so will romantics looking for a colonial twilight. As you approach through the ocher waters of the silt-heavy Pearl River estuary, the reality of modern Macau is unavoidable. High-rise apartments and office blocks mask the hillsides, multistory factories cover land reclaimed from the sea, and construction hammers insist that this is no longer a sleepy old town.

The modern prosperity comes from taxes on gambling and the export of textiles, toys, electronics, furniture, luggage, ceramics, and artificial flowers. Like Hong Kong, Macau is a duty-free port where anyone can set up a business with minimal taxation or government restrictions. As a result, there is little evidence of city planning and many of the new skyscrapers are grotesque. However, some building projects have benefited Macau. These include the University of East Asia and the racetrack on Taipa Island, a handsome handful of good hotels, and a number of superbly restored or re-created historical buildings.

Relations with China have never been better, with ever-increasing two-way trade and joint ventures in Zhongshan, the neighboring Chinese county. Macau's close proximity to China also makes it a popular gateway for excursions across the border. Following the Sino-British agreement to hand Hong Kong back to China in 1997, the Portuguese negotiated the resumption of Chinese sovereignty over Macau, which will take place on December 20, 1999.

Macau has a population of about 450,000, and most live in the 2.5 square miles (6.5 sq km) of the mainland peninsula, with small communities on the mostly rural islands of Taipa and Coloane. About 95% of the inhabitants are Chinese, many of them of long-standing residence. About 7,000 people speak Portuguese as their first language, but only a few come from Portugal, the others being Macanese from old established Eurasian families. The more transient residents are expatriate Europeans, Americans, and Australasians, plus a few hundred Vietnamese refugees and several thousand nightclub hostesses from Thailand and the Philippines. Although Portuguese is the official language, and Cantonese the most widely spoken, English is generally understood in places frequented by tourists.

Essential Information

Arriving and Departing

The Hong Kong–Macau route is possibly the busiest international water highway in the world, with more than 6 million round-trip passages a year, or a daily average of over 16,000. The crossing procedure is very efficient, but this is not to say it's problem-free. Tickets are hard to get on weekends and public holidays, when the Hong Kong gamblers travel en masse. And services are disrupted when typhoons are in the area.

Travel Documents Visas are *not* required by Portuguese citizens or nationals of the United States, Canada, the United Kingdom, Australia, New Zealand, France, West Germany, Austria, Belgium, the

Netherlands, Switzerland, Sweden, Denmark, Norway, Italy, Greece, Spain, Japan, Thailand, the Philippines, Malaysia, South Korea, Ireland, Singapore, Brazil (up to a six-month stay), or Hong Kong residents. There is unlimited stay for Chinese, 20 days for non-Chinese. Other nationals need visas, available on arrival: HK$145 for individuals, HK$290 for a family, and HK$72.50 for group members. Visas are good for one or two visits within 20 days.

Tickets Travel agents and most Hong Kong hotels can arrange for tickets. There are also 11 Ticketmate computer-booking outlets in Hong Kong that sell tickets up to 28 days in advance for the Jetfoils headed for Macau. They are located in Exchange Square (Central, Hong Kong Island) and the major Mass Transit Railway (MTR) stations. It's best to get the return ticket at the same time because it can be inconvenient to do so in Macau. If you change your mind about the time of your return, you can go to the harbor and return on a stand-by basis. Tickets can also be booked in Hong Kong by phone and with credit cards (Jetfoil, tel. 859–6596, AE, DC, V; Jetcats, tel. 523–2136, AE, V). There is a HK$22 departure tax from Hong Kong, none from Macau.

By Boat The vast majority of sailings for Macau use the Macau Terminal in the Shun Tak Centre (200 Connaught Rd.), a 10-minute walk west of Hong Kong's Central District.

Booking offices for all shipping companies, most Macau hotels and travel agents, excursions to China, and the Macau Tourist Information Bureau (MTIB) are located in the Shun Tak Centre.

In many cases information is hard to obtain over the phone; it's best to call the MTIB (tel. 540–8180).

A fleet of Boeing Jetfoils provides the most popular service between Hong Kong and Macau. Carrying about 260 passengers, these craft ride comfortably on jet-propelled hulls at 40 knots and make the 40-mile trip in about an hour. Beer, soft drinks, and snacks are available on board, as are telephones and Macau's instant lottery tickets. Jetfoils depart at least every half hour from 7 AM to dusk, with frequent sailings between 6:30 PM and 7 AM. The top deck of each vessel is first class, and there are nonsmoking sections on both decks.

Fares for first class are HK$92 on weekdays, HK$99 on weekends and public holidays, and HK$121 on the night service. Lower-deck fares are HK$78 weekdays, HK$85 weekends, and HK$103 at night. The Jetfoils are operated by Far East Jetfoil Company, a division of Shun Tak Shipping, which also operates some daytime services from the China Terminal on Kowloon side.

The other long-established company on the route is Hong Kong Macau Hydrofoil Company (HMH), which operates jet-propelled catamarans called Jetcats. The smaller vessels carry 215 passengers and make the trip in about 70 minutes, with 10 roundtrips a day. Fares are HK$62 weekdays, HK$72 weekends. Jumbocats—bigger boats—carry 306 passengers and take just over an hour, making nine roundtrips a day. Fares for small boats are HK$70 on weekdays, HK$78 on weekends; Jumbocats are HK$80 on weekdays, HK$88 on weekends.

The newest vessels on the Macau run are High Speed Ferries, which take about an hour and a half on five roundtrips daily between 8 AM and 10:30 PM. These sleek, comfortable craft have a sun deck and first-class lounge. On all three decks the seats are comfortable, there's Chinese-language TV and slot machines for entertainment, plus a variety of snacks and drinks. Fares are HK$62 first class, HK$48 tourist, HK$30 economy weekdays, HK$74, HK$60, and HK$45 weekends and public holidays. Bookings can be made at Ticketmate and the wharf.

Another service is by Sealink's hover-ferries. They carry 250 passengers and take about an hour. Fares are HK$55 weekdays, HK$68 weekends and holidays. They make eight roundtrips a day and, unlike those mentioned above, sail from the China Terminal on the Kowloon peninsula.

By Air   Helicopter service is available with at least four roundtrips a day. The 20-minute flights cost HK$830 weekdays, HK$930 weekends and public holidays. Bookings: Shun Tak Centre, tel. 859–3359; Macau Terminal, tel. 572–983.

Important Addresses and Numbers

Tourist   In Macau, the **Department of Tourism** offers information, ad-
Information   vice, maps, and brochures about the territory. It has an office at the arrival terminal, open 9 AM–6 PM every day. The main office is in Leal Senado Square, open 9–6 (tel. 315–566).

Probably more useful is the MTIB in Hong Kong. It has a wide range of maps, brochures, and up-to-the-minute information on hotels and transport. The office is located on the same floor as the wharf entrance. *Shun Tak Centre, tel. 540–8180; outside office hours, 540–8198. Open weekdays 9–5, Sat. 9–1.*

In addition, there is a Macau information desk at Hong Kong's Kai Tak Airport, just outside the Arrivals Hall. *Open daily 8 AM–10 PM.*

Business visitors to Macau can get information about all aspects of local commercial conditions from the Macau Business Centre, Edificio Ribeiro, in the square between the Praia Grande and Rua do Campo (tel. 881–949). For trade information call the Export Promotion Department (tel. 378–221).

Getting Around

In the old parts of town and shopping areas, walking is the best means of transportation. Here the streets are narrow, often under repair, and invariably crowded with vehicles weaving between sidewalk vendors and parked cars, so that pedestrians often make the fastest progress. Otherwise transport is varied, convenient, and often fun.

By Pedicab   This tricycle-drawn, two-seater carriage has been in business as long as there have been bicycles and paved roads in Macau, and a few look like originals. They cluster at the wharf and their drivers hustle for customers, usually offering guide services. In the past it was a pleasure to hire a pedicab for the ride from the wharf to downtown, but no longer. Construction along the Outer Harbour and the outrageous prices asked by today's drivers make it a hassle. To appreciate the pedicab, especially on a sunny day, take one along the Praia Grande and admire the avenue of ancient trees and the seascape of islands and fishing junks. The city center is not a congenial place for pedicabs, and the hilly districts are impossible. Of course you have to haggle, but you shouldn't pay more than HK$20 for a short trip.

By Taxi   There are usually plenty of taxis at the wharf, outside hotels, and cruising the streets. All are metered and most are air-conditioned and reasonably comfortable, but the cabbies speak little English and probably won't know the English or Portuguese names for places. It is highly recommended that you carry a bilingual map or name card in Chinese. The base charge is 5.50 patacas for the first 1,500 meters (about 1 mile), and 70 avos for each additional 250 meters (about ¼ mile). Drivers don't expect more than small change as a tip. For trips to Taipa there is a five-pataca surcharge, and to Coloane 10 patacas.

By Bus   The public buses that run around Macau are cheap—no more than 1.5 patacas in the city—and convenient. Most useful for visitors are services from the wharf: the 3A passes the Lisboa, Beverly Plaza, Sintra, and Metropole hotels before proceeding down the main street to the Inner Harbour; the 28C passes the Lisboa, Guia, and Royal hotels, Lou Lim Ioc Gardens, and Kun Iam Temple en route to the border. All routes are detailed on posts at bus stops. The others are those that commute between the city and the islands. Among those that serve Taipa, for 2 patacas, are some open-topped double-deckers, which provide a roller-coaster-like ride across the bridge. Less dramatic are the single-deck buses that go to Coloane village and Hac Sa beach, for 2.30–3 patacas. They stop outside the Lisboa. The other buses in town are replicas of 1920s London buses known as "Tour Machines." Their depot is at the wharf, and they can be hired for parties of up to nine people, for 200 patacas an hour. They are also often used to transfer groups to and from hotels. Finally, they ply set routes for 20 patacas a ticket good for all sections of the route. For information call 555–686, ext. 3004.

By Bicycle   Bicycles are available for rent at about 10 patacas an hour from shops near the Taipa bus station. The Hyatt Regency Hotel also has bikes for rent. They are newer and more modern but cost more.

By Hired Car   Self-drive Jeeplike mini vehicles called mokes are fun and ideal for touring. International and most national driving licenses are valid. Rates are HK$260–HK$280 for 24 hours weekdays, HK$290–HK$320 weekends; special packages in conjunction with hotels are available. For Macau Mokes contact 543–4190 or Ticketmate in Hong Kong, or the office at the wharf in Macau (tel. 378–851). For Avis Mokes call 542–2189 in Hong Kong, or their office in the Mandarin Oriental hotel (tel. 567–888).

Guided Tours

Regular and customized tours, for individuals and groups, by bus or car, are easily arranged in Macau, and provide the maximum amount of sightseeing in a short space of time.

There are two basic tours. One covers mainland Macau with stops at the Chinese border, Kun Iam Temple, St. Paul's, and Penha Hill. It lasts about 3½ hours. By bus it costs HK$67 for one to three passengers, HK$62 each for four or more, and includes lunch. By car, the cost is HK$150 for one, HK$100 each for two or more. The other standard tour consists of a two-hour trip to the islands across the bridge, to see old Chinese villages, temples, beaches, the Jockey Club, and the University of East Asia. The bus tour costs HK$15 each for four or more.

Aerial touring has taken off in Macau, with Ultra-light planes available for 10-minute flights at HK$300 each (tel. 307–343).

The most comfortable way to tour is by chauffeur-driven car. For a maximum of four passengers it costs HK$100 an hour. Taxis can also be rented for touring. Depending on your bargaining powers, the cost will be HK$80 or more an hour (*see* Getting Around in Essential Information, above).

Most people book tours with Macau agents while in Hong Kong or through travel agents before leaving home. If you do it this way, you will have transport from Hong Kong to Macau arranged for you and your guide waiting in the arrival hall. There are many licensed tour operators in Macau. Among those specializing in English-speaking visitors, and who have offices in Hong Kong, are **Able Tours** (Hoi Kwong Building, Travessa do Pe. Narciso, Macau, tel. 566–938; in Hong Kong, 8 Connaught Rd. West, tel. 545–9993); **Estoril Tours** (Lisboa Hotel, Macau, tel. 573–614; in Hong Kong, Macau Wharf, tel. 559–1028); **International Tourism** (9 Travessa do Pe. Narciso, Macau, tel. 287–522; in Hong Kong, 143 Connaught Rd., tel. 541–2011); **Macau Tours** (9 Ave. da Amizade, Macau, tel. 385–555; in Hong Kong, 387 Des Voeux Rd., tel. 542–2338); and **Sintra Tours** (Sintra Hotel, Macau, tel. 85878; in Hong Kong, Macau Wharf, tel. 540–8028).

Exploring Macau

Like any territory with a long, eventful past, Macau is packed with points of interest that overlap and overlay each other. For those who would rather explore than sightsee, we have divided Macau into the following areas, which can be seen separately or back to back.

The Outer Harbor

Numbers in the margin correspond with points of interest on the Macau map.

The history of Portuguese Macau almost came to an end at this spot in 1622, when the Dutch fleet landed a large invasion force to capture the rich port. From here the troops attacked Guia and Monte forts, only to be defeated by a ragtag army of Jesuit priests, Portuguese soldiers, and African slaves.

❶ Today the **Outer Harbour** is designed to welcome all arrivals. On the mile-long (1.6 km) avenue from the wharf are the Man-
❷ darin Oriental, Presidente, and Lisboa hotels, the **Jai Alai Sta-**
❸ **dium** and entertainment center, the new **Macau Forum** for conferences and sports events, and the grandstand for the annual motor and motorcycle Grand Prix events.

❹ Overlooking the harbor are the slopes of **Guia Hill**, embossed with new homes, a convent, and a hospital, and topped with a fort and the oldest lighthouse on the China coast, still a beacon for ships. The seascape presents a changing panorama, with fishing junks bobbing through the quiet, ocher water, ferries

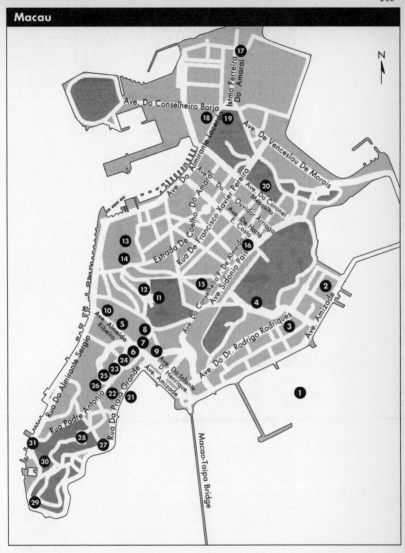

A-Ma Temple, **30**
Avenida Almeida
Ribeiro, **5**
Bela Vista Hotel, **27**
Bishop's Palace, **28**
Camões Grotto and
Garden, **13**
Canidrome, **18**
Dom Pedro, **23**
Guia Hill, **4**

Jai Alai Stadium, **2**
Kun Iam Temple, **20**
Leal Senado, **6**
Lin Fung Miu, **19**
Lou Lim Ieoc
Garden, **15**
Macau Forum, **3**
Maritime Museum, **31**
Memorial Home of Dr.
Sun Yat-Sen, **16**
Monte Hill, **11**

Old Protestant
Cemetery, **14**
Outer Harbour, **1**
Palacio, **22**
Portas do Cerco, **17**
Post Office, **9**
Pousada de São
Tiago, **29**
Praia Grande, **21**
Rua Cinco do
Outubro, **10**

St. Augustine, **24**
St. Lawrence, **26**
St. Paul's, **12**
Santa Casa da
Misericordia, **7**
São Domingos
Church, **8**
Seminary of St.
Joseph's, **25**

chugging to Canton, and the arcs of white wake as foilborne vessels and hovercraft land and take off like giant waterfowl.

Another kind of aircraft used to appear in the outer harbor: the flying clippers of Pan American Airways, which gave Macau a brief, and accidental, place in aviation history. On April 28, 1937, the Hong Kong Clipper left Manila on a flight that would inaugurate air service between the West Coast of the United States and China. The plane was supposed to land in Hong Kong, but at the last minute the British authorities held back landing permission, in order to gain rights for their own Imperial Airways. The seaplane landed in Macau and was greeted by most of the population before flying on to Hong Kong. The service continued intermittently until the outbreak of war; the Pan Am terminal stood on the site now occupied by the Mandarin Oriental Hotel.

Downtown

In theory, Macau is small enough to allow a visitor to cover all of the main attractions in a day, and with unswerving determination you could do it. However, it's almost impossible to resist the casual pace of Macau, where meals are enjoyed at leisure and traffic slows to pedicab or pedestrian speed in many parts of town. For a relatively straightforward introduction to the many-layered and often contradictory character of the city, you
❺ can stroll the mile (1.6 km) or so of the main street, **Avenida Almeida Ribeiro,** generally known by its Chinese name, **Sanmalo.** It begins a short walk from the Lisboa and ends at the floating casino in the inner harbor.

Within this short distance you find colonial Portugal, traditional China, and modern Asia locked in architectural and social embrace. Logically, it is an unworkable misalliance; in Macau it's an enduring marriage of convenience. One reason is that buildings, institutions, and even lifestyles have survived because enough people wanted them to, not because their preservation was officially decreed. Sanmalo might look and sound casually chaotic, but it works.

Like a European city, the focal point of this downtown is a large square with a fountain and plaza surrounded by several impres-
❻ sive buildings. The **Leal Senado** (Loyal Senate) has a classically simple facade, garden courtyard, and Edwardian council chambers. The Senate acts as a municipal government, taking care of parks, garbage collection, the police force, and traffic regulations.

The library in the Leal Senado, a superb copy of a classic Portuguese library, contains possibly the best collection of books in English about China's history, society, economy, and culture. Much was inherited from the British- and American-managed Chinese Customs House. In addition, the library has some rare books from the early days of the Portuguese empire and bound copies of old Macau newspapers. Scholars and others are welcome to browse or study. *Open Mon.–Sat. 1–7.*

❼ The Senate president is by tradition the president of the **Santa Casa da Misericordia** (Holy House of Mercy), the oldest Christian charity on the China Coast. Its headquarters occupy a handsome baroque building in the square, and its offices administer homes for the elderly, kitchens for the poor, clinics,

8 and a leprosarium. Behind the Santa Casa is the beautiful **São Domingos** church, with a magnificent altar.

9 The central **Post Office** and telephone exchange, as well as some handsome old commercial buildings with arcades at street level, are also in the square. (One of them has been restored to house the Government Tourist Office.) The São Domingos produce market, its narrow streets packed with stalls selling fruit, vegetables, and wholesale-price clothing from local factories, leads off the square.

Sanmalo has some regular clothing stores, but the majority of shoppers come here for gold jewelry, watches and clocks, Chinese and Western medicines, brandy, biscuits, and salted fish. Interspersed are banks, lawyers' offices, and the Central Hotel. Now a rather dingy, inexpensive place to stay, the Central used to contain the city's only casinos, where the *fan tan* (button game) attracted the high rollers and the top-floor brothel did a thriving business.

The heart of the old red-light district was Rua da Felicidade ("Street of Happiness"), which runs off Sanmalo. Few brothels have survived competition from sauna and massage parlors and have ended up being replaced by budget hotels and restaurants. The area does preserve the atmosphere of a prewar China-coast community, especially in the evening. After sunset, food stalls with stools and tiny tables are set out. Lights blaze from open-front restaurants, laundries, tailor shops, and family living rooms. The pungent smell of cooking pervades the streets, and it seems as if most of Macau's 450,000 people have fled their tiny apartments to eat out, relax, and socialize.

10 Another side street off Sanmalo worth a detour is **Rua Cinco do Outubro,** which contains one of the best-looking traditional Chinese medicine shops anywhere. The Farmacia Tai Ning Tong has an elaborately carved wood facade and a cavernous interior, its walls lined with huge apothecary jars of medicinal roots, deer horn, and other assorted marvels. In a corner are mortars and pestles for making potions to order.

The Old Citadel

11 The most remarkable early buildings in Macau were on **Monte Hill.** Built by the Jesuits, they included a fort, a college, and the collegiate church of the Mother of God, commonly known as **12** **St. Paul's.** By the early 17th century, the college had become a university for scholar-missionaries en route to the courts of China and Japan. The church was declared the most magnificent in Asia, and a small town of merchants, clerics, and craftsmen grew up around the Monte.

Today this area is the heart of old Macau for visitors and is easily reached from Senate Square via Rua da S. Domingos. The college was destroyed in a disastrous fire in 1835, and the ruins of the fort are now a quiet belvedere. Of the church, only the great stone facade remains, but it is less a ruin than a dramatic symbol of Macau and certainly the leading attraction.

Traditional craftsmen, still in business carving camphorwood chests and family shrines, hand-beating metal utensils, making barrels and mattresses, and weaving bird cages, still occupy the jumble of narrow streets below the church. Tercena and Estalagens are the most interesting streets.

Following either Rua de S. Paulo or Tercena, you reach Praça
⑬ Luis de Camões and the **Camões Grotto and Garden,** today
Macau's most popular public park, frequented from dawn to
dusk by people practicing t'ai chi ch'uan (shadowboxing), men
carrying their caged songbirds for a country walk, young lovers, students, and groups huddled over games of Chinese
chess.

The garden was originally the private grounds of the former
Camões Museum (now Orient Foundation offices), and in 1785
was used by French cartographer La Perouse for a small obser-
vatory aimed at China. The garden was taken over by the city
in 1886, when a heroic bronze bust of Camões, Portugal's greatest poet (who spent some years in Macau), was installed in a
rocky alcove. Nearby a wall of stone slabs is inscribed with
poems praising Camões and Macau by various contemporary
writers. *Open dawn–dusk.*

⑭ The **Old Protestant Cemetery,** a "corner of some foreign field"
for over 150 Americans and British, is opposite the entrance to
the garden. It is a well-kept and tranquil retreat, where tombstones recall the troubles and triumphs of Westerners in 19th-
century China. Some of the names are familiar: George
Chinnery; Captain Henry Churchill, great granduncle of Sir
Winston; Joseph Adams, grandson of John Adams, the second
U.S. president; Robert Morrison, who translated the Bible
into Chinese; Thomas Beale, the opium king; and traders
James B. Endicott and Samuel Proctor. In addition, there are
graves of sailors who were victims of battle, accident, or dis-
ease.

Restoration Row

One of the most incredible, and illogical, aspects of Macau is the
physical survival of so much of its past. Given the city's shortage of land, revenue, and investment possibilities, it would
have made economic sense to follow Hong Kong's lead and replace old buildings and gardens with high-rise office and apartment blocks. It's true that this has frequently happened, the
most glaring example being the Praia Grande, but history is
more than holding its own. One reason is the Macanese power of
positive procrastination, which infuriates businessmen today
as it doubtless did the would-be developers of the past. It's not
that the government and public enterprises are not enthusias-
tic about development projects, it's that they rarely get past
the discussion stages.

Happily for Macau's heritage, when it comes to maintaining
public buildings procrastination is overcome by family pride,
and every year or two buildings are given a new coat of white or
pastel wash and generally spruced up. In some cases, such as
the governor's residence and the government palace, the interiors have been redecorated and air-conditioned. Following suit,
all of the churches and Chinese temples have also been restored
to their old splendor.

Conservation and common sense don't always go together, but
there is an outstanding example of such a match in Macau's
Restoration Row. Actually it is a row of houses built in the
1920s in symmetrical arcadian style, on the **Avenida do
Conselheiro Ferreira de Almeida,** a block or so from the Royal
hotel. The owners of the houses were persuaded to forego huge

profits and sell to the government. The houses were then converted into homes for the Archives, the National Library, the Education Department, and university offices. The exteriors were extensively repaired and the interiors transformed. In the case of the library, the building had to be completely gutted to accommodate the stacks and rooms for the vast collection of old books. The Archives building has space for researchers and a small auditorium.

(15) Continuing along the avenue, you come to Estrada de Adolfo Loureiro and the **Lou Lim Ieoc Garden,** a classic Chinese garden modeled on those of old Soochow. It was built in the 19th century by a wealthy Chinese merchant named Lou. With the decline of the Lou family fortunes early this century, the house was sold and became a school. The garden fell into ruin until it was taken over by the city in 1974 and totally restored. Enclosed by a wall, it is a miniaturized landscape with miniforests of bamboo and flowering bushes, a mountain of sculpted concrete, and a small lake filled with lotus and golden carp. A traditional nine-turn bridge zigzags (to deter evil spirits, which can move only in straight lines) across the lake to a colonial-style pavilion with a wide veranda. This is used occasionally for exhibitions and concerts. *Admission: 1 pataca. Open dawn–dusk.*

(16) Another place of interest in this area is the **Memorial Home of Dr. Sun Yatsen.** Dr. Sun, father of the 1911 Chinese revolution, worked as a physician in Macau from 1892 to 1894, and some of his family stayed here after his death. The memorial home, in strange mock-Moorish style, was built in the mid-1930s. It contains some interesting photographs, books, and souvenirs of Sun and his long years of exile in different parts of the world. *1 Rua Ferreira do Amaral. Admission free. Open weekdays 10–1, weekends 10–1 and 3–5. Closed Tues.*

On the Doorstep of China

(17) The date of Mesquita's victory (1849) and a solemn quotation from Camões are inscribed on the stone gate—**Portas do Cerco**—that leads to China. Today the gate is closed at night, but throughout the day it is used by a steady stream of two-way traffic. From China come farmers carrying morning-fresh produce in bamboo baskets or on trucks, along with Chinese officials involved in joint business ventures and Macau and Hong Kong residents returning from visits with their families. From Macau the traffic consists of bus loads of tourists and groups of businesspeople.

(18) (19) Close by the border are two very different attractions. On one side is the **Canidrome,** where greyhound races are enthusiastically followed. On the other side of the road is the **Lin Fung Miu,** or Temple of the Lotus. In the old days this used to provide overnight accommodations for mandarins traveling between Macau and Canton. Today it is visited for its exquisite facade of clay bas-reliefs and classic architecture.

(20) **Kun Iam Temple,** nearby on the Avenida do Coronel Mesquita, should not be missed. A Buddhist temple, it has a wealth of statuary and decoration and a courtyard with a stone table where the first Sino-American treaty was signed in 1844 by the Viceroy of Canton and President John Tyler's envoy, Caleb Cushing.

Peninsula Macau

The narrow, hilly peninsula stretching from the main street to Barra Point and the Pousada de Sao Tiago is quintessential Macau, very Portuguese and very Chinese, ancient and uncomfortably modern. It is bounded on one side by the **Praia Grande** and its extension, Avenida da Republica, a graceful, banyan-shaded boulevard where people fish from the sea wall or play Chinese chess. Unfortunately, parts of the promenade have been taken over by parked cars, but there are also plenty of benches and the traffic is well diluted by pedicabs.

The cargo and fishing wharfs of the inner harbor, with their traditional Chinese shop houses—the ground floors occupied by ship's chandlers, net makers, ironmongers, and shops selling spices and salted fish—are on the opposite side of the peninsula.

In between there are several areas of historic or scenic interest. One is Largo de Sto. Agostinho, or St. Augustine Square, which is reached by climbing the steep street next to the Senate, or from the Praia Grande and the pink-and-white **Palacio,** which houses government offices.

Taking the Travessa do Paiva to the right of the Palacio, you turn right along Rua de São Lourenco to the dimple-stone ramp to the square, which looks as if it came all of a piece from 19th-century Portugal. To the left is the **Dom Pedro V** theater, modeled after a European court theater. Opposite is the imposing church of **St. Augustine,** and next door is Casa Ricci, offices for one of the most active Catholic charities in Macau. Across the square is the **Seminary of St. Joseph's,** home of preeminent local historian and living legend Father Manuel Teixeira and a collection of religious art by 17th-century European and Japanese painters. The baroque chapel is now open to the public Thursday–Tuesday 10–4. The Entrance is on Rua do Seminario. Completing the scene is the memorial home of Sir Robert Hotung, the Hong Kong millionaire, who gave his house to the city in thanks for giving him refuge during the Pacific War.

Retracing your steps down the ramp and continuing along the Rua de São Lourenco, you reach the elegant twin-tower church of **St. Lawrence** and the Salesian Institute, a technical school that stands on part of the site of the headquarters of the British East India Company. From here you can return to the Praia Grande and follow it to the Calcada do Bom Parto to the **Bela Vista Hotel,** a century-old landmark that is currently being transformed into a luxury inn.

Farther up the hill is one of the best lookouts in Macau, the courtyard of the **Bishop's Palace** and Penha Chapel. The palace is always closed but the chapel is open daily 10–4. On the site of the original 1622 structure, the present building was constructed in 1935 and is dedicated to Our Lady of Penha, patroness of seafarers.

At the far end of the peninsula is Barra Point with the **Pousada de São Tiago,** a Portuguese inn built into the ruined foundations of a 17th-century fort (*see* Lodging, below), the **A-Ma Temple,** Macau's oldest and most venerated place of worship, and the new **Maritime Museum.** This gem of a museum has been a consistent favorite since its doors opened at the end of 1987. It is ideally located, where the first Chinese and later first Portuguese made landfall, and it is housed in an imaginatively restored colonial house facing the harbor. The old number one wharf was restored to provide a pier for a fishing junk, tug, dragon boat, sampan, a working replica of the pirate-chasing lorchas, and a copy of one of the "flower boat" floating pleasure palaces that once sailed along the China coast. Inside the museum are displays of the local fishing industry, models of historic vessels, charts of great voyages by Portuguese and Chinese explorers, a relief model of 17th-century Macau and the story in lantern-show style of the A-Ma Temple, navigational aids such as an original paraffin lamp once used in the Guia lighthouse, and much, much more. *Admission 5 patacas adults, 3 patacas children. Open 10–5:30. Closed Tues.*

Taipa Island

Numbers in the margin correspond with points of interest on the Taipa and Coloane Islands map.

Linked to the city by the graceful 1.6-mile (2.5-km) bridge, Taipa can be reached by bus (including a double-decker with open-top roof deck) or taxi. Some residents jog over it daily. Up until the end of the 19th century, Taipa was two islands and provided a sheltered anchorage where clipper ships and East India-men could load and unload cargoes, which were then carried by junks and barges to and from Canton. Gradually the islands were joined by river silt and land reclamation, but Taipa, with its mansions—one of which now houses a museum—offers a reminder of the old days.

Taipa and Coloane, its neighbor, are Macau's New Territories, having been ceded by China only in 1887. Until the building of the bridge, both islands led a somnolent existence, interrupted only by occasional pirate raids. Taipa's economy depended on the raising of ducks and the manufacture of firecrackers. There are still some duck farms to be seen, but the courtyarded firecracker factories have closed, unable to compete with China.

❶ The **village of Taipa** is a tight maze of houses and shops in the traditional mold. It is changing, due to the island's new prosperity, and now boasts banks, a two-story municipal market, air-conditioned shops, and several excellent restaurants. Below the church of Our Lady of Carmel is the **Taipa House Mus-** ❷ **eum.** This finely restored 1920s mansion contains authentic period furniture, decorations, and furnishings that recapture the atmosphere and lifestyle of a middle-class Macanese family in the early part of the century. *Taipa Praia. Admission free. Open 9–1 and 3–5. Closed Mon.*

❸ Another restored building worth a visit is the **Pou Tai Un Temple,** a short walk from the Hyatt Regency. It is famed for its vegetarian restaurant (the vegetables are grown in an adjoining garden), and has been embellished with a new yellow tile pavilion and statue of the Buddhist goddess of mercy.

For Buddhists, Taoists, and Confucians, Taipa is a favored, last, earthly address. They are buried or their bones stored in ❹ the massive **United Chinese Cemetery,** which covers the cliff on the northeastern coast of the island. It is lavishly decorated with colored tiles and assorted religious images. Off-shore you

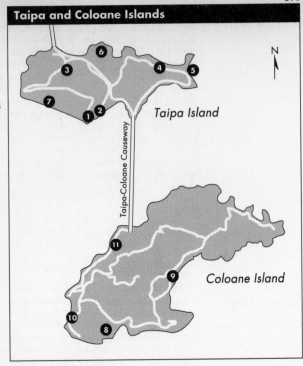

Taipa and Coloane Islands

Taipa Island

Taipa-Coloane Causeway

Coloane Island

N

➎ can see the site of the planned **Macau International Airport,**
scheduled for a late 1993 opening.

The northeast section of Taipa provides a stunning contrast,
thanks to a recent building boom. Just across the bridge is the
➏ luxurious Hyatt Hotel and the hilltop **University of East Asia.**
Directly facing the bridge is a monument sculpted with images
from Macau's history. On the western side of the island is the
➐ raceway of the **Macau Jockey Club,** 50 acres of reclaimed land
with an ultramodern, five-story grandstand, and track.

Coloane Island

Situated at the end of a 1.5-mile (2.4-km) causeway from Taipa,
the larger, hillier island of Coloane has so far been spared from
development. About a 25-minute drive from the city, it is generally considered to be remote. This makes it a popular spot for
➑ relaxed holidays, especially at the attractive 22-room **Pousada
de Coloane.** There is a long beach below the pousada and anoth-
➒ er at **Hac Sa** (Black Sands). Both are clean, although the water
is Pearl River ocher. There are plenty of cafés for food and
drink. A first-class hotel and championship golf course, to be
managed by Westin, are under construction north of Hac Sa
Beach.

The village of Coloane, with its old tile-roof houses, the Tam
➓ Kong Temple, and the **Chapel of St. Francis Xavier,** are interesting to overseas visitors. The picturesque chapel, with its
cream-and-white facade and bell tower, was built in 1928. Outside its door is a monument surrounded by cannon balls com-

memorating the local defeat of a pirate band in 1910, Macau's last encounter with old-style pirates. There are some important relics inside the chapel. The most sacred is an arm bone of St. Francis Xavier, who died in 1552 on an island 50 miles (80 km) from here while waiting to begin his mission in China. The bone, now in an ornate silver reliquary, was destined for his church in Japan, but by then the Japanese had closed their doors on the Christian church.

Other relics are the bones of the martyrs of Nagasaki and those of Vietnamese Christians executed in the early 17th century. By a strange irony, although it is not so strange for Macau, Coloane has a small Vietnamese community of boat people who fled their country and now await resettlement in a large, open camp administered by the Catholic church.

⓫ Coloane Park, on the west coast of the island, is the newest of Macau's natural preserves. Its centerpiece is a walk-in aviary containing more than 200 species of birds, including the rare Palawan peacock and the crested white pheasant. Nearby is a pond with black swans, a playground, the "1999" restaurant, a picnic area, and a nature trail around the hillside. Developed by the Forestry Department, the park has an impressive collection of exotic trees and shrubs. *Admission free for park, 5 patacas for aviary. Open 9–7.*

Historic Sites

With more than four centuries of history-making, it's not surprising that Macau has a wealth of historic buildings. What is remarkable is how well they have survived the assault of time, climate, and schemes for modernization. One reason is that they have all been in constant and practical use. They are also valued as part of a proud heritage and so are regularly restored and redecorated, even as they are obscured by graceless skyscrapers and gimcrack architecture.

St. Paul's (São Paulo) has long been a popular symbol of Macau. The richly carved baroque facade is all that remains of what was called "the greatest church in Asia." Built between 1602 and 1627 by exiled Japanese Christians and local craftsmen under the direction of Jesuits, St. Paul's was the collegiate church for the Jesuit college, which was the first Western-style university in Asia. Such scholars as Matteo Ricci and Adam Van Schall studied here before going to the court in Peking. The church fell into disuse when the Jesuits were expelled in 1762. Later, the army was billeted in the college, and in 1835 a fire destroyed everything except the facade.

Monte Fort, on the hill overlooking St. Paul's, was also built by the Jesuits and completed in 1623. In 1622, the year before it was completed, the fort was the scene of Macau's most famous battle. The Dutch, jealous of Portugal's power in Asia, invaded the territory, which was protected by a small force of soldiers, African slaves, and priests. As the Dutch closed in on Monte, a lucky cannon shot, fired by one of the priests, hit the enemy's powder supply and in the ensuing confusion the Dutch were driven back to sea. In 1626, the first full-time governor of Macau evicted the Jesuits from the fort. For the next century-and-a-half it was the residence and office of Macau's governors. The fort's buildings were destroyed in the 1835 fire, but the great walls remain, along with their cannon. Today the fort is a popular belvedere for residents and tourists, with an information office. Its gates are open from 7 AM to dusk.

The Loyal Senate (Leal Senado) stands in the heart of the city, on the main street facing a European-style square. It is a superb example of colonial architecture, with a simple, elegant facade dating from 1876. The main building was constructed in the late 18th century to house the senate of leading citizens who were at the time far more powerful than the governors, who served their short terms and then returned to Portugal. Today the senate, with some elected and some appointed members, acts as the municipal government, with its president holding the same power as a mayor. Inside the building, a beautiful stone staircase leads to a wrought-iron gate and a charming garden. The upper floor contains the senate chambers and the original national library, modeled on that of Mafra in Portugal. The foyer and garden are open during working hours, and there are art and history exhibitions in the foyer and adjoining galleries.

Holy House of Mercy (Santa Casa da Misericordia) stands in the square opposite the senate. Behind the imposing white facade are the headquarters of the first Western charity in Asia. Founded in 1569, it established orphanages, clinics, homes for the aged, free food supplies for the poor, and a leprosarium. On the second floor (open during office hours) is a reception room with paintings of benefactress Marta Merop and Macau's first bishop, Dom Belchior, as well as the latter's cross and skull.

St. Dominic's (São Domingos), Largo de São Domingos, adjoining senate square, is possibly the most beautiful church in Macau, with a magnificent cream-and-white baroque altar of graceful columns, fine statues, and a forest of candles and flower vases. Built in the 17th century by the Dominicans, it has a stormy history. In 1644 a Portuguese officer involved in civil strife was murdered by a mob at the altar during mass. In 1707 the church was besieged by the governor's troops when the Dominicans sided with the Pope against the Jesuits over a controversy as to whether or not ancestor worship should be permitted among Chinese Christian converts. After three days, the soldiers broke down the doors and briefly imprisoned the priests. Today those doors are open only during services; at other times, visitors should ring the bell on the green gate next to the entrance.

Guia Fort and Lighthouse, built in the 1630s, is on the highest point in Macau. Several roads lead up to the fort. The gate is open from 7 AM to dusk, and the views from the fort's platform are truly panoramic. Within the fort is the lighthouse, erected in 1865 and the oldest on the China coast, and a small, simple, white-stone chapel, built in 1707 and dedicated to Our Lady of Guia. The fort is used by the Marine Police. When there are typhoons in the area, typhoon signals in the form of specially shaped black metal baskets are hoisted on a yardarm on the platform. Permission is needed to enter the lighthouse and chapel (not easy, but you can ask the Department of Tourism to try).

The Border Gate (Portas do Cerco) marks the traditional boundary of Macau. Beyond is the Chinese border town of Gongbei. The present gate was built in 1870 and bears the arms of Portugal's navy and artillery, along with a quotation from

Camões, which reads, in translation: "Honor your country for it looks after you." On either side of the gate is written the date 1849. This commemorates the year when the governor, Ferreira do Amaral (whose statue used to stand outside the Lisboa Hotel), was assassinated by the Chinese. The local warlord planned to invade Macau but a Macanese colonel, Nicolau Mesquita, with 37 men, slipped across the border and captured the Chinese fort. Today there is a steady flow of vegetable farmers, businessmen, and tourists at the gate. *Open daily 7–9.*

Temple of the Lotus (Lin Fung Miu), Ave. do Almirante Lacerda, is close to the border gate. This superb temple, dedicated to both Buddhist and Taoist deities, was built in 1592 and used for overnight accommodations by mandarins traveling between Macau and Canton. It is famous for its facade of intricate clay bas-reliefs depicting mythological and historical scenes and an interior frieze of colorful writhing dragons. *Open dawn–dusk.*

Kun Iam Temple (Kun Iam Tong), Avenida do Coronel Mesquita, is in the north of the city. This Buddhist temple, dedicated to Kun Iam (also known as Kwan Yin), the goddess of mercy, was founded in the 13th century. The present buildings are richly endowed with carvings, porcelain figurines, statues, old scrolls, antique furniture, and ritual objects. The temple is best known among Western visitors for the stone table in the courtyard, where, on July 3, 1844, the first Sino-American treaty was signed by the Viceroy of Canton and the United States envoy, Caleb Cushing. The temple has a large number of funeral chapels, where you can see the offerings of paper cars, airplanes, luggage, and money, which are burned to accompany the souls of the dead. *Open dawn–dusk.*

Dom Pedro V Theater, Largo de Sto. Agostinho, is on the hill above the Praia Grande and behind the Loyal Senate. The oldest Western theater on the China coast, it was built in 1859 in the style of a European court theater. Until World War II, it was in regular use with local performers and international artists. In recent years it has been extensively restored and equipped with sophisticated stage lighting. It is now used for concerts and other entertainment, such as plays in Macanese. Although not officially open to visitors during the day, one of the doors is usually open and no one objects to people looking around at the marvelously Victorian foyer and auditorium. The facade is also very fine.

St. Augustine's (Sto. Agostinho) is in the Largo de Sto. Agostinho, opposite the theater. This superb baroque building dates from 1814, when it replaced the burned-out 17th-century original. In the marble-clad high altar is the large statue of Our Lord of Passos, which is carried through the streets on the first day of Lent. Among the tombs in the church is that of Maria de Moura, a romantic heroine who in 1710 married the man she loved, even though he had lost an arm when attacked by another of her suitors. She died in childbirth and is buried with her baby and her husband's arm. The church is open daily.

St. Joseph's (São Jose), also in Largo de Sto. Agostinho, was once an important seminary with a superb church. Today it is in great need of repair and houses only Father Manuel Teixeira, Macau's resident historian, and some brilliantly restored 16th-century paintings. The church, a gem of cruciform Baroque design, is open 10–4 daily except Wednesday.

Government Palace, Praia Grande, a distinctive pink-and-white mansion that contains the offices of the governor and his ministers, was built in 1849 by Macau's greatest architect Tomas de Aquino. Unfortunately, the public is not permitted inside to see the regal banquet hall and dining room. The exterior is very impressive.

Government House (Palacio de Santa Sancha) was also built by Aquino, and it shows the same mastery of elegant, simple lines. Surrounded by attractive gardens, it is the residence of the governor, and it is closed to the public. But the house can be easily seen from the road.

Penha Hill, above the Bela Vista on the highest point of the narrow peninsula, is the dominant landmark for arrivals by sea. At one time it was crowned with a church, where seafarers would worship before setting out. The present building is the bishop's residence and includes a small chapel built in 1935, which is open daily 10–4.

Temple of A-Ma (A-Ma Miu) is at the far end of the peninsula. Dating from the early 16th century, this is the most picturesque temple in Macau, with ornate prayer halls and pavilions built among the giant boulders of the waterfront hillside. The rocks are inscribed with red calligraphy telling the story of A-Ma (also known as Tin Hau), the favorite goddess of fishermen, who allegedly saved a humble junk from a storm. One of the many Chinese names for the area was Bay of A-Ma, or A-Ma Gau, and when the Portuguese arrived they adopted it as Macau. The temple is open dawn to dusk.

Shopping

At first glance, Macau is a poor country cousin to Hong Kong when it comes to shopping. Most stores are small and open to the street, the clerks might be eating snacks at the counter, and the merchandise is likely to be haphazardly arranged. There is also very little for sale here that isn't available in far greater abundance and variety in Hong Kong.

So why shop in Macau? First, the shopping areas are much more compact. Second, sales staff are in general much more pleasant and relaxed (although their command of English might not be as good as in Hong Kong). And, most important, many goods are cheaper. Like Hong Kong, Macau is a duty-free port for almost all items. But, unlike the British territory, commercial rents are reasonable and wages low, keeping overheads to a minimum.

Macau's shops are open every day of the year, except for a short holiday after Chinese New Year for family-run businesses. Opening hours vary according to the type of shop, but usually extend into mid-evening. Major credit cards are generally accepted, but not for the best discounts. Friendly bargaining is expected, and is done by asking for the "best price," which produces discounts of 10% or more. Larger discounts on expensive items should be treated with suspicion. Macau has its share of phony antiques, fake name-brand watches, and other rip-offs. Be sure to shop around, check the guarantee on name brands (sometimes fakes come with misspellings), and be sure to get receipts for expensive items.

The major shopping districts of Macau are the main street, Avenida Almeida Ribeiro, commonly known by its Chinese name Sanmalo; Mercadores and its side streets; Cinco de Outubro; and Rua do Campo. One of the pleasures of shopping here is the shop names that reflect Macau's dual heritage, for example, *Pastelarias Mei Mun* (pastry shops), *Relojoaria Tat On* (watches and clocks), and *Sapatarias Joao Leong* (shoes).

Antiques

The days of discovering treasures from the Ming among the Ching Chinoiserie in Macau's antiques shops are long gone, but there are still plenty of old and interesting pieces available. Collectors of old porcelain can find some well-preserved bowls and other simple Ming ware once used as ballast in trading ships. Prices for such genuine items run into the hundreds or thousands of dollars. Far cheaper are the ornate vases, stools, and dishware from the late Ching period—China's Victorian era, which are in vogue. This style of pottery is still very popular among the Chinese and a lot of so-called Ching is faithfully reproduced today in China, Hong Kong, and Macau. Many of these copies are excellent and hard to distinguish from their antique cousins.

Over the years, dealers and collectors have made profitable trips to Macau, so it's interesting to ask where new supplies of antiques are coming from. The standard answer used to be "from an old Macau family" that was emigrating or had fallen on hard times. Today there is another explanation: They are brought out of China by legal and illegal immigrants in lieu of capital or foreign currency. Most of these smuggled items are small but some are rare and precious. Among them are such things as 2,000-year-old bronze money in the shape of knives, later types of coins with holes in the middle, jade *pi* (discs), ivory figurines, and old jewelry. In addition, you can still sometimes find Exportware porcelain, made for the European market in 19th-century China, and old bonds from the early 20th century.

Antiques shops that have earned excellent reputations over the years include the two stores of **Veng Meng** (114 Ave. Almeida Ribeiro and 8 Travessa do Pagode), **Wing Tai** (1A Almeida Ribeiro), and **The Antique House** (opposite Kun Iam Temple at 11 Ave. Coronel Mesquita). *All are open 9–6.*

Clothing

There are many shops in Macau that sell casual and sports clothes for men and women at bargain prices. Most are made in Macau or Hong Kong and carry big-name labels. In some cases these are fakes, but more often they are genuine overruns or rejects from local factories that manufacture, under license, garments for Yves Saint Laurent, Cacharel, Van Heusen, Adidas, Gloria Vanderbilt, and many others. Name-brand jeans cost about HK$150 and shirts HK$120. There are also padded jackets, sweaters, jogging suits, windbreakers, and a very wide range of clothes for children and infants at very low prices. The best shopping areas are on Rua do Campo or around

Mercadores. For the very best bargains you should visit the street markets of São Domingos (off Leal Senado Square) and Cinco de Outubro. Credit cards are accepted at larger shops.

Crafts

Many traditional Chinese crafts are followed in Macau, and the best place to watch the craftsmen at work is along Tercena and Estalagens. These old streets are lined with three-story shophouses with open-front workshops on the ground floor (living quarters and offices are above). Some shops produce beautifully carved chests and other furniture made of mahogany, camphorwood, and redwood, some inlaid with marble or mother-of-pearl. Other craftsmen make bamboo bird cages, family altars, "lucky" door plaques, and colorful sandals. Macau also makes modern furniture, lacquer screens, modern and traditional Chinese pottery, and ceremonial items such as lion dance costumes, giant incense coils, and temple offerings.

Gold and Jewelry

Macau's jewelry shops are not as lavish as those in downtown Hong Kong, but they offer much better prices. Each store displays the current price of gold per *tael* (1.2 troy ounces), which changes from day to day or even hour to hour according to the Hong Kong Gold Exchange. Some counters contain 14- and 18-carat jewelry, such as chains, earrings, pendants, brooches, rings, and bangles. There are also ornaments set with pearls or precious stones (usually made in Hong Kong), as well as pieces of costume jewelry and fanciful traditional Chinese items. Most important, however, are the counters with 24-carat jewelry and gold in the form of coins and tiny bars, which come with assays from a Swiss bank. Pure gold is very popular with the Chinese as an investment and as a hedge against the vagaries of the stock exchange and currency fluctuations.

Prices for gold items are based on the day's price plus a small percentage profit, so a limited amount of bargaining is possible.

Among the best known are: **Tai Fung** (36 Ave. Almeida Ribeiro), **Chow Sang Sang** (58 Ave. Almeida Ribeiro), **Pou Fong** (91 Ave. Almeida Ribeiro), **Sheong Hei** (Ave. Almeida Ribeiro). *All are open 9–7. The staffs are helpful and English-speaking.* *AE, DC, MC, V.*

Sports

For most regular visitors to Macau, the sporting life means playing the casinos, but there are plenty of other sports, albeit often with gambling on the side. The Macanese are keen on team sports and give creditable performances at interport soccer and field hockey matches. In addition to traditional annual events such as the Grand Prix, there are also international table tennis championships. Many events are held in the new Macau Forum. Participant sports activities have also increased, with some excellent routes for joggers and sports facilities in hotels.

Dragon Boat Racing

This newest of international sports derives from an ancient Chinese festival in which fishing communities would compete in long, shallow boats with dragon heads and tails, in honor of a poet who drowned himself to protest official corruption. At the time, about 2,000 years ago, his friends took to boats and pounded their oars in the water while beating drums to scare away the fish who would have eaten the poet's body. The festival and races have been revived in recent years in many parts of Asia, with teams from Hong Kong, Nagasaki, Singapore, Thailand, Malaysia, and Macau, plus crews from Australia, the United States, Europe, and China's Guangdong Province. The races are held in the Outer Harbour, where the waterfront provides a natural grandstand for spectators. The Dragon Boat Festival takes place on the fifth day of the fifth moon (usually some time in June) and is attended by a flotilla of fishing junks decorated with silk banners, and fishing families beating drums and setting off firecrackers.

Golf

Until the opening of the Westin resort on Coloane it will not be possible to play golf in Macau, but the Zhongshan and Zhuhai international-standard clubs are just a short distance across the border (*see* Essential Information in Chapter 10).

Greyhound Racing

The dogs are very popular with residents and Hong Kong gamblers. The races are held in the scenic, open-air Canidrome, close to the Chinese border. Most dogs are imported from Australia. The 10,000-seat stadium has rows and rows of betting windows and stalls for food and drink. Multi-million dollar purses are not unheard of and special events, such as Irish Nights, occur routinely. *Ave. General Castelo Branco. Races, 8 PM, Tues., Thurs., weekends, holidays, year-round. Admission: 2 patacas for public stands, 5 patacas for members' stand, 80 patacas for 6-seat box.*

Horse Racing

The raceway, built for Asia's first trotting track, is located on three million square feet of reclaimed land close to the Hyatt Regency Hotel.

The Macau Trotting Club spared no expense in building the facility. The five-story grandstand can accommodate 15,000 people, 6,000 of them in air-conditioned comfort. There are restaurants, bars, and some of the most sophisticated betting equipment available. Unfortunately, trotting races did not bring in sufficient revenue and so the Macau Jockey Club was formed. The track was greatly enlarged and upgraded for year-round racing each weekend and midweek, and timed not to clash with Hong Kong races. Summer meetings are held in the evenings. For details check with hotel desks.

Motor Racing

The Macau Grand Prix takes place on the third or fourth weekend in November. From the beginning of the week, the city is shattered with supercharged engines testing the 3.8-mile (6-km) Guia Circuit, which follows the city roads along the Outer Harbour to Guia Hill and around the reservoir. The route is as challenging as that of Monaco, with rapid gear changes demanded at the right-angle Statue Corner, the Dona Maria bend, and the Melco hairpin.

The Grand Prix was first staged in 1953 and the standard of performance has now reached world class. Today cars achieve speeds of 140 miles per hour (224 kph) on the straightaways, with the lap record approaching 2 minutes 20 seconds. The premier event is the Formula Three championship, with cars brought in from around the world for what is now the official World Cup of Formula Three racing, where winners qualify for Formula One licenses. There are also races for motorcycles and production cars. Many internationally famous drivers have raced here, including Alan Jones, Ricardo Patrese, and Keke Rosberg.

Hotel bookings during the Grand Prix are made long in advance, and the weekend should be avoided by anyone not interested in motor racing.

Running

The 26-mile (41.6-km) Macau Marathon takes place in November or early December. All are welcome to try the fairly grueling course beginning and ending with the Macau-Taipa bridge and including the roads around both islands.

Stadium Sports

Since the opening of the Macau Forum's multipurpose hall, it has been possible to stage a variety of sporting events here. The world table tennis and roller hockey championships have been held here, as have regional basketball and badminton matches. Visitors interested should check with their hotel front desk staff to find out if something special is on.

Tennis and Squash

Both the Hyatt Regency and Mandarin Oriental hotels have tennis and squash courts for use by guests. At the Hyatt there is also a tennis coach.

Dining

Although East and West have clashed in many respects, when it came to cooking there was instant rapprochement and it happened in Macau. By the time the Portuguese arrived, they had learned a lot about the eating habits of countries throughout their new empire. They adopted many of the ingredients grown and used in the Americas and Africa, and brought them to China. The Portuguese were the first to introduce China to peanuts, green beans, pineapples, lettuce, sweet potatoes, and shrimp paste, as well as a variety of spices from Africa and India. In China, the Portuguese discovered tea, rhubarb, tangerines, ginger, soy sauce, and the Cantonese art of fast frying to seal in the flavor.

Over the centuries a unique Macanese cuisine developed, with dishes adapted from Portugal, Brazil, Mozambique, Goa, Malacca, and of course, China. Today some ingredients are imported, but most are available, fresh each day, from the bountiful waters south of Macau and the rich farmland just across the China border. A good example of Macanese food is the strangely named Portuguese chicken, which would be an exotic alien in Europe. It consists of chunks of chicken baked with potatoes, coconut, tomato, olive oil, curry, olives, and saffron. Extremely popular family dishes include *minchi* (minced pork and diced potatoes panfried with soy), pork baked with tamarind, and duckling cooked in its own blood, all of which are served with rice.

The favorites of Portuguese cuisine are regular menu items. The beloved *bacalhau* (codfish), is served baked, boiled, grilled, deep fried with potato, or stewed with onion, garlic, and eggs. Portuguese sardines, country soups such as *caldo verde* and *sopa alentejana*, and dishes of rabbit are on the menus of many restaurants. Sharing the bill of fare are colonial favorites: from Brazil come *feijoadas*, stews of beans, pork, spicy sausage, and vegetables; Mozambique was the origin of African chicken, baked or grilled in fiery *piri-piri* peppers. In addition, some kitchens prepare baked quail, curried crab, and the delectable Macau sole that rivals its Dover cousin. And then there are the giant prawns that are served in a spicy sauce—one of Macau's special dining pleasures.

Not surprisingly, Chinese restaurants predominate in Macau. In addition, there are several restaurants offering excellent Japanese, Thai, Korean, Indonesian, and even Burmese meals, not to mention grills and various fast-food outlets. Visitors should take the unique opportunity of dining Macau-style. Food prices here are generally so reasonable that it's well nigh impossible to categorize restaurants by price except at the very top and bottom of the market.

One of the best bargains in Macau is wine, particularly the delicious Portuguese *vinho verde*, a slightly sparkling wine, and some reds and whites, such as the Dao family of wines. Restaurant wine prices range from 23 patacas (the same as in the wine shops) at the inexpensive **Riquexo** to 90 patacas a bottle at the **Mandarin Oriental Grill**. The average price is 50 patacas a bottle. Except in hotels, beer and spirits—including some powerful Portuguese brandies—are very reasonably priced.

All restaurants are open every day of the year except, for some, a few days' holiday after Chinese New Year. In most cases there is no afternoon closure for cleaning, and both lunches and dinners tend to be leisurely affairs, with no one urged to hurry up and leave. Most people order wine, relax, look at the menu, note what other diners are eating, talk to the waiter, and then make their decision. Dress is informal, and nowhere are jackets and ties required. The Department of Tourism's brochure, "Eating Out in Macau," is very useful.

The most highly recommended restaurants are indicated with a star. ★

At press time there were 7.8 patacas to the U.S. dollar.

Category	Cost*
Expensive	over 150 patacas
Moderate	50–150 patacas
Inexpensive	under 50 patacas

*per person including service

The following credit card abbreviations are used: AE, American Express; DC, Diners Club; MC, MasterCard; V, Visa.

Macanese-Portuguese

Expensive **Fortaleza.** The setting of this exquisite restaurant would be reason enough to dine here. Located in the traditional Portuguese inn built into the 17th-century Barra fortress, it offers vistas, between the branches of gnarled trees, onto an idyllic seascape of green islands and sailing junks. The decor and atmosphere recall the days of the Portuguese empire, with crystal lamps, hand-carved mahogany furniture, blue and white tiles, and plush drapes. The food is almost as marvelous, with a good selection of classic Macanese dishes, such as baked codfish, quail, and spicy prawns, and Continental dishes, too. Service is attentive, and prices expensive only by Macau standards. *Pousada de Sao Tiago, Ave. Republica, tel. 78111. Reservations recommended for evenings. Dress: informal. AE, DC, MC, V.*

Moderate **Afonso's.** This is one of the most attractively designed restaurants in Macau. It is horseshoe-shaped, with Portuguese tiles on the wall, floral cushions on the rattan chairs, spotless table linen, and dishware made to order in Europe. Picture windows frame the gardens outside, and there is space for musicians when the hotel has promotions such as "April in Portugal." The menu is imaginative and the prices reasonable, with entrees costing about 50 patacas. The menu is a good balance of Macanese favorites, such as spicy prawns, and regional Portuguese dishes, including *açorda* bread, seafood soup, and *frango na pucara*, chicken in a clay pot. There is an excellent wine list and the service is cheerful and efficient. *Hyatt Regency Hotel, Taipa Island, tel. 321234. Reservations recommended. Dress: informal. AE, DC, MC, V.*

A Galera. This is the new A Galera, very different but just as good as the one that used to be in the hotel basement. It is an elegant, handsomely decorated restaurant, with blue-and-white-tile wall panels, black-and-white-tile floors, pearl-gray table linen, Wedgewood dishware, a bar with high-back armchairs, and views of the S. Francisco fortress. The atmosphere and menu indicate high prices, but in fact this is not so. Main courses, such as *bacalhau a bras* (codfish cooked in a skillet with rice, olives, egg, and onion) and squid stuffed with spiced meat, cost around 70 patacas; rich, homemade soups are 14 patacas and dessert souffles 15 patacas. As for wine, there is *vinho verde* and reds and whites for 60 patacas a bottle. *Lisboa Hotel, 3rd floor of new wing, tel. 577–666 ext. 1103. Reservations not necessary. Dress: informal. AE, DC, MC, V.*

★ **A Lorcha.** Opened in 1989, near the Maritime Museum, this Portuguese restaurant has become a firm favorite with demanding locals. Come here for casseroles at extremely reasonable prices and first-class service. *289 Rua do Almirante Sergio, tel. 313193. Reservations recommended. Dress: informal. MC, V. Closed Tues.*

★ **Balichao.** Opened in 1991 in the city's northern suburbs this Portuguese restaurant is, by general consent, the most originally elegant in town, with a tented ceiling, antique-filled walls, rattan furniture, and Canton floor tiles. The menu is equally unusual, with great casseroles and dishes served with "balichao" shrimp paste. *Hoi Fu, Est. de Cacilhas 93, tel. 566000. Reservations recommended. Dress: informal. AE, MC, V.*

Fat Siu Lau. Opened in 1903, this is the oldest European restaurant in Macau and one which has maintained the highest standards of food and service. Years ago it looked like the average Chinese cafe, but now each of its three floors is elegantly furnished and decorated. The ground floor seems to have been transported from Portugal. The walls of bare brick are partly covered with white stucco, blue tiles, and green vines. There is also a false half-roof with Cantonese tiles. The menu is tried and true. Regulars automatically order the roast pigeon (50 patacas) Fat Siu Lau made famous. Other favorites are African chicken (46 patacas), sardines (33 patacas), and ox breast with herbs (25 patacas). A large carafe of wine runs 28 patacas. *64 Rua da Felicidade, tel. 573–580. Reservations not necessary. Dress: informal. No credit cards.*

Flamingo. Designed like a European pavilion, with verandas on three sides, this restaurant is ideally located in the gardens of the Taipa Island Resort. There are no flamingos, but there are some very well-fed ducks in the surrounding pond. At night there is music by a Filipino group in the main room, with its Portuguese decor. At all times there is a wonderfully carefree atmosphere, and Flamingo has the greatest bread (a whole fresh cottage loaf) in Asia. The menu is very varied and reasonably priced. *Taipa Island Resort, Hyatt Regency Hotel, tel. 321234, ext. 1874. Reservations recommended on sunny days and weekend evenings. Dress: informal. AE, DC, MC, V.*

Galo. This new restaurant proves what can be done, with flair and dedication, to transform a traditional Taipa village house into a delight for all the senses. The owners—he was with the Portuguese military, she (his wife) is Macanese—gutted the two-story building. Then they decorated it in bright Iberian colors and added Macanese touches, such as Chinese rattan hats for lamp shades and big porcelain plant pots, plus a fireplace and country-style bar. The food is also country-style. One specialty is from Madeira and consists of chunks of orange-flavored lamb on a suspended skewer; others include *pipis*, rice with chicken in a hot sauce (15 patacas), codfish salad with tomatoes and green olives (25 patacas), and curry crabs. Topping off the pleasure of dining here are scenes of village life viewed through the lattice windows. *47 Rua do Cunha, Taipa Island, tel. 327423. Reservations not necessary. Dress: informal. No credit cards.*

Henri's Galley. Situated on the banyan-lined waterfront (with some tables on the sidewalk), this is a favorite with local residents and visitors from Hong Kong. The decor reflects owner Henri Wong's former career as a ship's steward. There is a coiled blue rope pattern on the ceiling, pictures of old ships on the walls, and red and green lights to keep passengers on an even keel. The food is consistently good, with probably the biggest and best spicy prawns in town, delicious African and Portuguese chicken (54 patacas), Portuguese soups (15 patacas), and fried rice, complete with hot Portuguese sausage. Wines are 50 patacas a bottle. *4 Avenida da Republica, tel. 556251. Reservations recommended especially on weekends. Dress: informal. MC, V.*

Pinocchio's. Until the opening of the Hyatt Hotel, the only reason most visitors went to Taipa was to eat at this restaurant. Owned by a former marine policeman (Senhor Pina, which explains the name), it has grown rather gracelessly from the original small, air-conditioned rooms and open courtyard. Now the courtyard is covered with a corrugated tin roof and lighted with harsh fluorescent strips. However, there's no better place for curry crabs, baked quail, and steamed shrimps. Other specials are a superlative leg of lamb and roast suckling pig, which have to be ordered in advance. The atmosphere is country café, the service often casual, and little English is spoken. *4 Rua do Sol, Taipa Island, tel. 327128. Reservations essential on weekends. Dress: informal. No credit cards. Closed Mon.*

Pousada de Coloane. This is 20 minutes by car from the city, by Macau standards a long, long way to go for a meal, but many residents and Hong Kong regulars consider it well worth the trip. The setting is fine, with a large open terrace outside the restaurant. When the weather is good, an alfresco lunch overlooking the beach and water is marvelous. For indoor dining, the restaurant is reminiscent of many in Lisbon, with dark wood panels, colorful tile floors, and folk art decorations. Service can be rather haphazard, but the food is usually excellent. Among the specialties are feijoadas, grilled sardines, and stuffed squid. Best of all is the Sunday buffet, with a great selection of Macanese dishes for only 85 patacas per person. Regular meals cost less than 100 patacas, including wine. *Praia de Cheoc Van, Coloane Island, tel. 328144. Reservations not necessary. Dress: informal. MC, V.*

Solmar. For many, many years the Solmar has been an unofficial club for local Portuguese and Macanese men, who gather here to drink strong coffee and gossip. It has a pleasantly lived-in atmosphere and a good range of dishes. Service can be slow, but the meals are worth waiting for, especially the baked Portuguese chicken and spicy African chicken (each 55 patacas). Wine is 66 patacas a bottle. *11 Praia Grande, opposite the Metropole Hotel, tel. 574-391. Reservations not necessary. Dress: informal. No credit cards.*

Inexpensive **Riquexo.** This self-service cafe was created by and for lovers of authentic Macanese food at family prices. Each day half a dozen dishes are prepared in private kitchens and delivered to the Riquexo (Portuguese for rickshaw and pronounced the same) in large tureens, which are kept heated in the restaurant. Beer and wine (regulars have their own bottles in the big refrigerator) are offered at little more than shop prices, as well as soups, salads, and desserts. The place is bright and basic, with the atmosphere of a family get-together. The staff doesn't speak much English but is very helpful. Prices average 40 patacas a meal, including wine. The best entrees are the first to go. *69 Sidonio Pais, tel. 565655. No reservations. Dress: informal. No credit cards. Lunch only.*

Asian

Expensive **Ginza.** As befits a member of the Dai-Ichi group, the Royal's Japanese restaurant has an elegant, classic simplicity, with tatami rooms, sushi and tempura counters, and grill-topped tables for teppanyaki. There are a variety of set meals as well as à la carte, and prices are relatively reasonable, about 180 patacas per person for a full meal with beer or sake. *Royal Hotel, tel. 568412. Reservations recommended. Dress: informal. AE, DC, MC, V.*

Moderate **Chiu Chau.** This is probably the best, and certainly most sumptuous, restaurant in Macau serving the Chiu Chow cuisine of Swatow. Many Hong Kong and Thai Chinese (and therefore many gambling visitors to Macau) are originally from Swatow Province. The food is richer than Cantonese and more spicy, with thick, strong shark's fin soup, chicken in hot *chinjew* sauce, and crabs in chicken sauce. *Lisboa Hotel, tel. 577666, ext. 83001. Reservations not necessary except on weekends. Dress: informal. AE, DC, MC, V.*

Ease Garden. Locals say this restaurant offers the best dim sum in town as well as other excellent Cantonese fare. It is attractively decorated in garden style and the staff is eager to please. *11 Rua Dr. P. J. Lobo, behind the Sintra Hotel, tel. 562–328. Reservations not necessary. Dress: informal. AE, DC, MC, V.*

Four Five Six. Lovers of Shanghainese food flock to this restaurant, where the specialties are lacquered duck, braised eel, and chicken broiled in rice wine, plus steamed crabs during the winter. The atmosphere is generally cheerful, noisy, and welcoming. *Lisboa Hotel, mezzanine of new wing, tel. 388474. Reservations recommended on weekends. Dress: informal. AE, DC, MC, V.*

Long Kei. This is one of the oldest and most popular Cantonese restaurants in Macau. It has a huge menu, plus daily specials of the best dishes (printed only in Chinese, so ask the waiter to translate). Like all good Chinese restaurants in this part of the world, it is noisy and apparently chaotic, with no attempt at glamour or sophistication. The total focus is the food and few will be disappointed here. *7 Largo do Senado, tel. 573–970. No reservations. Dress: informal. No credit cards.*

Royal Canton. This large, attractively decorated Cantonese restaurant is very popular with locals and visiting groups, who use it for family parties and celebrations, as well as for breakfast and morning dim sum. The menu is very extensive and the service friendly and efficient. *Royal Hotel, tel. 552222. Reservations not necessary. Dress: informal. AE, DC, MC, V.*

Lodging

A decade ago Macau's accommodations were, at best, merely adequate. But in recent years, the situation has changed dramatically with the opening of several hotels that are of high international standards. These can be booked worldwide through offices overseas or in Hong Kong. Macau's hotels depend on occupancy by Hong Kong residents, who often make plans to visit at the last moment, so business fluctuates with weather conditions and holidays. This means that sizeable discounts are usually available for midweek stays. These are best obtained through Hong Kong travel agents or at the hotel itself.

Macau also has two Portuguese *pousadas* (inns), modeled after the national inns of Portugal, with distinctive Macanese elements incorporated.

In general, hotels listed as *Expensive* are of the highest international standard, with swimming pools and health clubs, meeting rooms for conferences and parties, fine restaurants, public areas that are design showcases, business centers, and guest rooms with all the modern comforts and conveniences. Those in the *Moderate* category are efficient, clean, and comfortable, with air-conditioning, color TV (with English and Chinese programs from Hong Kong as well as the local channel), room service, and restaurants. They cater primarily to gamblers, regular Hong Kong visitors, and budget tour groups. *Inexpensive* hotels tend to be old and spartan, but they are clean and safe.

The most highly recommended hotels are indicated with a star ★.

At press time there were 7.8 patacas to the U.S. dollar.

Category	Cost*
Expensive	800–1,200 patacas
Moderate	300–800 patacas
Inexpensive	under 300 patacas

per room; add 10% service and 5% tax

The following credit card abbreviations are used: AE, American Express; DC, Diners Club; MC, MasterCard; V, Visa.

Expensive

★ **Hyatt Regency and Taipa Island Resort.** Opened in early 1983, the Hyatt is the first in Asia to have guest rooms that were fully prefabricated (in the United States) and shipped as modules. They conform to Hyatt Regency's high standards, with all the modern conveniences and attractive furnishings. The public areas were built in Macau to designs by Dale Keller, and they combine the best of Iberian architecture and Chinese decor. The foyer is a spacious lounge with white arches, masses of potted plants, and fabulous Chinese lacquer panels. Beyond is the coffee shop, an aptly named Greenhouse salon, a hideaway bar, and Afonso's Portuguese restaurant. A small casino is located off the lobby. The Taipa Resort, which adjoins the hotel, has a complete health spa, with different baths, massage and beauty treatments; facilities for tennis, squash, and ball games; a large pool and botanical garden; a jogging track; and the marvelous Flamingo Macanese veranda restaurant. The hotel is close to the race track, and operates a shuttle-bus service to the wharf and Lisboa. The hotel is very popular with Hong Kong families. *Taipa Island, tel. 321234, in Hong Kong 559–0168, elsewhere Hyatt Hotels Reservations. 365 rooms with bath. Facilities: restaurants, bars, casino, health spa, outdoor pool, 2 squash courts, 4 tennis courts, sauna, whirlpool, gym, massage, beauty parlor/barber, baby-sitting, car rental, tours, shuttle bus service to wharf. AE, DC, MC, V.*
Mandarin Oriental. Built on the site of the old Pan Am seaplane

terminal, with marvelous views of the Pearl River and islands, this is a beautifully designed and furnished hotel. Its lobby features reproductions of Portuguese art and antiques, the Grill Room has a wood ceiling inlaid with small oil paintings, and the Cafe Girassol could have been transported from the Algarve. The Bar da Guia is probably the most elegant drinking spot in town, and the casino is certainly the most exclusive. Recreation facilities consist of two pools, tennis and squash courts, and a health club, all overlooking the outer harbor. The guest rooms have marble bathrooms and teak furniture. *Avenida da Amizade, tel. 567–888, in Hong Kong 548–7676, elsewhere Mandarin Oriental reservation offices. 438 rooms with bath. Facilities: restaurants, bars, casino, 2 outdoor pools, 2 tennis courts, 2 squash courts, gym, sauna, massage, beauty parlor, car rental, tours, shuttle bus to wharf. AE, DC, MC, V.*

★ **Pousada de São Tiago.** This is as much a leading tourist attraction as a place to stay. It is a traditional Portuguese inn that was built, with enormous imagination and dedication, into the ruins of a 17th-century fortress. For instance, the ancient trees that had taken over the fort were not cut down but incorporated into the design, and the position of their roots dictated the shape of the coffee shop and terrace. A classic European fountain plays over the site of the old but still operative water cistern, and the small restored chapel of *S. Tiago* (St. James) can be hired for weddings. Furnishings, made to order in Portugal, include mahogany period furniture, blue-and-white-tile walls, and crystal lamps, plus terra-cotta floor tiles from China and carpets woven in Hong Kong. The entrance is the original entry to the fort, and natural springs have been trained to flow down the rocky wall in tile channels on either side of the staircase. There is also a swimming pool, sun terrace, meeting room, and superb restaurant. Each of the rooms, complete with four-poster beds and marble bathrooms, has a balcony for great views with breakfast or cocktails. Rooms for weekends have to be booked in advance. *Avenida da Republica, tel. 378111, in Hong Kong 810–8332 and 739–1216. 23 rooms with bath. Facilities: restaurant, bar, terrace, outdoor pool, chapel, car rental. AE, DC, MC, V.*

Pousada Ritz. Opened in 1990, opposite the Bela Vista, this handsome inn commands fine views of Praia Grande Bay from balconied rooms and the spacious dining terrace. The restaurants serve Chinese and Continental meals. Recreational facilities include an indoor pool and gym, as well as a games room for billiards and darts. *Rua Comendador Kou Ho Neng, tel. 339–955. 12 rooms, 19 suites. Facilities: sauna, pool, gymnasium, restaurants. AE, DC, MC, V.*

Royal. The Royal has an excellent location, with fine views of Guia, the city, and Inner Harbour. It has a marble-clad lobby with a marble fountain and lounge, plus some excellent shops. In the basement are the health club, squash court, sauna rooms, and a karaoke bar. Upstairs is the glass-roof swimming pool and four restaurants: the Royal Canton for Chinese food, the Japanese Ginza, the Portuguese-Continental Vasco da Gama, and the coffee shop. The hotel has shuttle bus service to the wharf and casinos. *2 Estrada da Vitoria, tel. 552222, in Hong Kong 542–2033, elsewhere Dai-Ichi Hotels reservation offices. 380 rooms with bath. Facilities: restaurants, bar, lounge, indoor pool, squash court, sauna, gym, shuttle bus to wharf and casino. AE, DC, MC, V.*

Moderate

Beverly Plaza. Located in the new suburb behind the Lisboa, this hotel is managed by the China Travel Service, which has offices in the building. The hotel also has a shop with goods at bargain prices. Locals often shop here and ship their purchases to relatives in China. The hotel's lobby bar has become a popular rendezvous. *Avenida Dr. Rodrigues, tel. 337755, in Hong Kong 540-6333. 300 rooms. Facilities: Chinese and Western restaurants, bar. AE, DC, MC, V.*

Emperor New World. Scheduled to open at the end of 1991 beside the Outer Harbour, this Hong Kong-managed hotel has 402 rooms, two Chinese restaurants, a Portuguese bistro, coffee shop, and health club. *402 rooms. Ave. do Dr. Rodrigo Rodrigues, no tel. Facilities: 2 restaurants, health club, shops. AE, DC, MC, V.*

Guia. Situated on Guia Hill, this small hotel is excellent value for the money. *1 Estrada Engenheiro Trigo, tel. 513888. 89 rooms. Facilities: Chinese restaurant, coffee shop, disco, karaoke bar. AE, DC, MC, V.*

Lisboa. Rising above a two-story casino, with walls of mustard-color tiles, frilly white window frames, and a roof shaped like a giant roulette wheel, the main tower of the Lisboa has, for better or worse, become one of the popular symbols of Macau and is an inescapable landmark. A new wing houses the Crazy Paris Show, the superb A Galera restaurant, a nightclub, billiards hall, and raucous children's game room, plus an ostentatious collection of late Ching Dynasty art objects and a small, lobby-level exhibition area. The original tower has restaurants serving some of Macau's best cuisine of Chiu Chow province of China, Japan, and Shanghai. Also contained in the complex are a video arcade, a four-lane bowling center, a nonstop coffee shop, Macau's first Pizza Hut, some very good shops, a sauna, and a sometimes operative pool terrace. *Avenida da Amizade, tel. 577666, in Hong Kong 559-1028. 750 rooms with bath. Facilities: restaurants, bars, casino, game rooms, disco, theater, bowling center, sauna, outdoor pool, tours, shuttle bus to wharf. AE, DC, MC, V.*

Metropole. This centrally located hotel is managed by the China Travel Service. It has pleasant, comfortable rooms and an excellent Portuguese-Macanese restaurant. The hotel is popular with business travelers and China-bound groups. *63 Rua da Praia Grande, tel. 881-66, in Hong Kong 540-6333. 109 rooms with bath. Facilities: restaurant, coffee shop, supper club, China tour arrangements. MC, V.*

Pousada de Coloane. This *pousada* is a small, delightful resort inn. Among the delights are the huge terrace overlooking a good sandy beach, a pool, and a superb restaurant serving excellent Macanese and Portuguese food. The Sunday buffets (when weather permits) are renowned and, at 85 patacas per person, a great bargain. The rooms have good-size balconies and stocked refrigerators. This is a place for lazy vacations and, during the summer, it's usually packed with families from Hong Kong. There is a shuttle bus to and from the wharf. *Praia de Cheoc Van, Coloane Island, tel. 328144, in Hong Kong 730-1166. 22 rooms with bath. Facilities: restaurant, bar, terrace, outdoor pool. MC, V.*

Presidente. The Presidente has an excellent location and is very popular with Hong Kong visitors. It offers an agreeable lobby lounge, European and Chinese restaurants, the best Korean food in town, a sauna, and a great disco with a skylight roof. *Avenida da Amizade, tel. 553888, in Hong Kong 526–6873, elsewhere Utell International reservations offices. 340 rooms with bath. Facilities: restaurants, sauna, nightclub/disco. AE, DC, MC, V.*

Sintra. A sister hotel of the Lisboa, the Sintra is, in contrast, quiet, with few diversions apart from a sauna, nightclub, and European restaurant and bar. It is ideally located, overlooking the Praia Grande bay and within easy walking distance of the Lisboa and downtown. *Avenida Dom Joao 1V, tel. 851–11, in Hong Kong 540–8028. 236 rooms with bath. Facilities: 2 restaurants, tours, shuttle bus to casino. AE, DC, MC, V.*

Inexpensive

Central. In the very heart of town, this was once the home of Macau's only legal casino and best brothel. Now it is a budget hotel with clean but basic rooms and an excellent Chinese restaurant. *Avenida Almeida Ribeiro, tel. 77700. 160 rooms with bath. Facilities: restaurant. AE, MC, V.*

Grand. Pre-World War II hotel geared for the gamblers who frequent the nearby casinos, the Grand has an old-fashion atmosphere and good restaurants. *146 Avenida Almeida Ribeiro, tel. 579922. 90 rooms. Facilities: restaurants, nightclub/disco. No credit cards.*

East Asia. This newly renovated hotel is in the heart of the old town. *1 Rua da Madeira, tel. 572631. 98 rooms. Facilities: restaurant. AE, DC, MC, V.*

In addition, there are some small, old hotels and boarding houses called villas. They usually cater to Chinese visitors, so the staff generally speaks little English. However, they are clean and inexpensive, sometimes with private bath and TV. The Department of Tourism and Macau Tourist Information Bureau (MTIB) can provide details.

Nightlife

According to old movies and novels about the China coast, Macau was a city of opium dens, wild gambling, international spies, and slinky ladies of the night. It might come as a letdown to some visitors to find the city fairly somnolent after sunset. Most people spend their evenings at the casinos or over long dinners. There is, however, some action.

Lisboa Theater. Apart from a few concerts by visiting performers or shows by local artists, theater in Macau means the Crazy Paris Show at the Lisboa. This was first staged in the late 1970s and has become a popular fixture. The stripper-dancers come from Europe, Australia, and the Americas, while the choreographer and director are Parisian professionals. The show is very sophisticated and cleverly staged. By the end of most acts, the performers have shed their clothes, but there's nothing lewd about the show. In fact, half the audience is likely to be made up of female tourists. The acts are changed completely every few months, and are a tribute to the imagination of the director's team, with superb use of lights and music as well as the athletic prowess of the artists. One show-stopping act has become a regular. It features a woman, with apparently magical breath control, who does Esther Williams-type routines in a huge tank of water on stage—but, unlike the movie star, she wears no clothes. *Lisboa Hotel, 2nd floor, new wing, daily shows at 8:30 and 10 PM, with additional show on Sat. at 11:30 PM. Admission: HK$90 weekdays, HK$100 weekends and holidays. Tickets available at hotel desks, Hong Kong and Macau ferry terminals, and the theater.*

Discos/Nightclubs

The **Skylight** is a disco and nightclub, with floorshows three times nightly by English striptease artists. *Presidente Hotel, Ave. da Amizade, tel. 553888. Admission: 60 patacas; includes one drink. Open 6 PM–4 AM.*

The Lisboa's **Mikado** nightclub is a sleek, slinky place with hostesses, high-tech lighting and a lively crowd. *Lisboa Hotel, new wing, tel. 577666. Admission: 200 patacas; includes one drink. Open 9 PM–4 AM.*

China City, the most upscale nightcub in Macau, in the Jai Alai Stadium, attracts wealthy local and visiting Hong Kong businessmen and Japanese tourists. The club employs more than 300 hostesses (35 patacas for about 10 minutes of their company in the club), and has a live band and a dance floor. *Jai Alai Stadium, tel. 312333, Minimum HK$200. Open 6 PM–4 AM.*

The **Metropole** supper club, in the Metropole hotel, has a dance floor, live band, and medley of singers. It operates in the Chinese restaurant from 7 PM to after midnight. Cover charge is HK$15. *Metropole Hotel, tel. 388166.*

For those who want to dance and maybe have a meal without strobe lights and deafening music, there is the **Portos do Sol** in the Lisboa. It is an attractive room with a live band 8 PM–midnight, later on weekends. The minimum charge is 45 patacas on weekdays, 55 patacas on weekends. There is occasionally a floor show.

Casinos

The glamorous images summoned up by the word "casino" should be checked at the door with cameras before entering the Macau variety. Here you'll find no opulent floor shows, no free drinks, no jet-setters in evening dress, and no suave croupiers. What you do find is no-frills, no-holds-barred, no-questions-asked gambling. Open 24 hours a day, most of the rooms are noisy, smoky, shabby, and in constant use. The gamblers, mostly Hong Kong Chinese, are businesspeople, housewives, servants, factory workers, and students, united in their passion—and what a passion it is! There is almost certainly more money wagered, won, and lost in Macau's casinos than in any others in the world. The total amount is unknown except to Sociedade de Turismo e Diversoes de Macau (STDM), the syndicate that has the gambling franchise. In return for the franchise, STDM is paying the government a premium of HK$1.3 billion (about US$162.5 million) over a 10-year period, plus 26% to 30% of gross income, plus money to build homes for 2,000 families, provide new passenger ferries, and keep the harbor dredged. The syndicate does not complain, so judge the profits for yourself.

There are seven casinos in Macau: those in the *Lisboa*, *Mandarin Oriental*, and *Hyatt Regency* hotels, the *Jai Alai Stadium*, the *Jockey Club*, the *Kam Pek*, and the *Palacio de Macau*, usually known as the floating casino. The busiest is the two-story operation in the Lisboa, where the games are roulette, boule, Blackjack, Baccarat, keno, and the Chinese games *fan tan* and "big and small." There are also hundreds of slot machines, which the Chinese call "hungry tigers."

There are few limitations to gambling in Macau. No one under 18 is allowed in, although identity cards are not checked. Although there are posted betting limits, high rollers are not discouraged by such things. There are 24-hour money exchanges, but most gamblers use Hong Kong dollars.

The solid mass of players in the casinos might look rather unsophisticated, but they are as knowledgeable as any gamblers in the world. They are also more single-minded than most, eschewing alcohol and all but essential nourishment when at the tables. (Small bottles of chicken essence are much in evidence!) And they are superstitious. All of which adds up to certain "Macau Rules" and customs, which any serious visiting gambler should learn. The rules are printed out and available at the casinos, and there are two good books on the subject: *Gamblers Guide to Macau*, by Bert Okuley and Frederick King-Poole, and the *Macau Gambling Handbook*, by A-O-A publishers, both available in Hong Kong.

Baccarat has, in recent years, become a big status game for well-heeled gamblers from Hong Kong, who brag about losing a million as much as winning one. An admiring, envying crowd usually surrounds the baccarat tables, which occupy their own special corners. Minimum bets are HK$100 or HK$500, and the official maximum ranges from HK$35,000 to HK$300,000. In Macau the player cannot take the bank, and the fixed rules on drawing and standing are complex, making it completely a game of chance.

Big and Small is a traditional game in which you bet on combinations of numbers for big or small totals determined by rolled dice. The minimum bet is HK$20.

Blackjack is enormously popular in Macau and there are frequently dozens of people crowded around the players, often placing side bets. An uninitiated player might feel flattered to have others bet on his skill or luck—until he learns that by Macau rules anyone betting more than the player can call the hand. Otherwise the rules are based on American ones. The dealers, all women, must draw on 16 or less and stand on 17 or more. Minimum bets are HK$50, depending on the table. Many of the dealers are rude, surly, and greedy. In the Lisboa they take a cut of any winnings automatically, as a tip, and it's a battle to get it back. Players do, however, have a chance for revenge. No matter how bad a run of luck a dealer is having, she has to sit out her hour's stint.

Fan Tan is an ancient Chinese game which has, surprisingly, survived Western competition—surprising because it is so boringly simple. A pile of porcelain buttons is placed on the table and the croupier removes four at a time until one, two, three, or four are left. Players wager on the result, and some are so experienced that they know the answer long before the game ends.

Pacapio has replaced keno, a game which it in fact resembles. Punters choose four to 25 numbers from one to 80. Winning numbers are chosen by computer and appear, every half hour or so, on screens in the Lisboa and Jai Alai Stadium.

Roulette is based on the European system, with a single zero, but with some American touches. Players buy different-colored chips at an American-shaped table, and bets are collected, rather than frozen, when the zero appears. The minimum bet is HK$50.

Slot Machines line the walls of all five Western casinos, and seem in constant use. The newest attraction is a "mega-bucks" system with computer links to all casinos and million dollar pay-out possibilities.

The casino scene has gone upscale in recent years, with the opening of more elegant and exclusive rooms in the Mandarin Oriental and Hyatt Regency. Another change is the rejuvenation of the casino in the Jai Alai Stadium. It attracted few customers when located on the second floor; it has been spruced up and moved to a larger area on the ground floor where it is doing excellent business, especially with visitors who have time to spare before leaving for Hong Kong. Meanwhile, a new vessel has replaced the run-down old floating casino. It has one deck for slot machines and one for roulette, baccarat, and Black Jack; it does not have a restaurant.

The Kam Pek casino has moved from the old red-light district into a renovated building on the main street, and games now included roulette and Black Jack, as well as Chinese games. Unlike the other casinos, only patacas are used here.

The newest casino is located in the **Jockey Club** on Taipa. Consisting of five tables and 38 slot machines, it is open Saturday, Sunday, and race days, 11 AM to 3 AM.

10 Excursions to China

Introduction

by Shann Davies

When China opened its doors to foreign visitors in 1979, the response was overwhelming, and it was a rare first-time visitor in Hong Kong who didn't make a brief excursion across the border. Following the events of June 1989, tourism went into a sharp decline. Today tourism has picked up considerably, although it has not regained its previous strength.

The most popular destinations for both tourists and business travelers lie within the Pearl River delta of neighboring Guangdong (Canton) Province. Both geographically and economically, Hong Kong and Macau are intrinsic parts of the delta, which is one of the richest agricultural regions of China. Here two annual rice crops and a super-abundance of vegetables and fruit are produced, while the coastal waters yield bountiful catches of fish and seafood.

Ever since the first foreign traders, probably the Arabs, discovered the vast scope and possibilities of China, merchants have come to the "tradesmen's entrance" in the Pearl River delta: the port city of Guangzhou (Canton), which was sheltered and close to suppliers from the south and conveniently distant from the imperial authorities in the north. As a result, local merchants did not feel bound to obey the imperial ban on trade with Japan, which had been imposed because, the government declared, China needed nothing any foreign "barbarian" had to offer. When, in the mid-16th century, Portuguese trading adventurers arrived off the coast and suggested that they act as intermediaries between Guangzhou and the merchants of southern Japan (whose government had similarly banned trade with China), the Cantonese businessmen were delighted to accept.

With Guangzhou's approval, the tiny peninsula of Macau was settled by the Portuguese and quickly became a great international port, in time attracting traders from Britain, Europe, and America. By the early 19th century the Portuguese had gained a virtual monopoly on China's overseas trade.

When the Chinese objected to the opium sales that made the West's domination possible, the British went to war and won Hong Kong, which became a greater port than either Guangzhou or Macau.

With the 1984 signing of agreements between the Chinese government and those of Britain and Portugal, both territories are scheduled once again to come under Chinese sovereignty. History will have come full circle, and the future of Hong Kong and Macau will once more be that of the delta.

In terms of travel, it has always made sense to treat the delta as a unified destination. But even with liberalized travel, it has, until quite recently, been difficult to make the circuit because of poor roads, inadequate wharf facilities, and a scarcity of tourist accommodations. There are still some problems, with secondary roads impassable after heavy rains and occasional breakdowns in communications, but excursions of one to four days are now comfortably possible.

Essential Information

Arriving and Departing

Hong Kong–Zhuhai Hydrofoils make three round-trips a day to the pier at Jiuzhou, a journey of about 70 minutes. *Hong Kong China Hydrofoil Co., Hong Kong, tel. 523–2136. Cost: about HK$120 weekdays, HK$130 weekends.*

Hong Kong–Zhongshan Hydrofoils make four round-trips daily to Zhongshan harbor, close to Shiqi. *Chu Kong Shipping, Hong Kong, tel. 859–1591. Cost: HK$140.*

Hong Kong–Guangzhou **By Train:** There are four express trains a day, which take less than 2½ hours and cost *HK$176.*

By Ship: Two coastal ferries—*Xinghu* and *Tianhu*—make the journey every day, departing at 9 PM and arriving at about 7 AM. They have restaurants, and cabins of different classes. There is also hovercraft service to Huangpu in the outskirts of Guangzhou (fare HK$165).

By Plane: CAAC, the Chinese airline, has frequent flights, which take about 20 minutes and cost about HK$320 (plus HK$150 departure tax).

Hong Kong–Shenzhen **By Train:** There is commuter service by electric trains from Kowloon to the border at Lo Wu (HK$23.50).

By Bus: There is regular service by Citibus (tel. 736–3888) from various points in Hong Kong to Shenzhen city and tourist areas (Fares HK$40–HK$60).

By Ship: A pleasant 50-minute ride in a hydrofoil (Hong Kong China Hydrofoil) to Shekou is available.

Border formalities should pose little problem. In recent years, customs declarations and money have rarely been checked, and those on group visas have had to ask in order to get a stamp in their passports. At the Chinese arrival points there are money-exchange counters, and duty-free liquor and cigarettes are sold at bargain prices.

Visas

Everyone needs a visa to enter China. Individuals can obtain visas from CTS offices in Hong Kong for HK$130 (ready in 48 hours), HK$180 (rush service). One photograph is needed. For groups of 10 or more, travel agents get visas; you need only supply your passport number the day before the tour. In theory, it's also possible to get a visa on arrival in China, but it's safer not to rely on this.

Guided Tours

The vast majority of tourists on side trips to China take a regular guided tour, ranging from one to four days and using boats, buses, or trains. Tours offered by China Travel Service (CTS) and Hong Kong travel agents are designed to fit into any normal schedule. By far the most popular is to **Zhongshan** via **Macau,** which provides a full and interestingly diverse, if rather tiring, day. All one-day Zhongshan tours begin with an early departure from Hong Kong to Macau and a bus transfer

to the border at **Gongbei,** in the **Zhuhai Special Economic Zone.**
From here tour itineraries vary, but all spend time in **Cuiheng
Village,** to visit the house built by Sun Yatsen, hero of the 1911
revolution, and an excellent museum devoted to his life and
times.

Most tours visit the **Chung Shan Hot Springs Resort** for lunch
and an exploration of the resort's facilities. Some tours take
lunch in one of the ornate "neo-Ching Dynasty" resort hotels in
Zhuhai or at the elegant **Cuiheng Hotel.** Completing the itinerary is either a visit to a farming unit (formerly a commune) or a
kindergarten. In each case the lunch, of half a dozen Cantonese
dishes, is usually delicious (and accompanied by free beer and
soft drinks), and the tour offers a fascinating glimpse of ancestral China in confrontation with the modern Western world.
Tours return to Macau for a late afternoon trip back to Hong
Kong. The cost is about HK$600.

This Zhongshan tour is often combined with a day and night in
Macau, which makes for an excellent balance. The cost is about
HK$980, depending on the cost of your stay in a hotel in Macau.

The other established one-day China trip takes in the **Shenzhen
Special Economic Zone,** immediately across the border from
Hong Kong. This begins with a coach trip to Shenzhen and its
prime tourist attraction, known as **Mini Kingdom** or Splendid
China, which is a park containing 70 miniaturized historical or
scenic wonders of China, complete with a population of thou-
sands of porcelain figurines. The tour also includes visits to a
Hakka village, kindergarten, and market (HK$495 adults,
HK$415 children).

Shenzhen was interesting when it was one of the few places in
China open to foreigners. Now it looks and feels more like a
suburb of Hong Kong—complete with branches of McDonald's
and the Hongkong Bank. Nowadays most visitors are businesspeople, while tourists head for Mini Kingdom, the
Shenzhen Golf Club, or the resorts that cater to Hong Kong
families.

Given the geographic and historic unity of the delta region, it
would seem logical to have circular tours that included all
places of interest. Now that bridges have been built over the
numerous Pearl tributaries, and major roads upgraded, this
has become possible. The basic itinerary is a three-day tour,
beginning with a hydrofoil to Macau, a visit to Cuiheng, an
overnight stay in Shiqi, a day in Foshan, and a night and day in
Guangzhou before taking the express to Hong Kong. The cost is
about HK$1,690. There is also a four-day tour that adds on
Seven Star Crags. The cost is about HK$1,960.

The above examples represent the range of excursions now
available from Hong Kong. Prices quoted refer to rates per
person, double occupancy for overnight trips, during the week.
On weekends and public holidays, rates are slightly higher.
Most tours have daily or very frequent departures.

Some agents in Hong Kong selling excursions to China are: **Chi-
na Travel Service** (78 Connaught Rd., Central, tel. 853–3533; 27
Nathan Rd., Kowloon, tel. 721–1331); **Able Tours** (8 Connaught
Rd., Central, tel. 544–5656); **Estoril Tours** (Shun Tak Centre,
Central, tel. 559–1028); **International Tourism** (140 Connaught

Rd., Central, tel. 541–2011); **Macau Tours** (287 Des Voeux Rd., Central, tel. 542–2338).

Golf Resorts

Although it's quite possible to visit Zhongshan and Zhuhai independently by hired car and driver, most Westerners who do so are business travelers or golfers. The latter can choose from two of the best clubs in Asia.

The **Chung Shan Golf Club** is part of the Chung Shan Hotel Springs Resort complex. It was designed by Arnold Palmer's company and opened in 1984, with Palmer among the first to try it out. It is a 72-par, 5,991-meter course of rolling hills, streams, and tricky sand traps. Professionals who have competed in China's first international golf tournaments here declare it first-class, and local youngsters who have been trained here now make up what amounts to China's national team. The clubhouse, with gleaming mahogany paneling and elegant rattan furniture, was designed by a Filipino company. It has a bar, restaurant, sauna, and granite-walled pool, plus a pro shop with everything you'd expect to find in an American or Japanese club. Greens fees for visitors are HK$350 per day during the week, members only on weekends and public holidays. Bag carriers cost HK$80 a round, and a set of clubs rents for HK$100. Bookings, transport (via Macau or Jiuzhou), visas, and any required reservations at the resort can be arranged by Hong Kong and Macau agents or through the club's office (504 Pedder Bldg., 12 Pedder St., Hong Kong, tel. 521–0377).

The **Zhuhai International Golf Club** was established by Japan Golf Promotion Inc., in 1985. It is located on the coast in Zhuhai, close to the Macau border and Jiuzhou pier. The 72-par, 6,380-meter links course is beautifully laid out in a long valley, with awesome sand traps, lakes, and woods. The clubhouse is a Japanese version of an antebellum mansion of the U.S. South, with neoclassical columns and deep verandas. It is attractively furnished and offers a restaurant, bar, pro shop, and spa. Visitor greens fees are HK$350 weekdays, HK$500 weekends and holidays. Caddies cost HK$80 a round, and a set of clubs rents for HK$100. The Hong Kong agent is Creative Enterprises (Rm 1102, Wallpark Commercial Bldg., 10 Chatham Court, Kowloon, tel. 721–3848, fax 367–7112). ABC Travel (Silvercord, 30 Canton Rd., Kowloon, tel. 366–5333) offers a one-day package for HK$750 weekdays, HK$950 weekends, including transport from Hong Kong and 18 holes of golf. A two-day package adds an overnight stay and dinner at the Zhuhai resort, and another nine holes, for HK$1,400 weekdays, HK$1,800 weekends.

Exploring

Numbers in the margin correspond with points of interest on the Pearl River Delta map.

❶ Zhongshan/Zhuhai makes up the county that was known to the first western visitors as Heungshan ("fragrant mountain"). The name was changed to Chung Shan ("central mountain") in honor of Sun Yat-sen. Zhongshan is the new spelling. It covers 687 square miles (1,786 square kilometers) of the fertile

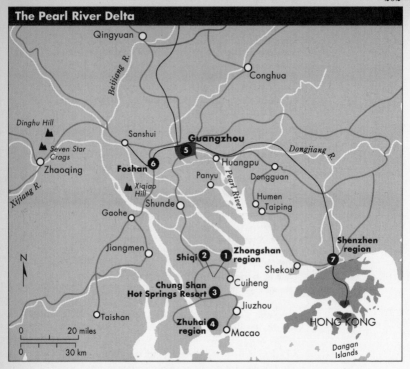

The Pearl River Delta

Pearl River delta and supports about 1.3 million people, many of them wealthy farmers who supply Macau with much of its fresh produce.

With substantial help from overseas Chinese investors, many new industries have been developed in recent years, mostly textiles, medicines, processed food, and electronic components. This prosperity contrasts starkly with the situation a century ago. At that time the mandarins benefited from nature's bounty, but the peasants who harvested it were kept in abject poverty. The same applied to much of China, but here the downtrodden had a way out—across the border to Macau and by coolie ship to the railroads of California and the gold mines of Australia.

The peasants left in the tens of thousands. Zhongshan's city fathers boast of the half million "native sons" now resident in lands around the globe. A few did come back, from a sense of patriotism and the desire to show off their newly acquired wealth. Throughout the county you can see some of the results: three- and four-story tower houses, shaped like American skyscrapers or European castles. More significantly, they brought back ideas of democracy and reform. Among them was Sun Yatsen, born in Cuiheng, who led the movement to overthrow the Manchus and become "father of the Chinese Republic."

For much of the past century, Zhongshan benefited from its overseas relatives, who sent funds when times were hard. However, during the Cultural Revolution the county suffered, since all positions of power were taken from locals and given to northerners who didn't have foreign contacts. These days the benefits are flowing again, and it seems every new hospital and auditorium was funded by cousins from Hong Kong or overseas. Others help to boost the flourishing local tourist industry when they come in search of their roots.

Cuiheng, where Sun Yatsen was born in 1866, is on every Zhongshan tour. Its major attractions are contained in a memorial park. One attraction is the house that Sun built for his parents during a visit in 1892. It is a fine example of China coast architecture, with European-style verandas that face west. This is bad geomancy for traditional Chinese, and it underscored Sun's reputation for rebellion. The interior, however, is traditional, with high-ceiling rooms, ancestral plaques, gilded carvings, and heavy black-wood furniture that includes a roofed Chinese marriage bed. Next door is the excellent **Sun Yatsen Museum,** with rooms ranged around a patio, each showing the life and times of Sun as man and revolutionary. The exhibits are well chosen and displayed, with labels in English, Chinese, and Japanese. In addition, there are videos about Sun and Zhongshan.

Also in the park is the Sun Yatsen Memorial High School, with some splendid blue tile roofs and a traditional Chinese gateway. It was built in 1934 and has about 700 students. Across from the park is the 242-room Cuiheng Hotel, a gracefully designed resort with pool terrace and good Western and Chinese restaurants.

2 Shiqi (formerly spelled Shekkei) is the county capital and has been for 800 years an important market center and inland port. It is about 38 miles (60.8 kilometers) from Macau and 49 miles (78.4 kilometers) from Guangzhou, and thus a convenient stopover on excursions of the delta area (*see* Dining and Lodging, below).

The busy town of 100,000 sits astride the **Qi River,** where a cantilever bridge is opened twice a day (or when a ship's captain pays) to allow freighters to pass. Along the riverbanks are floating restaurants, and the riverside roads are taken up by open cafés and sidewalk shops, which are particularly active and colorful in the evenings. The symbol and landmark of the town is a Ming Dynasty **pagoda,** standing in a hillside park where the paths are paved with 19th-century tombstones.

The newest attraction of Shiqi is the superb **Sun Yatsen Memorial Hall,** built for US$1.3 million by a Hong Kong tycoon. It consists of three linked, pagoda-shape towers, topped with imperial-yellow tile roofs. Inside is a 1,400-seat auditorium used for concerts, and exhibition halls showing Zhongshan products and history. Also worth a visit is the newly restored **Xishan Temple,** with prayer halls around a courtyard, close to the downtown area. Some tours include a visit to a Shiqi kindergarten, where the children give a charming show.

3 Chung Shan Hot Springs Resort is more than a place to stay. Built by a Hong Kong millionaire, it is included as a stopover for lunch on many day tours, so visitors have a chance to explore the complex. The 350 guest rooms are in low-rise blocks or in classical pavilions that perch beside willow-screened, carp- and lotus-filled ponds. There is a huge Chinese restaurant with a series of ornately furnished rooms. There is also a small western café and bar. Outside are extensive grounds containing a swimming pool, shooting range, horseback-riding ring, and shopping center. And to justify the name, there are four bathrooms fed by hot spring water piped in from a neighboring valley.

4 Zhuhai was one of the first Special Economic Zones set up in 1980 with special liberal laws to encourage foreign investment. The zone has been extended from an original 5 square miles (13 square kilometers) to 46 square miles (121 square kilometers), complete with a long coastline and many small off-shore islands.

Zhuhai has proved an economic success, producing textiles, glassware, TV parts, computer discs, and an award-winning beer. However, the main industry is tourism. Every day hundreds of western visitors cross from Macau and observe hundreds of Chinese tourists, often from remote provinces, who are observing them in return. Domestic tourists come to Zhongshan to pay their respects to Sun Yatsen, and then they explore the shops and restaurants of Zhuhai, usually pausing to gaze across at Macau.

There is almost nothing old in Zhuhai, which is very proud of its factories and super highway, but the past is not forgotten. It can be found in the **Zhuhai Resort,** which was modeled on the highly ornate style of late Qing—China's Victorian era. Here a large Chinese restaurant boasts walls of windows etched with pictures of birds, flowers, and scenes from legend. This resort also has pavilions, ponds, and winding bridges.

5 Guangzhou is still better known as Canton, an English corruption of the Portuguese version of the Chinese name. With a strategic location on the South China coast, it has been a major trading port for almost 2,000 years. It received cargoes from the Spice Islands, India, and the Middle East long before Europe knew China existed. It was also the port of export for silk, and centuries ago, it began holding semiannual fairs at which the silk was bartered for spices, silver, and sandalwood. From the time the Portuguese settled Macau, Guangzhou became the prime meeting place of East and West. During the 19th century it was a business home for British, American and European traders.

Throughout its history Guangzhou has shown a rebellious character, and the Cantonese have frequently been at odds with the rulers in the north. Exposure to western ideas made them more independent, and it is no surprise that the 1911 revolution and the organization of the Chinese Communist party both started here.

Today the majority of foreign visitors to Guangzhou are attending trade fairs or are otherwise involved in business. Tourists rarely spend more than a day in the city. Although there are some interesting attractions, Guangzhou is best combined with tours of other parts of the delta. Of the tourist sights, **Shamian Island** appeals to those who know something of its history. This is where western traders set up shop when the island was a sand spit in the Pearl River, linked to the city by bridges that were closed at night. The traders built fine mansions, churches, and even a cricket pitch. Quite a number of the buildings have been renovated to house government and business offices, hotels, and shops, while others have been converted into small factories and apartments.

Of general interest is **Yuexiu Park,** with its array of Krupp cannons, and the 14th-century Zhenhai Tower, which contains the Municipal Museum (open daily 8:30–5:30). The museum offers a comprehensive display of the city's history from 200 BC to the present, unfortunately with labels only in Chinese. Nearby is the modern statue of five goats with sheaves of corn in their mouths. Legend has it that the goats were sent from heaven with gifts of cereals; they have been adopted as the symbol of the city. Sun Yatsen is, of course, honored where he studied medicine and later celebrated the birth of the Chinese Republic. The Memorial Hall dedicated to him, built in 1925, contains a 5,000-seat auditorium.

One of Guangzhou's several memorial parks celebrates the uprisings that culminated in the 1911 revolution; it is built around the mausoleum containing the remains of 72 martyrs. Another park is dedicated to those who died in the uprising of local Communists in 1927. The **Peasant Movement Institute** is a monument to an early Communist organization. In 1924 Mao Zedong and his comrades set up schools to teach their doctrine. The Guangzhou Institute, housed in a Ming Dynasty Confucian temple, has been restored to recapture the atmosphere of a revolutionary cell.

There are other sites of interest, such as the **Chen Family Institute,** with some magnificent porcelain friezes and stone carvings; the 11th-century Zen Buddhist **Temple of the Six Banyans** with its 196-foot-high pagoda (open 8–5:30); the 7th-century **Huaisheng Mosque** (closed to tourists during services), which was once a beacon for ships; and the **Roman Catholic Cathedral,** built in the 1860s and again active after years as a warehouse. The other attraction of the city is its food. Although in general not as good as those served in Hong Kong, Cantonese meals can be enjoyed in the leading hotels and several traditional pavilion-style restaurants (*see* Dining and Lodging, below).

6 **Foshan,** which translates as "Buddha Mountain," is 12½ miles (20 kilometers) southwest of Guangzhou and on the main circuit of the delta region. The drive takes less than 30 minutes on the new expressway. The city's history goes back 1,200 years. At one time it was an important religious center with a population of a million. Today, after centuries of obscurity, it is again a prosperous town with numerous joint enterprises involving overseas cousins.

The legacy of the past has been well preserved in Foshan, and the city's **Ancestral Hall,** with its brilliantly decorated prayer halls and astonishing porcelain murals, is beautifully maintained. To fully appreciate the porcelain figurines, you can visit **Siwan** and watch craftsmen making them. Some figurines are on sale. Equally skilled workers are found in the Folk Art Center, where intricate paper cutouts are made by hand. Chinese lanterns, fishbone carvings, and other handicrafts are also produced here and are on sale at extremely reasonable prices. *Open daily 8–6.*

7 **Shenzhen/Shekou** was another of the initial Special Economic Zones, and Shenzhen (Shumchun in Cantonese) was the first "instant China" destination. Since then it has developed at such a rapid rate that it's very like Hong Kong. Today most tourists to Shenzhen are Chinese from Hong Kong engaged in business or on family holidays at lavish but moderately priced resort hotels. Local and foreign tourists are drawn to the brilliant **Mini Kingdom** park, and golfers head for the 18-hole golf course.

Dining and Lodging

The vast majority of foreigners making excursions to destinations in the Pearl River delta are on escorted tours and therefore have no choice in the restaurants and hotels visited. A growing minority, however, are independent travelers, usually visiting the golf clubs, the town of Shiqi, or the provincial capital Guangzhou. Because the best restaurants are generally found in hotels and resorts, they are included in the following lodging list.

Category	Cost*
Expensive	US$70–$100
Moderate	US$40–$70
Inexpensive	US$40

double room; add 10% service

The following credit card abbreviations are used: AE, American Express; DC, Diners Club; MC, MasterCard; and V, Visa.

Zhongshan/Zhuhai

Chung Shan Hot Springs Resort. This vast recreational complex includes horseback riding, golf, shooting, swimming, and tennis. The Chinese restaurant, which is used by many tour groups, has good food and efficient service. The hotel is 15 miles (24 kilometers) from Macau. *Zhongshan, tel. 686888; in Hong Kong, 521–0377. 350 rooms with bath. Facilities: pool, tennis courts, riding, golf, shops, hot spring baths. AE, MC, V. Moderate.*

Fuhua Hotel. Situated beside the river, this high rise offers superb views. The Chinese restaurant, located in its own pavilion with stylishly furnished rooms, serves excellent food. *Sunwen Xi Lu, Shiqi, tel. 822034. 380 rooms with bath. Facilities: pool, disco, restaurant, sauna, bowling alley, shops. AE, V. Moderate.*

Shichingshan Resort. This very attractive hotel with spacious hillside gardens, opposite the Zhuhai Convention Center, has good restaurants serving both Chinese and Western food. *Zhuhai, tel. 332582, in Macau, 553888. 115 rooms with bath. Facilities: swimming pools, tennis courts, shopping center. AE, DC, MC, V. Moderate.*

Zhongshan International Hotel. This 20-story tower, topped with a revolving restaurant, has become a landmark of downtown Shiqi. Its rooms, restaurants, and service are of international tourist standard. *2 Zhongshan Lu, Shiqi, tel. 824788. 369 rooms with bath. Facilities: pool, karaoke lounge, sauna, billiards room, 10-pin bowling. AE, MC, V. Moderate.*

Zhuhai Resort. This is a delightful reproduction of a Qing Dynasty courtyard mansion (*see* Exploring, above). The Jade City restaurant serves excellent Cantonese food, which is also available in private rooms. *Zhuhai, tel. 23718; in Macau, 552275. 200 rooms with bath. Facilities: restaurants, bar, pools, tennis courts, disco, conference rooms. AE, DC, V. Moderate.*

Cuiheng Hotel. Situated opposite the Sun Yatsen Memorial Park, this attractive hotel consists of low-rise wings and bungalows of contemporary, elegant design. It has landscaped gardens around the pool and a riding school next door. *Cuiheng Village, Zhongshan, tel. 824091. 242 rooms with bath. Facilities: restaurants, pool, disco. AE, V. Inexpensive.*

Gongbei Palace Hotel. Modeled on an imperial palace, this hotel sports brilliant mustard-colored tile roofs with upswept eaves. It is close to the Macau border and has good Chinese and western restaurants. *Gongbei, Zhuhai, tel. 886833. 210 rooms with bath. Facilities: pool, sauna, billiards room, shops. AE, V. Inexpensive.*

Guangzhou

China Hotel. This vast complex of a hotel, standing opposite the Trade Fair Exhibition Hall and the railroad station, is greatly favored by business visitors. It is expertly managed by Hong Kong–based New World Hotels. *Liuhua Lu, tel. 666888. 1,017 rooms with bath. Facilities: restaurants, theater, ballroom, shops, business center, pool, health center, bowling alley. AE, DC, MC, V. Expensive.*

Garden Hotel. The newest of the Big Three, managed by Lee Gardens International, is located in the eastern part of the city and boasts some spectacular gardens, including an artificial hill with a waterfall and pavilions. The hotel contains some fine antiques and modern artworks. *368 Huanshi Dong, tel. 338989. 1,000 rooms with bath. Facilities: pool, squash courts, health center, disco, business center, shopping arcade. AE, DC, MC, V. Expensive.*

White Swan. The first international hotel in town, the White Swan occupies a marvelous site, on historic Shamian Island beside the Pearl River. *Shamian Island, tel. 886968. 1,000 rooms with bath. Facilities: 12 restaurants, meeting rooms, pool, disco, health center, shopping arcades, post office, travel agencies, business center. AE, DC, MC, V. Expensive.*

Index

Personal Itinerary

Departure *Date*

Time

Transportation

Arrival *Date* *Time*

Departure *Date* *Time*

Transportation

Accommodations

Arrival *Date* *Time*

Departure *Date* *Time*

Transportation

Accommodations

Arrival *Date* *Time*

Departure *Date* *Time*

Transportation

Accommodations

Personal Itinerary

Arrival *Date*   *Time*

Departure *Date*   *Time*

Transportation

Accommodations

Arrival *Date*   *Time*

Departure *Date*   *Time*

Transportation

Accommodations

Arrival *Date*   *Time*

Departure *Date*   *Time*

Transportation

Accommodations

Arrival *Date*   *Time*

Departure *Date*   *Time*

Transportation

Accommodations

Personal Itinerary

Arrival *Date*   *Time*

Departure *Date*   *Time*

Transportation

Accommodations

Arrival *Date*   *Time*

Departure *Date*   *Time*

Transportation

Accommodations

Arrival *Date*   *Time*

Departure *Date*   *Time*

Transportation

Accommodations

Arrival *Date*   *Time*

Departure *Date*   *Time*

Transportation

Accommodations

Personal Itinerary

Arrival   *Date*   *Time*

Departure   *Date*   *Time*

Transportation

Accommodations

Arrival   *Date*   *Time*

Departure   *Date*   *Time*

Transportation

Accommodations

Arrival   *Date*   *Time*

Departure   *Date*   *Time*

Transportation

Accommodations

Arrival   *Date*   *Time*

Departure   *Date*   *Time*

Transportation

Accommodations

Personal Itinerary

Arrival *Date*   *Time*

Departure *Date*   *Time*

Transportation

Accommodations

Arrival *Date*   *Time*

Departure *Date*   *Time*

Transportation

Accommodations

Arrival *Date*   *Time*

Departure *Date*   *Time*

Transportation

Accommodations

Arrival *Date*   *Time*

Departure *Date*   *Time*

Transportation

Accommodations

Personal Itinerary

Arrival	*Date*	*Time*
Departure	*Date*	*Time*
Transportation		
Accommodations		

Arrival	*Date*	*Time*
Departure	*Date*	*Time*
Transportation		
Accommodations		

Arrival	*Date*	*Time*
Departure	*Date*	*Time*
Transportation		
Accommodations		

Arrival	*Date*	*Time*
Departure	*Date*	*Time*
Transportation		
Accommodations		

Personal Itinerary

Arrival   *Date*   *Time*

Departure   *Date*   *Time*

Transportation

Accommodations

Arrival   *Date*   *Time*

Departure   *Date*   *Time*

Transportation

Accommodations

Arrival   *Date*   *Time*

Departure   *Date*   *Time*

Transportation

Accommodations

Arrival   *Date*   *Time*

Departure   *Date*   *Time*

Transportation

Accommodations

Addresses

Name	*Name*
Address	*Address*
Telephone	*Telephone*
Name	*Name*
Address	*Address*
Telephone	*Telephone*
Name	*Name*
Address	*Address*
Telephone	*Telephone*
Name	*Name*
Address	*Address*
Telephone	*Telephone*
Name	*Name*
Address	*Address*
Telephone	*Telephone*
Name	*Name*
Address	*Address*
Telephone	*Telephone*
Name	*Name*
Address	*Address*
Telephone	*Telephone*
Name	*Name*
Address	*Address*
Telephone	*Telephone*

Addresses

Name	*Name*
Address	*Address*
Telephone	*Telephone*
Name	*Name*
Address	*Address*
Telephone	*Telephone*
Name	*Name*
Address	*Address*
Telephone	*Telephone*
Name	*Name*
Address	*Address*
Telephone	*Telephone*
Name	*Name*
Address	*Address*
Telephone	*Telephone*
Name	*Name*
Address	*Address*
Telephone	*Telephone*
Name	*Name*
Address	*Address*
Telephone	*Telephone*
Name	*Name*
Address	*Address*
Telephone	*Telephone*

Addresses

Name	Name
Address	Address
Telephone	Telephone
Name	Name
Address	Address
Telephone	Telephone
Name	Name
Address	Address
Telephone	Telephone
Name	Name
Address	Address
Telephone	Telephone
Name	Name
Address	Address
Telephone	Telephone
Name	Name
Address	Address
Telephone	Telephone
Name	Name
Address	Address
Telephone	Telephone
Name	Name
Address	Address
Telephone	Telephone

Notes

Fodor's Travel Guides

U.S. Guides

Alaska
Arizona
Boston
California
Cape Cod, Martha's
  Vineyard, Nantucket
The Carolinas & the
  Georgia Coast
The Chesapeake
  Region
Chicago
Colorado
Disney World & the
  Orlando Area
Florida
Hawaii

Las Vegas, Reno,
  Tahoe
Los Angeles
Maine, Vermont,
  New Hampshire
Maui
Miami & the
  Keys
National Parks
  of the West
New England
New Mexico
New Orleans
New York City
New York City
  (Pocket Guide)

Pacific North Coast
Philadelphia & the
  Pennsylvania
  Dutch Country
Puerto Rico
  (Pocket Guide)
The Rockies
San Diego
San Francisco
San Francisco
  (Pocket Guide)
The South
Santa Fe, Taos,
  Albuquerque
Seattle &
  Vancouver

Texas
USA
The U. S. & British
  Virgin Islands
The Upper Great
  Lakes Region
Vacations in
  New York State
Vacations on the
  Jersey Shore
Virginia & Maryland
Waikiki
Washington, D.C.
Washington, D.C.
  (Pocket Guide)

Foreign Guides

Acapulco
Amsterdam
Australia
Austria
The Bahamas
The Bahamas
  (Pocket Guide)
Baja & Mexico's Pacific
  Coast Resorts
Barbados
Barcelona, Madrid,
  Seville
Belgium &
  Luxembourg
Berlin
Bermuda
Brazil
Budapest
Budget Europe
Canada
Canada's Atlantic
  Provinces

Cancun, Cozumel,
  Yucatan Peninsula
Caribbean
Central America
China
Czechoslovakia
Eastern Europe
Egypt
Europe
Europe's Great Cities
France
Germany
Great Britain
Greece
The Himalayan
  Countries
Holland
Hong Kong
India
Ireland
Israel
Italy

Italy 's Great Cities
Jamaica
Japan
Kenya, Tanzania,
  Seychelles
Korea
London
London
  (Pocket Guide)
London Companion
Mexico
Mexico City
Montreal &
  Quebec City
Morocco
New Zealand
Norway
Nova Scotia,
  New Brunswick,
  Prince Edward
  Island
Paris

Paris (Pocket Guide)
Portugal
Rome
Scandinavia
Scandinavian Cities
Scotland
Singapore
South America
South Pacific
Southeast Asia
Soviet Union
Spain
Sweden
Switzerland
Sydney
Thailand
Tokyo
Toronto
Turkey
Vienna & the Danube
  Valley
Yugoslavia

Wall Street Journal Guides to Business Travel

Europe
International Cities
Pacific Rim
USA & Canada

Special-Interest Guides

Bed & Breakfast and
  Country Inn Guides:
  Mid-Atlantic Region
  New England
  The South
  The West

Cruises and Ports
  of Call
Healthy Escapes
Fodor's Flashmaps
  New York

Fodor's Flashmaps
  Washington, D.C.
Shopping in Europe
Skiing in the USA &
  Canada

Smart Shopper's
  Guide to London
Sunday in New York
Touring Europe
Touring USA